7/9/91

Dear Rick

Here is hoping Managing Growth
provides you with some help for the months.

Best Regards

Managing Growth
Keys to Success
for Expanding Companies

Guy E. Weismantel
J. Walter Kisling, Jr.

LIBERTY HOUSE®

LIBERTY HOUSE books are published by LIBERTY HOUSE, a division of TAB BOOKS Inc. Its trademark, consisting of the words "LIBERTY HOUSE" and the portrayal of Benjamin Franklin, is registered in the United States Patent and Trademark Office.

First Edition
First Printing

Copyright © 1990 by TAB BOOKS Inc.
Printed in the United States of America

Library of Congress Cataloging-in-Publication Data

Weismantel, Guy E.
    Managing growth : keys to success for expanding companies / by Guy E. Weismantel and Walter J. Kisling, Jr.
        p. cm.
    ISBN 0-8306-3051-1
    1. Small business--Management. 2. Small business enterprises--Management. I. Kisling, Walter J. II. Title.
HD62.7.W45 1989
658.4'063--dc20   89-13031
                                                                                                    CIP

TAB BOOKS Inc. offers software for sale.
For information and a catalog, please contact:

TAB Software Department
Blue Ridge Summit, PA 17294-0850

Questions regarding the content of this book
should be addressed to:

Reader Inquiry Branch
TAB BOOKS Inc.
Blue Ridge Summit, PA 17294-0214

Vice President & Editorial Director: David J. Conti
Book Editor: Jeanette S. Martin
Book Design: Jaclyn B. Saunders
Production: Katherine Brown

Contents

Introduction

MANY BUSINESS BOOKS ARE BASED ON THEORY, OTHERS ON CONCEPTS, AND still others on philosophy or theorem. Until now, very few texts specifically addressed the manager's need for *how-to* information. *Managing Growth: Keys to Success for Expanding Companies* is a book that fills this need by giving very practical, solution-oriented answers and planning ideas for virtually every potential problem area that a company encounters.

Managing Growth pays particular attention to expanding companies who are experiencing growth and are faced with dynamic changes in personnel, financing, planning, and goals. These are often called *emerging* companies and fall into one of two categories. First, the firm could be an older organization that—due to new management, new products, new directions or new markets—is entering a growth cycle. Second, the firm could be an embryo whose egg has matured and the offspring is beginning to grow while facing the new situations of the business world.

Rapidly developing businesses have problems and needs that are very different from those encountered by most businesses and for which owners and managers are usually unprepared. This book shows executives who are facing expansion and growth dynamics how to manage that growth and the problems it will always bring.

Growth-related complications—such as weak middle management or an inadequate financial report system—are dealt with realistically and concisely.

Solutions are discussed and are highlighted with checklists, guidelines, sample documents, evaluation forms, and questionnaires. These kinds of items make *Managing Growth* an invaluable resource for the reader.

Managing Growth developed out of the experiences of the co-authors, both of whom have experienced the situations discussed in this book in their own businesses.

Guy Weismantel is a chemical engineer and consultant. Walter Kisling is chairman and CEO of a very successful manufacturing company in St. Louis.

What differentiates this book from previous business books is that it offers concrete benefits: a hands-on approach tailored for executives who are trying to manage and control their growing business while not stunting that growth. *Managing Growth* deals with the everyday problems of growth as well as the strategy of maintaining growth.

In concept and approach, the book is aimed at emerging companies, small companies, and threshold companies who are faced with many problems, failures, and successes that don't fit the big-business approach to solutions. This book covers those "real world" aspects of business for growing companies by means of examples, checklists, and guidelines for firms experiencing metamorphosis.

The book carries chapters of practical, *how to* information using the following chapter format: Business Planning; Getting Good Managers, Developing Them, and Keeping Them; Overcoming Barriers to Communication; Overcoming Barriers to Innovation and Creativity; Financial Survival; Marketing; Managing the New or Emerging Company; Dealing with People Problems and Problem People; Turnarounds; Cashing Out; Relationship Management.

In Chapter 1, *Business Planning: Charting the Course and Leading the Way*, the reader is exposed to goals, planning, and growth. There is specific attention devoted to the mission statement and how to develop one. Checklists and action steps in initiation planning are coupled to integrating short-term planning with strategic planning. Tables and figures cover typical departmental objectives for an emerging company, yearly plans for a business unit, and dynamic developments that match your company to the emerging market.

Chapter 2, *Getting Good Managers, Developing Them, and Keeping Them*, is extremely important to the expanding company. The book points to real examples of hiring philosophy as well as creating the mold for entrepreneurial managers, testing an employee growth potential, and finding hidden talents in your organization.

Chapter 3, *Dealing With People Problems and Problem People*, covers a hiring strategy for emerging companies and how to build an emerging company staff in 6 month time frames. A special look at examples of employee appraisal is included.

In Chapter 4, *Marketing: What It Really Is and How to Do It,* the text goes into detailed due diligence tied to product planning and market research. These are tied to methods of sales that best fit an expanding company, how to rate market research, and how to perform a marketing audit. The ten commandments of competitive analysis play an important part of this chapter.

Chapter 5 covers *Relationship Management: The Key to Customer Satisfaction.* This is an essential aspect to running a new or an expanding company because it tells the reader how to supply a company with both needs and wants. It gives a seven step approach to relationship management covering everything from commitment to action to evaluation. This chapter gives illustrations and checklists on knowing your customer and knowing your customer's key people. It tells how to gauge your Customer Satisfaction Quotient (CSQ) in respect to your own relationship management skills.

Chapter 6 is called, *Financial Survival: You've Got to Be Resilient and Smart.* Besides special problems in budgeting and financing, the chapter defines what you need from accounting and from the weekly management report, and tips on selecting the right bank for your company.

Chapter 7, *Alone at The Helm: Managing the New or Emerging Companies,* deals with special managerial relationships with confidants, advisory boards, and consultants. It expands the breath of exposure into product development and commercialization as well as into international aspects of research and development. In addition, Chapter 9 digs into business diagnostics and paper flow. Checklists include such things as *Choosing An Advisory Board;* and *33 Possible Causes of Trouble In Growth Companies.*

Chapter 8 deals with *Overcoming Barriers to Communication.* Communication is a very important aspect of managing growth in an expanding or emerging company. There are both mechanical and physical barriers. The chapter explains how to meet the meeting problem head on with checklists of how to avoid rehashing old problems. It covers selecting an ad agency and performing a typical employee survey. Real examples are included.

In Chapter 9, *Overcoming Barriers to Innovation and Creativity,* the book deals esoterically with innovation and creativity in an emerging industry. It gives ways to turn on an innovative/creative program and how to manage innovation and creativity.

Chapter 10 on *Turnarounds: How to Get a Growing Company out of Trouble* is vital reading for the old company that is being rejuvenated for expansion as well as for the grass root plants that are involved with start up. Especially important are 25 tricks of the turnaround trade. They cover everything from acquiring a company and joint venturing to dumping problem accounts and using turnaround innovations. The chapter also covers 30 ways to turn a mature company into a growth company.

Chapter 11 on *Cashing Out: Selling the Company and Other Options* provides valuable reading to the family-owned company who wants to sell its assets. The options include partial redemption, an Employee Stock Ownership Plan (ESOP), going public, and other strategic cash-out alternatives. The chapter analyzes the best sale, acquisition or merger point (SAM Point), on one hand, and provides a sample of a work contract on the other. It gives one dozen reasons why businesses sell out, how to separate the buyers from the lookers, and various acquisition odds and milestones.

In conclusion, *Managing Growth* is a handbook and tool for every manager who has bottom-line responsibility. For privately held companies, for managers of small businesses or of large companies, for threshold companies, emerging industries, or old companies experiencing turnarounds, for educators and students, *Managing Growth* offers the information they need to get the job done.

1

Business Planning: Charting the Course and Leading the Way

PLANNING IS AN IMPERFECT SCIENCE, BUT AT THE SAME TIME IT IS THE foundation of success. It is one of the most difficult management functions. It involves a planning process that must be under constant review and with specific yearly objectives.

Some say, planning is the only characteristic in which a good manager should excel. In the list of management traits (plan, organize, staff, direct, control), good planning often undergirds the other functions.

A good planning program begins with a definition of what the company is and what its products are, as well as a definition of its market. Then comes the creation of the strategic plan for the company. The company then develops its operational goals, designed to contribute to succeeding in its strategies and meeting specific business objectives. The individual managers then develop their individual goals to help the company achieve its operational goals. Certain specific steps must be followed (Fig. 1-1).

Without some sort of plan, whether it's in the individual entrepreneur's head or on paper, a business doesn't go anywhere. What makes it even tougher is that psychologists tell us that only 10 percent of people in the world actually plan.

The Seven Planning Steps

1. Determine objectives (long- and short-range).

2. Determine the potential problems connected with each goal and the probable causes of the problems.

3. Design short-range goals (a step-by-step blueprint) to relate directly to the long-range goals.
   a. State each step as a specific goal.
   b. Explain what can be expected in return for the efforts expended.
   c. Show how each short-range goal relates to the long-range goal.
   d. Make a timetable for each step.
   e. Visualize each step. (If needed, mentally role play the activity in a fast-forward mode.)
   f. Generate a need to begin action.
   g. Mobilize yourself mentally.

4. Put it all on paper because:
   a. Writing a plan eliminates the danger of its being changed unconsciously by the passage of time.
   b. Written work can be more easily communicated to an individual personally as well as to others.
   c. Writing a thought is a great aid in remembering the idea.
   d. Writing a plan provides permanent unquestionable records.
   e. Writing a thought helps to recognize the inconsistencies and errors.
   f. Writing the thought allows it to be compared to others and it becomes easier to evaluate.
   g. The process of writing and of clarifying thinking helps to expand the thought and generate new ideas.

5. Organize the Plan. Organization is the process of dividing and matching short-range goals to the time and resources needed to achieve them.
   a. List the work to be accomplished.
   b. Divide the work into units.
   c. Define the goal of each step. Each step must be within the company's ability and should contribute to company goals and objectives.
   d. Set up timetables.
   e. Repeat and constantly review the plan.

6. Teach the plan and disseminate the information to every level of the organization.
   a. Managers should memorize it.
   b. When communicating the plan to employees, use the three-point teaching technique. First, tell them what you are going to tell them. Then tell them. Thirdly, tell them what you told them.
   c. Planning must consider all management functions, namely: plan, organize, staff, direct, and control.

7. Have someone critique the plan.

Fig. 1-1. Steps for planning goals.

BUSINESS REQUIREMENTS PLANNING IN AN EMERGING COMPANY

You can understand this problem as a result of a simple human nature. There are significant time constraints when managing a small or emerging company, so much so that formal planning adds to an already pressurized schedule.

It is not unusual for the manager of a small or emerging business to be sitting in his or her office, late at night and have these questions come to mind:

- Are we going to make it?
- Are we going the right direction?
- Which way are we going?
- How do we know which way to go?

Also, it is not unusual for this manager to be worrying more about how next week's payroll will be paid than about what will be happening ten years from now. Obviously, more than anything else, this manager has to be an optimist, and he or she has to be a survivor.

Planning helps to ensure that survival; however, the managers of an emerging company must be able to modify or change plans quickly because markets or business conditions can be extremely dynamic. With that thought in mind, an emerging company might have an advantage over its larger competitors in that it is flexible. The entrepreneurs who start businesses and make businesses grow are opportunists. Opportunists become that way by quickly taking advantage of a dynamic situation. Sometimes the decision to act itself is not the right one, but the opportunist can capture the moment and modify the decision to be correct and successful.

Being an opportunist, however, does not eliminate the need for planning. There is an old adage that "proper prior planning prevents poor performance." This slogan should be stamped on the forehead of every manager in an emerging company so that they see it each time they look in a mirror.

That reflection should be complemented, however, with good planning data. There is a rule of thumb that is extremely effective in setting any type of goal for your enterprise. The rule is to use three periods of history for each period you want to plan or forecast into the future.

Right away you can see a problem evolving. Some new or emerging companies don't have three meaningful periods of historical data. So, the emerging company, if it follows this rule, probably will encounter some problems in forecasting. New companies have ever-changing accounting and/or sales data. Furthermore, in some companies' records and documentation for past periods are incomplete, inconsistent, or (even worse) nonexistent. Depending on what is available, however, the manager must still act, and, in the process, he or she must develop a good set of objectives and goals for the accounting department so that data will be available for future planning cycles. Planning always requires good accounting information (Fig. 1-2).

Fig. 1-2. Planning requires good input data and communication.

In a small company, the information manager might also carry the title of president or general manager, i.e., a key manager wears the "communications" hat when considering the yearly business plan.

Marketing provides the first input to the plan so that the organization—whether service or manufacturing—can create the support needed to fulfill marketing objectives.

Financial needs must be evaluated in terms of priorities and availability of funds. Monthly reports should provide data comparisons for each account number in terms of budget vs. actual. These reports should also have a year-to-date summary. *Note*: In a small business, the key considerations in cash flow, cost-accounting, detailed reports, and budgeting become more crucial as a firm grows. Below sales of $200,000 annually, cash flow becomes a focal point of the Chief Executive Officer (CEO).

In manufacturing, materials planning is performed in concert with purchasing, especially when just-in-time (JIT) ordering is involved. In a service industry, timing is even more crucial. If a service industry cannot provide the service due to lack of parts, lack of personnel, or lack of anything, the order often goes to the competition.

Modern organizations often eliminate paperwork by relying on computer workstations for handling information. (This carries over even into placing orders at the local hamburger franchise.) In such an atmosphere, the data is handled on a central computer that provides easy access from several workstations. Programs should provide easy access by the CEO from the computer workstation in his or her office. Small businesses need this very much also, but it often requires too much capital and programming time to install and/or become user-friendly. However, it is not unusual for firms whose sales are as little as $200,000 annually to go to some form of central data bank with multiple access ports.

INITIATING THE PLANNING PROCESS

A plan is personal and individualistic, but sometimes an overriding theme within a company jumps out at you. That theme becomes the basis for building a strategic plan. Sometimes this theme is so dominant it cannot be ignored. For example, the president of a company with $22 million in sales and negative net worth was facing the problem of keeping the doors open. He sat down with the chairman of the board and developed ''The Strategy for Survival.''

After the company had weathered the survival storm for two years, the executives developed ''The Plan for Recovery'' and finally, ''The Plan for Growth.'' Each plan was made up of a series of action steps. These action steps included:

- Strategic planning
- Gathering information
- Reevaluating the plan
- Creating a mission statement
- Planning the action course
- Planning qualities
- Providing leadership
- Detailing the business plan
- Identifying individual/specific goals

Strategic Planning Action

Although a strategic theme might not be absolutely necessary, it does communicate to the people who work for you what the company's priorities are and where they (and the company) are going. If the theme is in writing, it jumps off the page to work for you and employees can more easily grasp the goals. To reach this point, you must analyze and understand what the driving forces are that make the company go. To some degree this is company culture.

Driving forces are the accomplishments that really motivate a chief executive and the top management group to achieve greater goals. Examples of driving forces include increasing income levels, increasing sales volumes, introducing new products, growing by acquisition, improving productivity, increasing inventory turns, and building new headquarters.

If the company is publicly owned, increasing dividends or stock prices might be what really enables the company to go. If it is an engineering-oriented company, the product-development and cost-reduction processes may be the buzz word for top management team to run.

If the CEO's background is finance, the driving force might be greater utilization and application of assets, management of receivables and inventories, and leveraging of bank debt, to name a few. Certainly then, the emerging company calls out for a balanced theme despite the background of the key executives. However, if you are at a subordinate level and charged with planning, it would be corporate suicide to try to deter the main driving force of the CEO.

The Strategic Planning Meeting

Once your company selects a theme and identifies the driving forces, it is probably ready to have its first strategic planning meeting. This is probably best accomplished away from the office.

If you can afford it, take your group to a resort or a conference center. If you can't, see if you can borrow a friend's condominium for a day.

Some managers don't believe in taking people away from the office to initiate a strategic planning session. Indeed this can be expensive, but it need not be. Although a resort atmosphere has its pros and cons, even a local hotel or other facility enables planners to isolate themselves.

A company with about $10 million in sales can typically take 14 people to a resort. This enables the group to mix a little recreation with the work. The top management will have to work hard during this planning meeting (and prior to the meeting to prepare for it), but you will find that middle and lower managers will really enjoy it. People enjoy being in on the ground floor of a company's future. They enjoy being part of a process like this one.

As a hint, be sure to get all the work done before the drinking starts. On one occasion a planning team stayed up so late one night they were too bleary-eyed the next morning to make their report. Similarly, planning for long working sessions after dinner is a mistake. If a restaurant is slow, or can't handle the group promptly, evening sessions accomplish very little.

Assuming you are having a two-day, one-night planning session, the following agenda makes sense:

1. Arrive before lunch and have a few introductory remarks by the chief executive officer, chief operating officer (COO), and the facilitator (if you have one).
2. After lunch break into separate brainstorming groups. Use groups of from five to seven people. In each group try to have people from a variety of disciplines and management levels.
3. The participants should be told in advance to address the following questions one at a time:

   - What are the corporate strengths?
   - What are the corporate weaknesses?
   - What is the company's business?
   - What do they do best?

- What is the company's market?
- What are the company's products?

4. After the groups address one question for a period of time, reconvene and list on a flip chart or blackboard what each group determined.

5. Reorganize the groups, again trying to maintain the balance of perhaps one officer in each group and one person from each discipline. (The organization of the groups should have been done in advance so that the establishment of the groups at the meeting is a simple task.)

6. Announce that at the first session the next morning the combined groups will address how to capitalize on the strengths and overcome the weaknesses. A secretary and a presenter should be in each group, established in advance.

7. The second day you review all the previous day's conclusions and have someone act as secretary to take notes, which are distributed after the meeting to all the participants.

You should try to use the strategic planning process as a tool to get the people in your organization from various departments working together to solve a common problem. If you are holding your meeting at a place that has some recreation facilities, it is a good opportunity to possibly break down some barriers between departments. Arrange your tennis groupings or golf foursomes so that people who perhaps don't get along very well at the office have a chance to play together and have their meals together.

Gathering Information

At some time in the future, your planning team will have to reassemble to reevaluate the result of their strategic planning session. Before that second planning meeting takes place, you will want to gather some historical data on sales by product line, profitability of product lines, inventory turns, market share, or whatever other statistics you feel are important. The president should be a believer in the theory that you should have three periods of history to examine for every one period you want to plan into the future.

If you feel your business can be compared with similar businesses, you might want to compile information on your competition. There are sources for these kinds of statistics and data including industrial and retail associations and marketing organizations. All this information should be distributed to attendees before the next meeting.

Reevaluation

Conduct a second meeting similar to the first. Break the planning team into brainstorming groups again. This time analyze the following type of questions:

- Why isn't your market share greater?
- Why isn't your profitability on certain products greater?
- Should you even be handling certain products considering sales volume and profitability?
- Should you drop some product lines?
- Are there other similar things to what you are doing well that you could be doing that you are not?
- Are there some things you are doing which are really inconsistent with what you have defined your business to be?

Again on the second day, review the results of the brainstorming sessions of the first day.

Mission Statements

Armed with the reams of information you have now derived from the first two meetings, management will begin to see what they should be doing and where they are going. The top management group should now begin to try to develop a mission statement. The preparation of a succinct mission statement that can fit on an $8^{1}/_{2}$-×-11-inch piece of paper is one major task that must be accomplished. When done, people are so proud of it that they often have it professionally printed, enlarged, framed, and hung in the lobby of each major business unit. Mission statements can be used in advertising and financial statements, and portions can be extracted to develop employee slogans and banners hung in the plant.

The mission statement (Fig. 1-3) should be agreed upon by all those participating in the planning meetings. The mission statement will meld all of the group together in a cohesive team that knows who they are and where they are going. The mission statement will also alleviate the need to redo again at a later day most of what was done in the first two meetings.

The company developing a mission statement for the first time may need some guidelines regarding what questions to consider (Fig. 1-4). The CEO should provide the initial guidance in this area to ensure that executives believe as he or she does. Initial input should come from the board of directors, if there is one.

Can one firm use another's mission statement? Rarely. That takes away the whole purpose of establishing a mission statement. The mission statement has to be developed the hard way because it applies only to your company. Once you have gone through this process and have a mission statement to refer to, it saves a great deal of time and trouble in developing policies and procedures or having to repeat an arduous strengths and weakness analysis. It is important, however, that top managers periodically explore the possibilities of any new significant strengths or weaknesses in your organization that need to be addressed.

Towards EXCELLENCE

PURPOSE

Multiplex's purpose is to continue to succeed and grow as a viable company through the constant attention to our customers' needs; our business is the satisfaction of customers through the marketing of beverage dispensing products manufactured to our strict specifications. Multiplex's products are sophisticated, unique in quality and design, and require the utilization of diverse manufacturing technology and processes.

MARKET

Multiplex's market is the discriminating customer interested in quality, delivery and service, both before and after the sale. Our market place is international and serves both industry and government.

MANAGEMENT

Multiplex's reputation has been achieved through dedication to a management system built around our greatest asset — our people. Multiplex's management system provides for:

1. Opportunities for ambitious people motivated by personal and corporate achievements, and the continuing challenges of the future.

2. Opportunities to contribute to the total management of the company through both formal and informal sharing of ideas.

3. A clear direction for individuals through Management By Objectives which provides understanding and the challenge to achieve predetermined goals.

4. Opportunities for personal recognition and self-satisfaction through the ability to measure progress toward goals, to correct deficiencies and to achieve results.

5. Opportunities to contribute within an organized structure without restrictions.

6. Personal and career growth through company sponsored education and career counseling.

7. A dedication to promotion from within wherever and whenever possible.

8. Opportunities for decision-making at all levels without abdication by Management.

9. Competitive salaries and monetary recognition for exceptional performance.

OWNERSHIP

Multiplex is a family-owned company. Since 1928 the family's companies have had a proud tradition of quality. The foundation of that tradition is our desire to listen to the customers' requests and to satisfy their needs. The owners of the company are primarily interested in corporate growth, together with viability. They feel that viability is maintained and the management system is perpetuated by growth through diversification. We continue to review corporate and product acquisition opportunities as well as new markets. The company aggressively funds research and development programs.

FACILITIES

The owners and all employees contribute to continued improvement of working conditions. Multiplex places the highest priority on safety. Continued facilities improvement will be funded through the reinvestment of depreciation and amortization, as well as through additional capital investment.

RESPONSIBILITY

Multiplex recognizes its responsibility to its employees, its customers, its suppliers and the community. The company actively supports charity and community projects. We encourage our employees to participate in civic and/or cultural activities, to become registered voters, and to make their wishes known to their elected representatives of government.

Fig. 1-3. A mission statement.

☞   What is our business?

☞   What are our products (now and in the future)?

☞   What is our market (geographically and by industry)?

☞   How do we set goals?

☞   How are people rewarded?

☞   How do our people participate in running the business?

☞   What are our stockholders objectives?

☞   What is our philosophy on reinvesting in the business?

☞   What are our responsibilities to the employees and to the community?

Fig. 1-4. A checklist for a mission statement (courtesy Multiplex).

Why is a mission statement needed? Because it succinctly summarizes the goals and the future of the company.

Other Operational Objectives

Although the discussion thus far has been on how to establish a strategic plan, there are some by-products of the process which will become evident. In an emerging company the corporate staff will probably find that they had some problems gathering the information needed for their second meeting. They will find weaknesses, inconsistencies, or incompletion in their records and documentation. Even worse, they might find that some of what you need for planning the business doesn't exist, and obviously you won't have three periods of history. These shortcomings should be documented, for it is the beginning of some operational objectives for the people and the departments responsible.

The Planning Course

It is now time for the chief executive officer to take what has been created in the first two meetings together with the mission statement and begin to develop a strategic plan in terms of where to go with the business and how to get there. Eventually this filters down into short-term objectives (Fig. 1-5). Before we begin to formulate a plan, it is important to examine some definitions and have an understanding of planning terminology. The word *strategy* comes from the Greek stratēgia generalship. It refers to the art of devising plans or stratagems to meet a goal.

A strategic plan and a long-range plan are similar. The strategic plan is more likely to plot the direction in which the company is going. The long-range plan might include some operational objectives, which are more likely to take longer than a year's term.

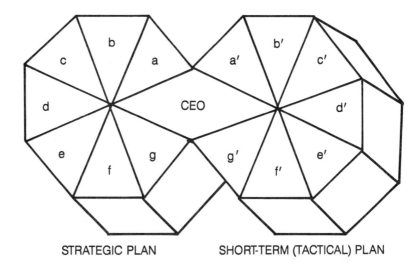

STRATEGIC PLAN   SHORT-TERM (TACTICAL) PLAN

a. Return On Investment (ROI) goals as designated by board of directors to provide return to stockholders
a'. Yearly sales, marketing, and cash flow objectives
b. Corporate growth goals
b'. Key account goals
c. Operational goals
c'. Productivity objectives
d. Relationship management objectives
d'. Customer satisfaction
e. Mission statement
e'. Meet personal and company yearly objectives
f. Community goals
f'. Public relations (PR) plan
g. Human resources and salary objectives
g'. Hiring goals, raises, and bonuses

Fig. 1-5. Integrating short-term planning with strategic planning.

Tactical plans are the steps taken to achieve the strategic or long-range plans. These differ from "ongoing" plans that are operational or business plans. They include such things as sales forecasts and budgetary objectives, and are generally for the period of the fiscal year. Short-range plans can be included in the operational or business plan but might last for a period of less than a year.

The chief executive officer's responsibility is the strategic thinking and strategic planning for the enterprise. His or her responsibility is to be constantly aware of what is going on in the environment outside of the company that can affect the company either positively or adversely. There is the responsibility of preserving the equity of the corporation. The CEO needs to protect the company from any outside forces, whether it is dependence on one customer or customer group, the effect of increasing interest rates, or the threat of product liability suits.

Planning Review

Strategic objectives as well as operational objectives or individual goals should be simple, consistent, measurable, and achievable. The strategic objectives should possess one other quality. They should be confidential. They should be on a "need-to-know" basis. After all, by definition they are established to take advantage of opportunities. You therefore would not want to provide your competition with your strategy.

The strategic objectives should be simple and concise. They should be tied into your theme as well as to the mission statement you have written. You could have as few as five but probably no more than eight strategic objectives. It should be easily memorized. As you communicate your objectives to your management team, they will pick up the theme and recall the mission statement. Terminology from the mission statement should be utilized periodically in your advertising, company newsletters, and talks with your employees. In so doing, the employees will pick up on the culture of the business, its purpose for being in business, and its objectives.

Since the strategic objectives are normally for 3 to 5 years, there should not be any significant changes unless, of course, a strategic objective is achieved. Companies therefore should adjust only to one or two of their strategic objectives each year to maintain that consistency and continuance.

In summary, then, strategic planning is the responsibility of the highest level of management. The mission statement is a condensation of the basic questions of who and what the company is. All questions do not have clear-cut perfect answers. If they did, you could control the future. In strategic planning, you want to control what you can and plan reactions for events that you can't control. The CEO's responsibility is to see that the company doesn't apply a strategy that endangers the company. Everyone will not plan equally or as enthusiastically.

The success of the strategic plan is often the result of the team effort in achieving the goals in the company's mission statement. The success of short-term tactical plans is directly related to early constructive feedback when agreed upon goals are not met.

Providing Leadership

The chief executive officer through action and communication wants to create "a sense of urgency." A sense of urgency is a drive to get it done. The people in the organization who plan their work and work their plans are the leaders. Obviously, more than anything else, the CEO has to be a positive, optimistic leader.

In the emerging company, the dominant characteristic is leadership by example. After all, it is the CEO who is responsible for the company. He or she is the one the employees look up to and, hopefully, respect.

To make the company go, the CEO cannot undersell him or herself. The company will only be as good as the boss thinks it is. In the emerging company it is the CEO who has made the total commitment, and when the company emerges, employees are more likely to do as the CEO does than as he or she says. If the employee knows that the boss comes early and stays late, the company is not likely to have a tardiness problem.

If the boss usually doesn't take the vacation he or she has coming, you can expect there will be few exceptions by the employees to the vacation policy. (This is an example and not a recommendation that the CEO not take a vacation.)

If the boss projects an image of warmth and professionalism, the employees will likely follow the example. If the boss wants the company to be sophisticated, it will be if the boss acts sophisticated.

The strength of our country is our democratic way of ruling. A corporation, however, is not a democracy. An emerging company cannot manage by committee. There are too many demands for the time of the leaders of an emerging company. Too many decisions need to be made, and right or wrong, the CEO is going to make those decisions.

It is the CEO, the leader of the emerging company, armed with the mission statement and a strategic plan who must develop an attitude within the company that "proper planning prevents poor performance." The CEO wants all of the operational employees to understand that that phrase is a part of the culture of the company.

The Business Plan

The next step in the planning process is for the chief operating officer, working with his or her staff, to develop the business plan or the operational plan for the year. These steps will be taken during the ensuing fiscal period to contribute to the ultimate success of the strategic plan.

Sales Forecast. The first step in establishing an operational plan is a sales forecast. This is the most difficult, but the most important, step in the operational plan. If the driving force within the company is marketing and/or growth, the sales forecast will be optimistic. The CEO and the COO had better monitor that sales forecast, applying experience as well as knowledge of the economic and industrial environment. But they need to do it in such a way as not to dampen the enthusiasm of the sales force.

In relating the sales forecast to the economy, the top management needs to understand whether their business leads or trails their industry and the general economy. They need to do a micro-economic analysis of what is happening in each of their market segments. Using historical data, the past year's sales must be analyzed to determine seasonality of sales during the year. If sales forecasting was easy, the multibillion-dollar automobile companies would not periodically end up with acres and acres of unsold automobiles.

Departmental Objectives. When a marketing and sales forecast is done, it is time for the chief operating officer, with his or her staff, to start establishing the individual departments' objectives.

There are many, many fundamental operational type goals that a company can establish (Table 1-1). Whatever the goals are, they should be stretching but achievable, measurable but above all clear and concise. They should fit onto one piece of $8^1/_2$-$\times$-11 paper.

Table 1-1. Typical Departmental Objectives for an Emerging Company.

Financial/Accounting	Production/Personnel	Sales/Service	Profitability
To reduce bank borrowing to a certain level.	To increase productivity—i.e., sales per employee to a certain level.	To complete the design, field testing, or introduction of a product by target dates.	To achieve a given level of profit.
To maintain Accounts Receivable at certain days outstanding.	To have some significant accomplishment completed by a certain date—i.e., the installation of a new computer, a news accounting systems, etc.	To improve customer service to a given level.	
	To hire a key individual in a position by a certain date.	To reduce customer complaints to a certain level.	
	To increase inventory turns to a certain level.	To achieve sales levels.	
			To achieve a safety goal in terms of accident frequency or severity rate.

As with the strategic goals, operational goals should be consistent from one year to the next. That way the staff begins to understand what is important to the company's success as well as what they are being measured and evaluated on—what is expected of them.

Unlike the strategic goals, the operational goals or yearly business plan should be printed, distributed, and communicated to all levels of management. It is from these operational goals that individual managers should prepare their individual goals. For a company undergoing dynamic growth, a typical document can be about 15 pages in length for a business unit doing $10 million per year in revenues.

Yearly Plans for a Business Unit* of an Emerging Company
Selling Pollution Control Equipment
(Summary of Yearly Objectives For Business Unit #1)

POLICY STATEMENT FOR THIS BUSINESS UNIT

To provide product services for commercial, industrial, and municipal use to control the water pollution. To be aware of existing and planned governmental regulations related to health and safety and how these existing or prospective regulations will affect our business objectives. This includes:

- Analyzing waste water permit applications.
- Consulting support.
- Assessing performance for key accounts.
- Monitoring new technology.
- Analyzing technically our products vs. the competition.
- Assessing technical/legal support.
- Continuing regulatory analysis.
- Setting standards to monitor and grade business activity.

BUSINESS UNIT GOALS FOR 1989

Identify and evaluate emerging markets for pumps and other fluid flow equipment.

Increase and maintain profitability by:

a. Bettering project management
b. Focusing marketing resources
c. Controlling overhead expenses
d. Reducing raw material costs.

---

*A "business unit" can be a division of a company or simply an *ad hoc* organizational structure for profitability and accounting purposes.

Increase revenues in real terms by capitalizing on company reputation and market position in several key areas. Be certain to identify the key area using specific market criteria.

ANALYSIS OF INTERNAL FACTORS

Strengths

- National reputation as leading pump manufacturer.
- Currently have 24 percent market share.
- Have broad support capabilities to sales.
- Have 14 regional offices.

- Provide services in:

  - Environmental area.
  - Handling hazardous material.
  - Dumps are widely accepted in the process industries, particularly those that will spend money in 1989.
  - Can provide pumps for power and utilities industry.
  - Government accepts our hardware and technology.

Weaknesses

- Poor communication with sales reps.
- Staff is getting old.

- Poor "cross-over" marketing increases sales expense.
- No engineering capability in sewage.
- Don't have experience in certain emerging markets.

Measurement Methods

- Check Recognition Rankings by using reports put out by *Chemical Engineering* Magazine.
- Check Market Share from Valve Manufacturing Association (VMA) reports.
- Develop and use relationship management scoring system to measure customer satisfaction.
- Prepare continuing education program in each area of weakness; send personnel to classes and have instructors report on before-and-after performance.
- Use consulting services to measure performance.

COMPARING EXTERNAL FACTORS

Opportunities	*Threats*

- Pump meets new ASME spec.

- Pump has very low emissions when used on organic liquids.
- Firms are turning to low maintenance hardware which we sell.
- Biotech processes must turn to this pump technology.

- New competition is expected from both U.S. and foreign competition.

- Capital expansion in our traditional industry sectors is limited.
- Energy prices introduces uncertainty in sales.
- Continued increased competition by small specialty firms in niche markets erode out high profit products.
- Market is volatile.
- Potential for legal entanglements with new pump introduction.

ASSUMPTION FOR 1989 PLAN

1. Economic conditions will remain in *status quo* so that new facilities in our traditional market industries will be limited.
2. California will pass regulations that will enhance sales of our units.
3. Municipal cuts in funding will not eliminate our accessibility to redesign engineering firms and to traditional government sector clients.
4. New grass roots plant is planned by our key customer.
5. Markets will grow in area where we are currently not selling.
6. Cost competition from large and small competitors will continue as a major problem.

1988 PERFORMANCE RECORD

- Had $10 million in sales.
- Had 8 percent before taxes.
- Had $10 million backlog at year's end.
- Had $9 million in proposals outstanding.
- Had 841 proposals were written and company received orders for 18 percent of those.
- Business unit made significant additions to its asset base.

BUSINESS UNIT SHORT-TERM OBJECTIVES

1. Revenue goals:
   1989: $12 million
   1990: $14 million
   1991: $17 million
   1992: $20 million
   1993: $25 million
2. Expand annual revenues and number of projects of this business unit in the power industry to 20.
3. Produce at least eight before income on revenues through 1993.
4. Produce $2.6 million revenue from new model pump in 1989.
5. Reduce number of proposals written and increase hit rate to 22 percent.
6. Initiate research and development project on pump to meet new emergency response requirements for chlorine.
7. Produce at least $2 million in 1989 in pumps for pollution control use.

NOTE: Do not list objectives that are inconsistent with the basic charter or mission statement of the enterprise.

RESOURCE REQUIREMENTS

Hardware needed:
- IBM PC/XT
- Additional Coatings Line

Staff additions:
- Six to eight chemical/mechanical engineers
- One additional computer programmer
- Power pump specialist for sales & service

Advertising and PR Program: $60,000

STRATEGIES FOR ACHIEVING SHORT-TERM OBJECTIVES

Objective	Strategy	Responsibility	Secondary Support
Produce $2.6 million in revenue from new model pump	Coordinate marketing effort to identify and follow up all bingo card leads in states, and initiate direct mail program with cooperation of sales reps.	C.J. Black	M.J. Lackey C.J. Ashbaugh
	Identify and implement new key accounts and assign key salesperson to these accounts to develop relationship management program.	C.J. Black	J.P. Powell M.G. Donald
Reduce number of proposals written and increase hit rate (winning based on value) to at least 22 percent	Analyze factors contributing to 1988 experience and change accordingly.	C.J. Black	M.R. Fleece
	Implement corrective improvements through policy development.	D.A. Beaumont	M.J. Smith
Initiate R&D project on new pump to meet EPA's emergency response requirements	Conduct screening and situational analysis of this market.	N.G. Gregory	D.A. Jones P.J. McCarthy
	Identify design improvements needed and assign responsibility for achieving them.	N.G. Gregory	R.D. Jones R.M. Bones

ADDITIONAL STRATEGIES FOR ACHIEVING FINANCIAL OBJECTIVES

Strategy	Primary Responsibility	Secondary Support
Establish contacts with current accounts in new sales territories.	R.N. Hoosier	M.R. Fleece J.M. Rose
Maintain/establish contacts with existing reps.	J.D. Road	W.R. Miller J.M. Rose
Identify key decision-makers in new target markets and plan and implement a marketing program.	R.N. Hoosier	M.R. Fleece J.B. Fisher
Explore opportunities for increased business unit support for overseas sales.	J.D. Road	W.R. Miller P.N. Knight
Renew contacts in governmental agencies in Washington, D.C.	P.N. Knight	R.L. Leo
Develop and implement plan for improved inter-office communication to duplicate sales made by one rep	R.L. Leo	M.D. Daniel N.J. Joseph
Write and implement a plan to pursue applications in the power industry	N.J. Joseph	M.D. Daniel

Individual Goals. An emerging company must pay close attention to the individual goals of its key employees to ensure they will stay contentedly with the company and grow with it. The individual goals should possess the same general qualities as the operational—i.e., stretching but achievable, measurable, consistent, and concise. Individual goals can and should include goals of a personal nature, such as promoting an understudy, completing an education course, and perhaps even changing a personality trait, i.e., to be more tolerant to those who answer to me or to have more empathy. The individual goals should be, for the most part, confidential between the employee and the supervisor.

The individual goals at the least should be a commitment from the individual manager that his or her department will do what is expected to achieve the operational objectives.

It is more important with individual goals than operational goals to be brief and concise. An individual should not have more than six or seven goals. For some reason a Management By Objectives (MBO) program for the goals of individuals always tends to get longer and more involved. If you are not careful, people's goals will become so complex that they won't remember the goals themselves. Some business plans for small companies are so large that they require loose-leaf binders. Who is going to remember in 3 months what is in it?

Try to avoid the MBO process that places a lot of issues and objectives down on paper, but do not tie them in with short-term and long-term goals.

Constant management of individual and corporate goals is crucial. It is management's responsibility to see that the achievement or failure to achieve an individual or corporate goal does not have a negative effect on the motivation of other people who might be affected by another's failure.

It is also important to see that changing situations and conditions or emergencies within the company do not have an effect on an individual's ability to achieve his or her goal. If this occurs, the goal, of course, must be changed.

It is also important that the individual have as much control as possible over the achievement of a goal. If an employee doesn't have total control over its achievement, the individual must be instructed to appraise the supervisor of problems he or she is having and the importance of correcting these problems. People can become pretty creative in terms of why they did not achieve their goals when it gets to the end of the year and bonus time.

Summary

To summarize this section on "Initiating the Planning Process," one should ask: What makes all these ideas, concepts, goals, and actions different in a small or emerging company vs. other businesses?"

- Much of the original planning efforts have to be done without background information.
- The effort is hampered by lack of people.
- The people involved in the effort are already overloaded.
- The changes taking place in business are often dynamic.
- The business is probably financially constrained.

The following section discusses ways to include and to overcome these problems as part of the planning process.

PLANNING THE METAMORPHOSIS FOR AN EMERGING COMPANY

The manager of a small or emerging company should *plan* before executing and *think* before planning. In many fast-growth situations (or in situations where a firm is simply trying to keep its head above water), managers are often reacting rather than acting toward a specific goal. Surprisingly, firms can continue to move in the right direction although totally out of control. It is not unusual in these situations to have one phone call after another that creates a new fire which must be put out or creates a new opportunity. We can avoid much of this trauma by planning—but first you must understand what is happening to you and your company. This is imperative if you expect to identify and to act to solve today's and tomorrow's problems, maintain profitability, and avoid staff turnovers.

Table 1-2. Four Stages of a Growth Cycle.

	I	II	III	IV
Number of Employees	1 to 2	6 to 15	15 to 50	50 to 100
Sales ($)	±$192,000	300,000 to 1,000,000	1,000,000 to 2,500,000	2,500,000 to 5,000,000
Company Structure	Usually a single proprietorship with support from family or outside services. Often carries "and associates" in title with associates being on call but paid on project basis.	Single proprietorship or partnership operating as a DBA (doing business as) or a corporation, often a Subchapter "S." Often a professional organization.	Partnership or corporation with some employees having limited ownership and profit-sharing. Family usually involved in running the business and in key management positions.	Usually a corporation (often public) having broader ownership that often extends outside the family. Some stock options available.
Ownership Structure	Family; organized and divided in a way to provide best tax benefits and cash flow.	Family with or without some investors; are close personally or in other business ventures.	Majority often owned by a few individuals. Initially tied to professional specialities (sales, finance, production). Organization has departmentalization.	Levels of management, to as many as 4. Professional management is hired and held accountable.
Management	Autocratic	Depends on owners' personalities. If one person has control, he or she can pretty much do what they want. Management may	Less control by a single individual. When families are involved, squabbles begin to occur, particularly in second-plus generations.	Ownership and management are often separate. MBO becomes important, as does accountability and

		appear systematic people-related, but owner still calls the shots.	Professional management is required but not always hired.	formalized departments. Policies and procedures become necessary.
Personnel	Family support, or use outside services from typing to legal.	Contract for legal and accounting services; need secretarial assistance; Rep support for sales.	Department heads are hired for key business functions such as finance and production.	Management of staff principles apply.
Pluses	Total flexibility to do what one wants to do and answers only to his or herself. Can get family involved. Has some tax advantages and, in some instances, can create own hours.	Size enables quick response to problems; in growth mode, new positions and responsibility appear.	Offers more chances for promotion; better security; more chance of financial success.	Move to professional management fosters opportunity and better return on investment; more opportunity for personal growth and business challenges.
Minuses	Individual is often alone—emotionally and physically. Has no one to bounce ideas off of, nor can family or associates appreciate the work load that must be handled. Often cash poor and credit hungry when business gets started. Problem of selling and doing the work, both.	Size can limit opportunity; morale is tied to personality of boss; limited access to technology and market. Firm is still sensitive to cash flow.	Communication problems increase; family-family and family-employee interface becomes critical with conflicts occurring. Employee morale problems surface.	Begins to develop some of the problems of larger businesses including that of overhead and increased costs of administration, morale, public relations, (internal and external). Conflicting management styles appear.

Growth: What Is It?

To manage the emerging company, you must understand the growth cycle and where you are in it (Table 1-2). Some things should be obvious, but one must be reminded of the obvious.

For example, in a single proprietorship in the field of consulting, or more specifically, a one-person office, billings are limited to about $192,000. How do you come up with that figure? First, you work 20 days a month and bill for 8 hours a day at $100 per hour. This gives $16,000 per month, or $192,000 per year.

Of course, many people cannot bill for every hour while others can bill more. You can play with these numbers, any way you want to move them up or down. And, for a very specialized service, we recognize that some fees are worth the price.

So, how does one get above the $192,000 boggie sales goal? You can increase daily rates charged to clients or you can grow in size by hiring more people. Growth implies that you have or are experiencing one or more of a dozen dynamic developments. They are:

1. Have a unique product that cannot be duplicated.
2. Provide a quality service or unique capability.
3. Have targeted and are part of a new or emerging market.
4. Have built a reputation that is expanding.
5. Are part of an economic boom.
6. Are tied to a governmental regulation that requires action.
7. Have initiated new marketing techniques:

   - Gone into exports.
   - Broadened sales effort geographically.
   - Hired an aggressive sales manager.
   - Added nationwide distributors.

8. Have referrals and repeat business beginning to pay off.
9. Are growing through an acquisition or merger.
10. Have improved your staff.
11. Have improved your management practices.
12. Have initiated a strong advertising and public relations program.

Of these dozen, being a part of an emerging market might be the most important. You can become a part of this market, by luck or by design through strategic planning, a facet of planning we have already discussed.

SMALL BUSINESS, BIG JOB GROWTH

In 1979, David L. Birch of the Massachusetts Institute of Technology published pioneering research on the structure of job generation process. Birch relied on a data file known as Dun's Market Identifier file (DMI) from Dun and Bradstreet. This database contained information on 5.6 million business establishments at four different points in time—1969, 1972, 1974, and 1976. From this source he was able to define and measure for each firm the processes by which change takes place, with emphasis on new formation, expansions, contractions, dissolutions, and movements. By aggregating firms at any given location, he was able to describe in considerable detail how economic change occurs in that location.

The results of this research were startling. Among the major findings were the following:

- Most of the variation in job growth among states and areas is due to differences in the rate of job generation (i.e., births and expansion of firms), not to differences in rates of job loss (i.e., deaths and contractions).

- Virtually no firms migrate from one area to another in the sense of physically relocating their operations. Branching, however, is quite important, particularly in manufacturing. It is differential branching, not physical migration, that causes many of the regional differences in job growth.

- The components of job change are sensitive to the business cycle. For most states, births and expansion of firms were fewer and deaths and contractions were more numerous during an economic downturn than during a preceeding upturn.

- Small firms, defined as those with 20 or fewer employees, generated 66 percent of all new jobs in the country during the early seventies. Middle-sized and large firms, on balance, provided few new jobs in relation to their size.

- On a regional basis, small firms generated all the net new jobs in the Northeast, 67 percent in the Midwest, 60 percent in the West, and 54 percent in the South.

Birch concluded, "The job generating firm tends to be small. It tends to be dynamic (or unstable, depending on your viewpoint)—the kind of firm that banks feel very uncomfortable about. It tends to be young."

From: "After Big Gains, Challenges for Small Business," Eleanor H. Erdevig, Chicago Fed Letter (March 1989): 1–3. Courtesy Federal Reserve Bank of Chicago.

Growth and Emerging Companies

There have been some startling findings regarding companies' growth. Although we hear of giants in employment, most job-generating firms tend to be small and dynamic—even unstable. These are the companies that are financially insecure. When you consider that emerging companies are quite often small companies in a growth cycle, top executive planning must pay attention to both short-term and long-term objectives. Here the value of the CEO gains importance. Strategic objectives, operational objectives, or individual goals should be simple, consistent, measurable, and achievable. A small error at the beginning puts you way off target in the future.

- On a regional basis, small firms generated all the net new jobs in the Northeast, 67 percent in the Midwest, 60 percent in the West, and 54 percent in the South.

Birch concluded, "The job generating firm tends to be small. It tends to be dynamic (or unstable, depending on your viewpoint)—the kind of firm that banks feel very uncomfortable about. It tends to be young."

Planning to Avoid a Depressed Industry

Who are today's hot growth companies? They are identified each year in *Business Week, INC Magazine, Fortune,* and other publications. Most of these emerging companies are firms with sales of under $150 million but with the honest potential for superior performance and return on capital investment. These range from retailers, who have been in and out of bankruptcy, to those offering infertility services and sperm banks. Today, in categorizing growth companies, we find them in the environmental area, computer-related activities, and services.

A creative manager will be able to identify a growth area before the news appears in print. The methodology of doing so involves using consultants, monitoring "mentions" of developing technology, assigning the task to a "futures" manager, or using Delphi techniques.

Looking, then, at depressed industries, in the early '80s many of them were hardware-oriented. The U.S. lost out to European and Japanese competitors. This is not to say firms on the downside of the bell curve are in a hopeless market, but the U.S. had simply fallen behind technologically in areas from plastic extruders to textile machinery, and the value of the dollar favored imports. In other industries such as shrimp growing or specialty chemicals, many consider overseas locations to avoid governmental red tape—often related to environmental constraints in the U.S.

The best way to be part of those growth markets is to identify them (using your own people or outside consultants) in advance and to *match your company to the market* (Fig. 1-6).

1. Determine for your company:
   - Strengths
   - Weaknesses
   - Where we are
   - Where we want to go
   - How we get there
   - Who will do the work
   - What our business is
   - What we do best

2. Formulate a mission statement tied to the emerging market you identify.

3. Set no more than seven strategic goals tied to the emerging market. In small companies and growing firms, strategic goals are usually confidential and not widely distributed. Managers can memorize and focus on seven goals without difficulty. (In large companies strategic goals are not confidential, but are the basis for teamwork and are distributed orderly.)

4. Formulate a yearly business plan aimed at the emerging market.
9/1	Strategic goals annually reviewed.
9/8	Additional personnel needs determined.
9/15	Sales forecast for year beginning 1/1/89 developed.
9/15	Cost center worksheets distributed.
9/15	Operational objectives for year distributed.
9/21	Personnel requests returned with job description.
10/15	Cost center budgets returned to finance.
10/15	Finance completed its forecast.
10/15	Management by objective (MBO) goals due by individuals.
11/7	Cost center budget requests due.
12/12	Management by objective (MBO) goals finalized.
12/22	Budget is printed and distributed.

Fig. 1-6. Match your company to the emerging market.

A key part of that endeavor is to *selectively choose your key accounts* and identify their needs and wants. (You do business with your friends.) Getting and holding business in an emerging industry demands that a company supply not only basic hardware or services, but all the other wants of the client that can only be gained by a close relationship management. It is surprising how many firms do not have specific target markets, target objectives, key account objectives, and money targets related to key accounts.

SUCCESSION PLANNING

This very crucial portion of the chapter has intentionally been left to the end. The principles and the values used for succession planning are foreign to the remainder of this chapter if your company is privately owned. Many of the considerations in succession planning are derived from estate planning.

The intent of this section is not to terrify the reader but, at the same time, not to ignore an issue that can be so crucial as to threaten a person's life's work. Succession planning is very, very tough and usually very, very personal.

If the success of the company hinges on one individual, the future of this person's family and the success of the company can be in jeopardy upon his or her demise. The following considerations should be taken into account as you think of succession planning:

- The CEO's chief responsibility is to maintain the equity and the value of the business.

- The issues that must be addressed for providing for the future of the company and the affected parties.

- The conflicts that can arise between an individual's business objectives and personal goals and, even more deeply, the conflicts between individuals as a result of the succession plan.

The CEO should realize that the lack of a succession plan puts everyone involved—employees, shareholders, descendants—all at risk.

Developing professional management is the best potential solution for a succession plan. Rather than have one person on whom the entire company hinges, the CEO or the chairperson of the board develops a cadre of quality people, each of whom can handle efficiently his or her respective chores and responsibilities. If this approach is taken, perhaps there will be one person who can be chosen as the successor to the throne. If that is not the case, an outside chairperson not involved in the everyday operations but with a keen responsible business sense can oversee a cadre of professionals.

In the elementary stages of developing a succession plan, the CEO should ask for whom he or she wishes to provide. Or is there anyone the CEO feels needs provision? What does he or she want to provide—jobs; liquidity; security? Then, what does the CEO have to work with?

Whatever the succession plan, it should be revised and fine-tuned annually. It may not be a good idea to identify who the successor to the chief executive officer might be. Times change and someone else might grow to be more qualified. After the potential successors for the staff are identified, the CEO should look to how well each of the members of this group continue to improve themselves through continuing education and development.

After reading the section on succession planning, you may elect, for more expanded options, to turn to chapter 11, "Cashing Out: Selling the Company and Other Options." If there are nonbusiness assets in your estate, they can have a bearing on some of the personal decisions you make. For example, if stock in the company is not the dominant part of the assets of your estate, you might be able to take a chance and identify a family member to be the successor.

If there are no family members, then obviously you need to look outside the family for a successor to run the company.

Later, when we discuss "Turnarounds" in chapter 10, we maintain trigger points, the probability of problems, the potential of the problems, and action plans. You might want to use the same strategy in your succession planning. Also, what will initiate the plan? Only the death of the owner, or will the plan be initiated while the owner is still active in the business?

As you assess your resources, if there is a potential heir, should you initiate training programs for that individual?

As you try to develop your succession plan, remember that both employees and potentially family members have expectations. Take into consideration any possible effect your choice of a successor might have on your employees or on your key customers. Examine what loyalties might exist to various people and to the company.

2

Getting Good Managers, Developing Them, and Keeping Them

YOU CAN HAVE THE BEST-LAID PLAN, BUT IF YOU DON'T HAVE ANYONE TO execute it, the plan is worthless.

A company business plan involves many facets; it starts with a sales forecast. From this sales forecast is developed a manning chart. Every facet of the business, be it sales, service, accounting, finance, manufacturing, data processing, or delivery, is going to be based on the sales forecast. Each of these operations has its own plan that first involves people; that is, a plan for the number and kind of people to do the job you need. In a new or small company undergoing dynamic growth, or in a firm involved in an emerging industry, the challenge of finding and hiring the right people—and sometimes being able to pay them—is the most serious problem a manager faces.

CREATING AN ORGANIZATION

Building a viable people organization is hard, tedious work. If you have a personnel manager, he or she will probably tell you that if half of the people hired work out, the department is doing a good job. However, most successful CEOs won't accept a .500 batting average, and consider an 80 percent success ratio as the minimum acceptable rate.

Many small businesses, on the other hand, don't have the luxury of a personnel manager, so other managers must wear the personnel hat. They could be the office manager or even the president of the firm. But, when the president of a small firm spends a day in the field on a project or as a sales representative, in legal meetings, or with environmental audits, he or she often lets the human resources task slide. Another reason for neglecting the task is that the firm doesn't have the money to hire the right people in the first place. Even large firms undergoing an expansion mode can have this problem.

Regardless of the size of the organization, of who identifies the personnel needs, or of who does the work, it is important that the emerging company devote planning and hiring attention to its human resource problems. It must be done effectively or it limits the company's potential to grow and to be profitable.

THE HIRING EVOLUTION

If we start with the basic one-person consulting firm (or any one-man or one-woman firm), a natural question is: "How much am I worth?" Fifty dollars per hour? One hundred dollars per hour? One thousand dollars per day? This places the upper limit on income until the company undertakes value-added project work.

The size of a project that one person can handle, or the territory one can cover, is limited. *Growth*, then, implies hiring the proper management for the emerging company.

The hiring evolution involves an analysis of what the company and of what the individual requires.

To begin with, the company itself must understand the job. This is particularly true when hiring high levels such as general manager or president. One company, for example, looked for a president for almost two years until they found (what they thought to be) the right person for the job. The glove of the company seemed to fit perfectly onto the hand of that individual.

Yet, in a short time, problems began to surface. First, the new president's personality and style was less people-oriented than previous managers who had held the slot. Second, bringing in a person from the outside, rather than promoting from within, disrupted the existing organization and hurt morale. Also, the emerging business was complicated and somewhat technical, so the president had to be able to deal with engineers in a complimentary manner; this becomes a stumbling block.

In a nutshell, the company would have been better off by promoting from within and backing the promotion with training and seminars leading to a manager whose style and compatibility was consistent with the company's.

Correspondingly, the company must closely consider whether it thinks the individual can do the work. This is much more important in an emerging company or small business than one that is established because of the closer physical and psychological working environment.

Without coming right out and asking the candidate, you need answers to these questions:

- Is this really a job that this individual will like to do?
- Are his or her goals consistent with the company's?
- Are the milestone charts and timetables for advancement of both the company and the individual complimentary?
- Can the individual really do the job, given the minimum staff that is usually available? (This becomes very important when bringing in new people who have worked for large companies and are used to having staff support.)
- Will the person, and his or her family, be happy doing this kind of work in the location assigned?
- For how long will they be happy?

Probably the most important point that can be made (on the company's side of the fence) is: Keep looking until you find the person that meets the criteria you set up in the first place. Do not simply hire the best candidate that applied.

Hire for the Future

Although hiring principles are important, a facet of employment just as important in an emerging company is: flexibility. During the dynamic changes that take place, companies experience a shift in focus, and management attention shifts with (or should shift with) the demands of today's problem. Hiring takes on an added dimension. You just don't hire the individual for what he or she must do today, but also for what the person will be asked to do 6 months or 2 years from now. That kind of strategic thinking leads to an ongoing successful management team. The good manager (that you hire) must be able to attend to all facets of the job, using a rifle approach to problems when it becomes necessary, rather than a shotgun approach.

From our earlier discussions, it is apparent that problems and difficulties exist in doing succession planning. Quite often an individual will be hired with the understanding of receiving successive promotions until he or she ultimately reaches a certain position. In some cases this includes the position of president or chairman. Some companies also ask managers, at the time of appraisal, to indicate who they are training to be their successor.

Both of those practices can be very dangerous unless handled properly. In the first instance, the individual who has set sights on a higher position can become a very valuable employee as he or she climbs through the succession steps, but the supervisor somewhere along the way begins to doubt whether the employee will be able to achieve the ultimate position. Now the supervisor has the choice of telling this individual that he or she really doesn't think the individual is going to be able to achieve that ultimate position (this task could best be done at the appraisal conference), or of not telling the individual, but at the last moment promoting someone else to the position, or finally, of promoting the individual to the position even though the supervisor is uncertain about this individual's ability to handle the job. If it is not handled properly, this succession plan could go down the tubes and you could lose one or more key people.

The best approach, probably, is not to make the ultimate promise to begin with. You might feel that you have to make the ultimate offer to get the employee, but don't forget what the end results could be. The reason that you change your mind might not be because of his or her performance or the fact that you chose the wrong person necessarily. Perhaps you tried to project too far into the future when you made the promise and, in the meantime, the employee has taken on the character of a problem employee.

In the other situation where each manager is asked to indicate who he or she is training as successor, the manager sometimes changes his or her mind every year. In the meantime, if it has been alluded to the subordinate, either in appraisal sessions or otherwise, that he or she is the heir apparent, you again box yourself into problems. Consequently, succession planning can be very, very difficult. It's probably a very appropriate subject to be discussed with confidants, in advisory board meetings, or with consultants. For sure, you should only review the plan with an employee step-by-step as you gain confidence in the individual based on proven performance and attitudes.

Who to Hire and Where to Find Them

It is fair to believe that the emerging company will experience new sets of specific problems relating to productivity, sales, marketing, government regulations, and other aspects of business. During those tempestuous times, the manager you hire should not be married to traditional values if they don't fit company needs. The manager of the emerging company (Fig. 2-1) should capitalize on new ideas, new concepts, and new marketing techniques without trying to follow old case histories (Fig. 2-2). The value of knowing these case histories avoids, of course, repeating the mistakes of others, but there are far fewer failure stories than there are of successes. People don't normally write about failures. If a new concept is ideal for your firm, don't be afraid to use it. If you are worried, fall back on the ol' reliable: common sense. To quote Perry Pascarella, editor-in-chief of *Industry Week*: "The best solutions are rooted in *common sense*, and they are not totally new."

One final note on the topic of hiring deserves attention; namely, lean and mean is a dual-edged sword. On the one hand, companies in an emerging industry are usually faced with cash flow considerations that necessitate a close con-

---

The Person Should:

☞ Be persistent and outgoing.

☞ Be open to new ideas.

☞ Be unafraid of failure, but stable enough to understand its dangers.

☞ Have a working understanding of marketing and finance.

☞ Be knowledgeable of the technical idiosyncrasies of the industry and your. company's products.

☞ Have a global perspective.

☞ Be able to cut through red tape.

☞ Genuinely care about his or her fellow employees.

☞ Show impeccable honesty at home and at business.

☞ Be respected.

☞ Abide by work-measurement habits for him- or herself as well as others.

☞ Accept errors without being corporal.

☞ Be a team player.

☞ Take or give criticism in an acceptable way.

☞ Surround his or herself with promotable people.

☞ Have good common sense.

☞ Not be addicted to alcohol or drugs.

☞ Find motivation intrinsic to the job.

☞ Have a history of successful work experience in dynamic companies.

☞ Be accepted as a leader both inside and outside the company.

At 5 points per trait, the goal of a company is to hire those that get all A's—90 or above.

Fig. 2-1. Creating the mold for entrepreneurial managers.

trol on salaries. On the other hand, too lean an organization does not give a company the ability to pick and choose from a new crop of potential managers. Thus, you are hampered by a personnel growth problem. When an emerging company needs people, it needs them fast, and thus you need a body bank. Yet, it is expensive to keep people ''on hand'' in the hope you will use them in the future.

There are ways to shift the ''body bank'' burden to someone else's pocketbook but doing so in a way that everyone benefits. Here are just a few ideas.

Donald M. Carlton
President

22 April 1989

Mr. Guy E. Weismantel
Weismantel International
P. O. Box 6269
Kingwood, TX 77325

Dear Guy:

In response to your recent letter, my thoughts on our approach to people management are as follows.

The basic approach at Radian to managing technical people is to encourage our people to do for the company what they do best--that is, what they like to do and what their skills permit them to do well. We discovered a need for this approach in 1973, after our company was four years old. The trigger for moving in this direction was the rapid growth of the company and the realization that a successful company had a variety of tasks to be accomplished, and it was important to find people capable of filling the various needs of the company.

To achieve the objective of ensuring that the various types of people contributed in a mutually supportive way, there are essentially three roles for technical people in the company: a purely technical role, a technical staff management role, and a marketing/program management role. It is clear that our company needs all three types, and with the management philosophy mentioned above, we were able to implement a policy of encouraging our people to follow the career path of their choice rather than forcing people into roles which were uncomfortable and therefore most assuredly unproductive.

Guy, your letter indicated that you wanted something brief. Please let me know if you need more.

Best regards,

Donald M. Carlton

DMC:pt

RADIAN
CORPORATION
8501 Mo-Pac Blvd. • P. O. Box 201088
Austin, TX 78720-1088 • (512) 454-4797

Fig. 2-2. Radian Corporation's hiring philosophy.

Use the Schools. Develop a plan in concert with local junior colleges, colleges, and universities that keeps you in touch with students whose goals and desires fit company needs. This can be done through partial scholarships, work programs, research and development (R&D) funding, or other means.

Tap Your Rep Organization. For companies selling through manufacturers representatives or distributors, it might be possible to find a person within these groups who will fit your company's needs but is pigeon-holed in his or her current slot at the rep. Some compensation to the rep may be in order if you raid his or her staff.

Create a Group of Independent Agents. One small energy company hired several people by setting them up as independent businesses (DBA's—doing business as) that were selling their services to the energy company. As time and dollars permit, they close the DBA and go onto the payroll full-time.

Rehire the Retired. The number and talent of retired people continues to go untapped in many cases. Yet, utilizing the services of a retired person who is knowledgeable in the industry to fill a slot for a given period of time—while the person in that slot moves onward—is an ideal way to help you through a growth period.

Use the Family. For short or long periods of time, small firms can utilize a spouse or others to get through a period of growth and to help relieve the pressure. Set some guidelines, however, so that the business and the family problems don't gravitate to personal complications.

Hire the Service Organization. If you have good talent in accounting where that manager can move up to vice president (VP), consider an accounting service to do the company payroll, books, and check writing. This is also true in other areas—e.g., toll processing some of your production until you can get the right people.

Pick up Services from Your Suppliers. Although it isn't possible in all industries, you can ask suppliers to perform some of your lab work, quality control (QC) work, etc., until you can get technical people. Many are anxious to do this if your formula uses their materials. A supplier might also have the talent you need to hire.

Cash In on Your Customer's Employees. Looking over those of your customer's can be a ticklish way to get employees, but in some cases it works; especially if the customer is trying to find a home for a person who has grown to a new level of responsibility, but has no slot at the current company.

Regardless of how or where you find the manager you hire, he or she should be *creative*!

Other Factors

Hire the individual's, not the resumés. What kind of background did they come from? What did their fathers do? Did their mother work? Did they have part-time or summer jobs to help defray the expense of their education? Are they happily married? Do they have a family? With some important jobs, it is also a good idea to meet the spouse. Having some idea of how home attitudes will affect a person's work can be important—especially in a dynamic company where you can't always consider the 8 hour day as standard.

Why the questions? You want to find out if these people come from a strong work ethic. You want to find out if they are well adjusted. You want to determine if their spouses are excited about them coming to work for your company. You want to try to determine what their value judgments are and how much common sense they have.

Depending on what the job is, you might want to try to ascertain their creativity level. This is difficult and again you need to dig beyond their resumé. Ask about hobbies. Dig into specifically what they did at their previous jobs. Explore what extra-curricular activities they participated in during school.

Depending on the size of your company, you might not have anyone on your staff who possesses these hiring skills. Regardless of the size of your company, there are certain jobs with which you, at a minimum, should be involved in the interviewing process.

If you already employ someone in your organization who is good at hiring people, you are in the minority. If your track record at hiring and retaining people isn't as good as you think it should be, you better look at your credibility through the eyes of the current employees Fig. 2-3. If you don't like the answers, get some outside help.

Many consulting firms make a business of polling employees with questions about their employers to get an opinion about morale, attitudes, or other business matters. Managers of a small company can perform a written or informal survey of their own to decide whether they are about to experience hiring or promotability problems. Check yourself.

How To Score:

Excellent:	+3	Poor:	−1
Very Good:	+2	Very Poor:	−2
Good:	+1	Terrible:	−3
Fair:	0		

Give your company a plus (+) score if you believe you are answering the questions in a positive mode. Give a negative (−) if you need improvement or have low promotability material.

Fig. 2-3. Testing employee growth potential.

Fig. 2-3. (Continued)

FOCUS	QUESTION	SCORE
Age	Many employees are elderly	_____
	Job tenure of staff is 5 years or over	_____
Attitude	Current employee's ideas don't fit new products and market focus; not motivated	_____
	Like the idea of growth and change that could lead to opportunity	_____
Awareness	Employees have firsthand knowledge of products and services	_____
	Future is problematic	_____
Company Traits	Financially stable	_____
	High morale and high degree of work satisfaction	_____
Competitive Spirit	Internal departmental squabbling	_____
	Team spirit	_____
Education	Technical competence and skill variety	_____
	Degreed people in key slots	_____
Outlook	Confident about company's future	_____
	People think strategically	_____
Personality Traits of Key Managers	Intelligent and broad-minded	
	Can take criticism and adjust to change	_____
Training	Abilities match needs	_____
	Aggressive program for continuing education	_____
Turnover	Lots of job changes and/or absenteeism	_____
	People leaving for unknown reasons	_____
Wages	Are above industry norm	_____
	Benefits package is flexible and suits needs of all ages of employees	_____

Total Your Score:

+60 to +72	Nominate yourself for an award!
+40 to +59	Pat yourself on the back.
+21 to +39	Doing OK.
+20 to −20	pH = 7.
−21 to −39	You have problems.
−40 to −59	BIG problems!
−60 to −72	Problems that are about to explode!

There are some good personnel consultants available. However, you are going to have to interview them just as if you were interviewing a prospective employee. You have to be sure that their values are similar to yours. It might take some trial and error before you find the right one.

Don't confuse personnel counselors with headhunters. A personnel organization can do any or all of the following:

- Prepare advertisements for jobs.
- Place advertisements in the proper periodicals at the right time.
- Receive applications.
- Screen applications.
- Conduct preliminary interviews.
- Test the applicants.
- Analyze your hiring practices.
- Analyze your turnover rates.
- Manage your unemployment compensation claims.
- Conduct exit interviews.

In selecting an organization to do this work, start with small projects until you reach a "comfort level" where you feel the results are meaningful. Be sure the organization is helping you.

As with any other skill, the more it is used, the better you get. It is not a bad idea to have someone get a transcript of the applicant's grades from high school or college. You would be surprised how many times you find that individuals never graduated from, or perhaps even attended, the schools they claim. If they lie before they start, you certainly don't need them in your organization. Small and emerging companies often let these checks slide. That is a mistake.

There is a lot of controversy about psychological testing. Large companies are more likely to abuse its employees with this kind of testing because it becomes impersonal. Yet if the tests are properly conducted, in a way that it appears as an extension of the interviewing process, an applicant who would refuse probably would have some stability hang-ups.

Even more important than the value of the test in the hiring process is the help the results can give you in subsequent years in terms of managing the individual. Your experience will prove that the test results will give you insight necessary for getting over a problem that developed later with an employee. This insight has helped in numerous cases to save an existing employee.

Be your own judge, but be careful in testing. Be certain the results are kept confidential. Be selective in choosing those who are tested as well as those who conduct the test. For an emerging company, salaried employees are likely candidates.

Truly small companies might not have the money for testing or consulting, so they should turn to services that are free. For example, many good people end up in the unemployment lines. A visit to the various state offices of Human Resources (HR) explaining your needs can be rewarding. Some of these government placement people take on an assignment more aggressively than someone you would pay to do the screening and hiring. These HR offices can be extremely useful if you are looking for a person in a new city where you hope to expand. They can come up with a local individual who has been calling on clients in the same market area that you intend to develop, and who has the educational background you need.

Also, look to the retired and to the "40 plus" for assistance. So many good people have been put out to pasture—especially during the past 5 years—that there is a crop of talent out there just waiting to be picked. One company hired a retired engineer as an independent agent to handle a sales territory on a part-time basis. On commission only, both the company and the individual were happy with the arrangement, and it was lucrative.

Pre-employment physicals that include drug testing are not only common, but recommended. If you are going to spend a lot of money on health care for your employees, spend it where you can develop loyalty and security—on employees who have been with you for awhile. Yearly physical exams are recommended for key employees. Take good care of yourself!

HIRING EXPERIENCES AND PRACTICES

You will get the best people to staff your organization if you can plan your requirements and not be in a hurry to fill the vacancies. You will also get your best applicants from referrals and not from the rolls of the unemployed.

In the mid-seventies, a corporate strategic planning meeting at a $10 million/year company pointed out that one of the divisions needed to create the position of general manager. Did the job require someone strong in manufacturing, marketing, finance, or a combination? One candidate, referred by a local trade association, seemed to be ideal (by the way, trade organizations can be a very good source for quality people). In this case, the individual was currently employed but was unhappy. Today he is the president of the company.

How do you "get good" at picking people? It isn't intuition. It is a reflex action by consistently being exposed to quality people. For example, if you are so inclined and have the time, you can improve your own personnel and hiring skills and expand your hiring network by helping quality people who are out of work.

You don't develop an 80 percent success ratio in keeping people nor build a good management team by hiring the first candidate with a good smile, a line of malarkey, and a pleasing personality. Also, it is ideological to think you can build your organization by promotion from within. If you try strictly promoting from within, you are bound to be guilty of "The Peter Principle." If you don't remember the definition of the Peter Principle, it is roughly that an individual works his or her way to a level of incompetence.

Also, you don't build an 80 percent success ratio without commitment. Agreed, bad times can lead to decreased staffing, but some companies actually think it is good to lay off people and have turnover. They preach that it gives them some fresh ideas and prevents the organization from getting stale. Hogwash! You can't develop any loyalty or dedication to the company and what it stands for in an era of insecurity. One very unusual experience proves this point.

A young man had been laid off from his position in the engineering department of a medium-sized company. After a preliminary interview with a new firm, the firm made him an offer telling him to think about it. When he called back a week later, he had already been called back to his previous employer. It turned out that his company was negotiating with a union representing its factory workers. In an effort to demonstrate that times were tough, the company laid off a third of their salaried workforce. The union came to terms and the company called back the laid off employees. This young man, who was 26 years old and single, lost all faith in the company. He felt insecure and uncertain about a future with a company that would treat its people that way. Imagine the trauma that must have been created with an employee who had three or four dependents. This company is not committed to an 80 percent success ration of keeping employees.

There is a growing trend for companies to use service organizations. We have had pretty good success with this over the past years. We even find that from part-time help, companies will get the same people back. Usually they are people who, for some reason or another, don't want a full-time job, and besides, we are not looking for a full-time employee. Companies many times look for service organizations to perform some of the functions after hours, such as janitorial and maintenance functions. It is a lot easier than running a second shift.

By definition, a team is a group that works and plays together. Your management team should work together helping each other without concern or worry about whose specific job it is, but with motivation to achieve the corporate objectives. When one person succeeds, everyone benefits.

Often the best way to view the team and its assignments is with an organizational chart. Although there is some truth to the theory that organizational charts polarize the job and deter conservative effort, it is still a good management-hiring planning tool. This is particularly true when the chart is used to determine the makeup of the team needed to achieve the company's strategic and operational objectives. The organizational chart need not be a published document. Some managers prefer to restrict its distribution on a need-to-know basis. This gives flexibility in job and project assignments.

The organizational chart can become a part of a business plan and the basis for the job descriptions. If you come up with a new organizational chart that you feel is appropriate for implementing business plans, some new positions will appear. Do not be in a rush to fill these positions. Furthermore, don't get caught in the "bamboo syndrome" where every segment of the organization creates a new organization around itself (Table 2-1).

While we are on the subject of team and organization building and before we talk about compensation, we have a few suggestions on the interviewing process. The interview should not be rushed. It should be private and without interruptions, preferably one-on-one or two-on-one. However, if you are bringing a new employee on board who is in a key position, he or she will receive greater reception if your key people talk to and agree on the person as opposed to him or her being your handpicked person.

You should also address the question of credibility. In that area, one interviewing technique that has proved successful for many years is to downplay the job. Tell a candidate how bad the job is, how demanding it is, and what problems occur. The result is that the individual can never say that he or she was sold a bill of goods or given a snow job. The worse that can happen is that the employee will be more satisfied in the position than he or she expected.

At some point, an emerging company should establish a salary structure for the organization. Then you don't have to negotiate compensation. You have to hire the candidate within the salary structure you have or you will disrupt the entire organization. If the candidate, on the other hand, has to take substantially less than what he or she is currently earning, the person will have adjustment difficulties in his or her personal life that will affect his or her ability to perform.

COMPENSATION

Although any theory on compensation is certain to create arguments, here are some facets of the problem of the real key to building an emerging organization. This key is to motivate people and to develop teamwork coupled to an incentive plan that includes strategic goals, operational goals, and individual goals. The secret to making an incentive plan like this work is making sure that people understand how it operates. At the same time, design the plan to be discretionary to the extent where it is not an entitlement program, but where the individual's performance in the eyes of management is a significant part of the reward.

The best plan is one where the people share in the achievement of the company's profit goals. It is best to tie this achievement factor to a percentage of profit on sales which is constant from year to year, e.g., 10 percent. Tying this portion of the incentive plan to a budget figure can be very disruptive. There are internal as well as external factors that affect the budget.

The portion of the individual's bonus that is based upon profitability should

Table 2-1. Developing a Stable Organization.

	I	II
Structure	Minimize line & staff, maximize talents of managers and employees.	Improve efficiency through departmentalization. Pay attention to keeping high morale. Keep lean.
Relationships	Minimize paperwork and duplication of efforts; communicate.	Maximize span of control to keep number of managers to a minimum. Improve communication.
Dynamics	Use management by objectives; and delegate.	Do not get bogged down with red tape or "busy" work. Create coordinated autonomy. Keep pruning or reassigning unnecessary staff.
Functions	Split duties among managers; avoid "Bamboo" effect.*	Group people through matrix organization to minimize specialties required. Matrixing can lead to "double-bossing" (or even triple-bossing, etc.) and can actually lead to a growth in staff that is unnecessary, then the manager is faced with trimming people off the payroll.
Wages	Be financially stern, but create potential for people to get rich.	Avoid dropping salaries below industry average; pay incentive bonuses willingly. Don't keep upping the "boggie" of commission salesmen.

*With bamboo, each segment of the plant, by itself, is capable of creating a new plant and expanding into new ground. In an organization, keep chopping back the bamboo to avoid having an organization grow when it shouldn't.

not be linear. In other words, the employee should not receive half of this portion of the bonus if the company only earns half of what its profit goal was. At the same time, if the company earns more than its profit goal, there should be some extra reward for that achievement. Participation in the profits in this fashion encourages employees to help you tighten the belt when things are slim; and when things are good, you should spend money for people and equipment to ensure a good next year.

The second part of an individual's bonus should be based on achievement of his or her individual goals. As described earlier, the individual should set four or five measurable goals. Based on the achievement of these measurable goals, he or she should be rewarded. It is quite possible then for the company not to achieve its profit target even when an employee had done everything within his or her power and everything the employee set out to do to make this contribution, and thus should benefit under this part of the bonus program.

An individual's performance should have a greater percentage of a total bonus available than the bonus that is paid for the corporate achievement. The reasoning is, if the achievement of the profit objective by the company is the larger portion, you will be paying out large bonuses to people whose performance was mediocre. Wages should remain the major portion of the compensation package.

WAGE POLICIES

It takes quite a bit of work initially to establish the wage rate for various jobs. Each of the jobs in your company has to be evaluated on the basis of its requirements and its responsibilities. Based on the analysis, the jobs are put into different classifications. The classifications are compared and analyzed for balance and equity. The salary range is established for each job classification. Once the program is established it can be maintained with a minimum of effort. Larger companies actually establish a point system when doing job evaluations.

You try to start each employee within the salary range for his or her job and classification. There are always exceptions, however. You may start someone below the entry level rate because the individual lacks experience, but has expressed confidence that he or she can do the job. You could hire the individual on a 90 day probation with the understanding that after the probation, if the individual has shown that he or she can handle the job, the salary will be increased to a starting range. On the other hand, you can start a person high in the range with the understanding that he or she will be promoted to a different position after a period of time.

The base wage rate for a job is only part of a good salary program. Fringe benefits are an important part of a compensation package. Let's imagine you had a group of neighbors talking over the back fence. One of the gentlemen is in his

50s, a second is newly married, a third has three children—an 8-, 10-, and 12-year-old. The fourth is in his early 40s with a sick wife. They are comparing fringe benefits. The gentleman with the sick wife has 5 weeks vacation but is unhappy with his medical insurance. The young newlywed has not yet qualified for 2 weeks vacation, but has a totally comprehensive medical plan. The individual with three children works for a company with a very generous profit-sharing plan but no dental insurance. The man in his 50s has a medical plan that has a good dental program, but his company doesn't have a retirement plan.

Generally, when employees with different companies compare their fringe benefit package, none of them come away from the discussion happy. There is an attempt being made today with flexible fringe benefits where the employee can pick and choose what he or she wants. The jury is still out on how this is going to work. For emerging companies, it is best to have a definite package that is documented and easily understood.

Be a believer that rank has its privileges. Depending upon how long the employee has been with you and what his or her position is in the company, the person should have greater fringe benefits. If you have a union, your salaried employees' fringes should be better than those of the hourly employees. This will always give the union employees an incentive to work hard and move up and out of the hourly rank and into the salaried employee rank. If you have a union, you want to resist ever providing the pension plan that the union proposes. Provide your own pension plan and control it yourself.

For many organizations, the best type of pension plan is a profit-sharing plan. (Portable pensions are okay.) You, and an employer, can't be expected to provide what the federal government hasn't been able to. Social security was supposed to take care of people's retirement. People have to do something for themselves. A profit-sharing plan provides this flexibility. The employees thus have an incentive to see that the company succeeds. If they do, they see the benefits going into their fund to provide retirement benefits. If the company has some lean years, employees continue to try, but at the same time realize they had better contribute something themselves to their retirement plan. The Individual Retirement Accounts (IRAs) were an attempt by government to allow people to do something for themselves to compliment their social security benefits. But what the government giveth, the government taketh away. If an employer tried doing that, he or she would be fined and sent to jail.

PERSONAL DYNAMICS

In an emerging company the phenomena of ''magnetic polar separation'' occurs. Employees gravitate toward one pole or another depending upon their attitudes, desires, willingness, and ability to accept change. On one side you will find a group that likes the fast-track, responds to challenge, and aggressively pursues the new opportunities that constantly occur. On the other hand is a group that is complacent and happy to work a simple 8 hour shift and/or finds themselves asked to do things beyond their abilities.

It is not unusual, especially in large companies, for managers to keep the latter employee well into a decade of service before taking action that helps both the employee and the company. This action could include training, retraining, reassigning, or even firing. Pigeon-holing is not a good answer for an emerging company because everyone has to be able to make a contribution toward growth.

Also, when an individual doesn't carry his or her own weight, the company must hire people to do the job the manager should be doing. This can lead to crazy compensation schemes and red-circling, i.e., creating an overpaid job slot. This is expensive and a no-no for the emerging company.

Another problem faced in emerging companies is that projects are often done by teams. This makes it hard to identify the driving force behind the team and to detail what each team member has contributed. You can measure the team performance, but not the performance of each individual. To ensure that you understand which management cream comes to the top, sit in on meetings or read minutes, or ask for tapes of the proceedings to form personnel observations during or after the fact.

Small firms, growth firms, and emerging companies will find hidden talent within their own organizations if they only look for it. One company (following Henry J. Kaiser's principle of "find a need and fill it"), began to make a chemical product here in the U.S. where it found a monopoly of one supplier. The company took a young man, without sales experience, and made him National Sales Manager. Outsiders criticized the decision; however, in two years the man had set up a national sales network of reps and distributors and led the company into a situation where production levels could not keep up with demand. As people marveled, saying, "I didn't know you could do that," the CEO smiled and continued to give a secretary the purchasing manager's job and lifted young engineers into plant manager slots. Many of these young dynamos don't know the meaning of the word *Can't*! You, too, should discover the capabilities of people that are right under your nose.

When performing an employee evaluation, whether formal or informal, look for the person that:

- Is creative (often a good sense of humor identifies the creative person).
- Stands out as a leader (sometimes a person's physical size, both large and small, lends itself to leadership).
- Has a desire to change things that can lead to improvements.
- Understands the implications of actions.
- Volunteers to accept challenges.
- Is willing to take risks.

- Does not demean other people, but capitalizes on their good points.
- Recognizes his or her own strengths and weaknesses.
- Provides inspiration to others.
- Has firm goals set for his or herself to include milestone charts to reach those goals.

PERFORMANCE AND MOTIVATION

Large corporations pay a lot of attention to compensation and performance at top levels of management but only give lip service to rewarding middle managers and first-line supervisors. An emerging company should be different—first of all, to keep good people; secondly, to avoid the horrendous expense of training new people; and thirdly, to ensure employees have true commitment. Commitment is not just a matter of money (although compensations and perks are important to eliminate the potential for good people to ''shop around''), but it also is a matter of fulfilling career interests and motivation (Fig. 2-4).

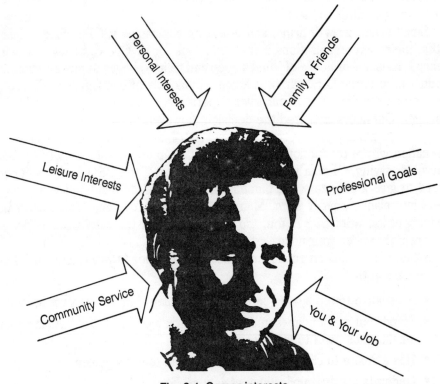

Fig. 2-4. Career interests.

Trying to motivate people is like trying to hit a moving target. Why? Because each person is unique, has different career interests, has different personal and family interests, and wants or accepts different things from life. Keep in mind that at higher levels of management money is not necessarily a motivator. Once a person has adequate compensation for basic needs, job motivation often comes from other facets of work.

Just how important is it to find these motivation facets? Very! Motivation is the seedling of performance, or lack of it, whether it be managers, employees, team, family, or whatever. The other aspect of performance is: ability. No matter how motivated a person is, if the ability is lacking, the results can be less than desired. The same is true of someone who has all the ability in the world, but lacks the motivation to do what you desire.

An emerging company must match abilities to company needs. Motivation, however, is tied to the way you treat people. This implies, then, that you really need to know a person and what makes him or her tick. It is a lot like internal relationship management. Indeed, we sometimes get so involved in trying to produce a product we forget about our people as people.

Many psychologists believe each person has a hierarchy of needs beginning with physiological (needs of the body). This continues from the lowest level and progresses through safety (both physical and emotional), social (to belong), esteem (recognition by others), to growth (or self-actualization) at the highest level. The reason for really knowing your people is to understand their needs and nourish them, therefore creating a climate for motivation and releasing the energy that would have been spent trying to satisfy that need. An emerging company should point to satisfying those needs by achieving company-related goals.

As a start, motivation, and its sibling known as satisfaction, often come by way of achievement. But it is not just achievement that motivates or satisfies but achievement *that is formally recognized*. Responsibility and growth, which are related directly to the job you give a person, should provide the road to achievement and the destination policies that appropriately reward this achievement (as a formal company policy). Without this, you have the potential to cause dissatisfaction.

Keep in mind that managerial attitudes become employee attitudes. If troubles develop, you should go through a process of introspection. If people problems keep reappearing, it is possible that the only common denominator is: you! In that case, the introspection process should include a close look at those relationships that exist between people problems and performance—between you and your employees (Fig. 2-5).

Take, for example, someone who constantly comes to work late. A manager might first think that the individual lacks personal values or doesn't care about attendance or punctuality. Consider, for a moment, that the interpersonal relationship between you and that person might not be so great. When people do not

☞ Do you present a good role model?

☞ Or are you considered a slavedriver?

☞ Have you successfully handled conflicts among subordinates?

☞ Are you honest with your employees in all matters?

☞ Do you fire people rather than help them improve?

☞ Are your employees' workload expectations the same as your own?

☞ Or do you expect them to ignore the time clock (as you do), but don't reward them accordingly?

☞ Do you feel giving them a job and benefits is enough?

☞ Do you know the right way to socialize with employees?

☞ Do you have the respect of your employees?

☞ Are you supportive during trying personal problems?

☞ Are you communicating (both ways) to your employees? (Or is all information from management downward?)

☞ Do you analyze the feedback you get so that employees see action?

☞ Can you be criticized?

☞ Is your door open for personal and business discussions?

☞ Are you using performance appraisals that really mean something to the employee and not just to the company?

☞ Are you promoting from within?

☞ Are you giving personal and financial recognition for employee achievements?

☞ Are you planting the seeds for promotability and executive status?

☞ Are you training assistants who can take the jobs of their bosses as the boss moves upward?

Fig. 2-5. Creating motivated/loyal employees: A checklist.

like a job, they quit; when a person doesn't like their boss, they stay away from the job—which strains the relationship even more—and the process is repeated. On the surface, the employee might not seem motivated on the job because performance was poor. Looking beyond the obvious, the problem might be one of relationships, and you may have control over that relationship and could take positive action.

On the other hand, in a dynamic organization you do lose people when a company grows, for a variety of reasons. Managers should not try to convince a person to stay with the company if the individual has concluded on his or her own that it is time to leave. What the manager should do is point out all the positive facets of the company and ensure that the individual makes the decision to stay or leave. In one case, a middle manager convinced a young engineer to stay with the company, only to leave the company himself 8 months later. This was quite upsetting to the individual who had been convinced to stay.

This brings us back to the aspect of motivation that is different for the emerging company, namely, doing something about motivation despite the grueling, demanding schedule that most managers experience. In summary, get to know your people; really know them and their needs. Unsatisfied needs are strong motivators. Nourish those needs to release energy to do things you want done. A satisfied need is not a motivator. Be sure there is an organizational climate that will promote personal growth and development. Have a balanced concern for people and productivity. Remember: Every employee is a profit center. Prevent dissatisfaction by nipping it in the bud using two-way communication and evaluate your communications to make sure it is two way.

A VALUABLE SECRETARY

One of the most valuable assets to any small company, and one that is the most often overlooked, is a really *super* secretary.

This position can make or break a company. She or he will be the first contact that people make with your company either on the telephone or when they enter your front door. The impression that your secretary makes is often the impression that people take with them and judge your whole operation by. If your secretary is friendly, knowledgeable, and willing to put out extra effort, your customer leaves with a "good" feeling about doing business with you. On the other hand, if she or he is discourteous, rude, lacking in knowledge on even the simple questions a customer might ask, that customer will leave with an unsettled feeling about your company's abilities.

Not only does the secretary rank high in the customer relations department, but he or she is also an extremely valuable asset in keeping the "nagging" office problems off your desk and in freeing your time for the major decisions. For example, if you don't have a reliable secretary who can make judgement calls like, "when to call the plumber," or is not able to "field" incoming calls or "walk-ins" on a day when you have a proposal or bid to get out, then you are spending "empty" time on the phone or talking to a person who really could wait until next week. A "top dollar" secretary should also be able to handle many of the "office decisions" and the smoothing over of any ruffled feathers that might exist among your employees.

Your secretary should be your right arm and fill in the gaps that your time won't permit you to do. Give her or him the freedom to make some decisions and you will be pleasantly surprised at the results.

On this premise, you would be wise not to short cut and hire the cheapest typist that you can find, but spend the extra dollars for a *quality* employee. The small company does not have the freedom in cash flow to hire someone who can't diversify his or her talents. Often the exceptional secretary will serve as the "unofficial office manager" and eliminate the need for hiring an additional person and leave you, the boss, in the position of spending your time on the growth of your business.

3

Dealing with People Problems and Problem People

THE SUCCESS OF ANY ENTERPRISE IS HEAVILY DEPENDENT UPON THE QUALITY of people in the organization. A common characteristic of the excellent company is the recognition of social responsibility. Social responsibility starts with treating employees fairly and recognizing the dependence that families of employees, as well as the employees themselves, have on the company.

AVOIDING TURNOVERS

If you incur high turnover in your organization, it is a good indication that you have people problems. Some large businesses feel that turnover is healthy; that a revolving door creates new ideas and brings in fresh approaches. The authors never concurred with this latter concept, particularly in the small- to medium-sized companies. High turnover breeds *more* turnover.

Hiring and firing is expensive and disruptive. You should operate under the principle that if a person doesn't work out, it is for one of several reasons. To start, you either hired the wrong person or you failed to train them properly. Also, when people become insecure, they lack faith in the company, and you lose people that you don't want to lose. Keep in mind that for the small emerging company, training and selecting is time consuming and expensive; therefore, you should take steps to avoid turnover. But the question is: Just what are those steps? (Fig. 3-1).

Utilize appraisal meetings to identify personnel problems and interview employees when they are given a bonus check. Cash in hand loosens the tongue. Watch for warning signals of employee-employee conflict.

What are your short and long term goals?

APPRAISAL

Ensure there is goal compatibility.

Come to grips with problems causing friction.

Send employee to outside seminar that focuses on needs.

What's wrong with the company?

BONUS

Be responsive to legitimate complaints.

Check to see if employee is receiving support to meet his or her business objectives.

What is your biggest problem?

APPRAISAL

Do you need to change your behavior pattern toward employee?

Identify hostility or anger.

Get to root of absentee problems.

JANUARY   MARCH   JULY

Fig. 3-1. Steps to avoid turnover.

Three of those steps that can help to nip the people problem in the bud are:

1. Include social input into your goal structure. (Recognize that the employee is part of a family and has needs outside the company.)

2. Match the "people factor" to your business forecast. (Don't put a person in the wrong slot. The employee who is sales-oriented should not be confined to the office or plant.)

3. Provide a financial overlay to ensure that your budget capability matches your payroll requirements. (It does no good to offer compensation and a benefit package that is really beyond the capability of a small or emerging company.)

These three steps are easier said than done. To begin with, most small and emerging companies don't even have a hiring strategy (Fig. 3-2). It is not an easy task to develop one either. Yet an entrepreneur, or business-builder, must recognize that the key to success might well be in exploiting technological innovation or providing a service based on creating a stable business organization that avoids turnover.

---

1. Use headhunters cautiously.
   - Using headhunters is a very expensive and many times an unnecessary step in hiring people.

2. Develop a referral network.
   - Use trade associations, friends, and other employees to pinpoint good people for now or in the future.

3. Keep track of competent people.
   - When you are not hiring, keep a file of "resumés-worth-keeping" of those people who are good candidates.

4. Initiate a policy for incoming employees.
   - Some key employees should take psychological exams; all employees take physical exams.
   - New hourly employees are more accident prone; train them properly.

5. Don't keep the incompetent.
   - Rate employees when hired; poor quality people often go for the easy jobs.
   - Remember, the inept employee makes the same demands for salary, insurance, and fringe benefits as does the competent.
   - Incompetent people cost you more and are harder to get rid of the longer you keep them.

Fig. 3-2. A hiring strategy for small and emerging companies.

The Matrix Organization

To create such an organization means that the "slot" on the organizational chart is more than a box with a job description. Often, what is *not* in a job description is the key to making an organization work, and nontangibles become important in avoiding people problems. The authors recommend that emerging companies try to use a matrix organization that is common to the defense and aerospace industries. In a matrix organization (Fig. 3-3), employees learn to work under a variety of conditions on any type of project. This is true from a manufacturing company to a dry cleaning establishment. In a matrix, an employee is not limited to one project nor limited by the constraints of a traditional organizational chart. The latter can be relegated to use as a planning tool but need not be published. Why? People then limit their thinking of what they can or should be doing.

For example, the job box can describe the line of authority, but cannot describe the interpersonal relationships that will exist among the staff. Yet, somehow the simpatico must be premeasured before you commit to hiring. Large companies use psychological testing, but a smaller company might have to rely on judgements made from interviews and on a thorough investigation of the employee's work history. Ask for and *check references*, and talk to former employers.

Project Manager A		Project Manager B		Project Manager C		

Employees

R	S	T	U	V	W	X
R′	S′	T′	U′	V′	W′	X′
R″	S″	T″	U″	V″	W″	X″

Employees of various disciplines (R, S, T, U, V, W, X) are working for one or more project managers at the same time, depending on the need of the project. For example, at one time the following staff might be:

PROJECT A   Manager A, plus R, S′, S″, T, W, and X
PROJECT B   Manager B, plus R′, R″, X′, X″
PROJECT C   Manager C, plus S, T′, T″, U, U″, V

The IMPORTANT thing to remember about a matrix organization is that matrixing—if used to excess—can lead to over-staffing, over-bossing (literally and physically) and overwork.

Fig. 3-3. One kind of matrix organization.

In growing companies, even the president might tidy up the men's room (or women's room). So, in filling a vacancy, you have to answer a lot of questions that are not on the employment form, like: Is this spot for a prima donna? If "sophistication" is the "air" that a prospective employee gives, the job is not right for him or her if the person has to empty his or her own wastebasket.

Aside from the personal nature of an emerging business, the organizational structure itself often leads to people problems. For example, one small consulting firm never has three women secretaries in the same office. The firm feels that two would eventually take sides against the other, and the continuity of the office procedures would always break down.

Although this may be an exaggeration, it serves as an oversimplification of what really can happen in offices where there are many secretaries and office personnel. The secret to avoiding "breakdowns" is to have a strong, firm, fair office manager (Fig. 3-4) who follows hiring principles and office procedures that are consistent with a high company morality, which, unfortunately, is not always the case.

Crime and immorality steal projects from any company, and small or emerging companies can ill afford these losses in dollars or time. Losses take place in

---

Traits:

• Fair, firm, and strong-willed.

• Competent to do any office job.

Attitudes:

• Won't put up with absenteeism or incompetence.

• Will let people go in a hurry if they don't handle their workload.

Relationships:

• Understands the needs of managers and matches the right people to give the support needed.

• Stands up for office staff vs. managers when managers expect too much.

• Comes down hard on hanky panky or wasted time.

Capabilities:

• Knows how to delegate, train, and distribute workloads and create a "team" to handle large or special projects.

Fig. 3-4. The office manager in an emerging company.

small ways (like employees taking pencils or simply wasting time), but there are outright crimes that are extremely costly. These include kickbacks to employees for order placement for collateral or equipment—a definite concern because emerging companies in a growth mode are buying a lot of new hardware or services.

A more subtle loss is sex at the office, a problem that cannot only disrupt productivity, but also lead to personnel problems. Office affairs lead to so much gossip among the other employees that they, too, become involved in the wasting-of-time problem.

In these cases, the action taken runs from firing the person on the spot to consultation and review. In almost every case it is best to get rid of these kinds of problem employees. The problems they can create are excessive, not to mention being potential lawsuits.

Growth rates that are too fast lead to hiring people who don't fit the mood of the company's future because hiring does not involve assurances of "shared values"—i.e., people's personal goals don't really match company goals, desires, or capabilities. This leads to organizational problems or to organizational successes.

Also, while many threshold companies are happy to have a building and space to work, the CEO should understand that organizational and people problems can be caused by things as simple as office or plant layout (a physical problem) as well as the human interface (a personal or personnel problem).

For example, CF Braun & Co. Alhambra, California, built an office building where each person had an individual office with a solid oak door and insulated for sound. The idea behind this is to isolate people to avoid tête-à-têtes and to force concentration on projects on your desk.

Although this might seem extreme for some firms, it illustrates that the emerging company should give thought to the people/hardware/office relationship. This is particularly true now that many activities center around the computer and copying machine.

One Houston-based company that is growing at 30 percent per year, provides a good illustration of what happens to a company when it burgeons in size.

- Original managers lost control of hiring.
- Facilities didn't match needs.
- Helter-skelter hiring put on bodies just to get the job done.
- Quality of people dropped.
- Young, aggressive sales force came aboard and marketing expenses ran rampant.
- Hanky panky (formal and informal) was born.
- Offices and office equipment were constantly moving to fit into space available.

- Inefficiencies cropped up everywhere, but people were too busy to do anything about it.
- With the bottom line still booming, no strategic thinking was given to people problems or to the physical plant to support them.
- Drug use was extensive.

In this current "people" discussion, we have generally assumed that the company has an adequate cash flow and can pay someone to do the personal/personnel job that has to be done. Unfortunately, this is not always the real case.

Improvisation

In the real world many small or emerging businesses are struggling to make ends meet and don't have the cash flow to hire anyone, much less the *right* person (who can often come at a high price). Then, you have to improvise.

Improvisation comes in the form of an "incubation period" of:

- Hiring outside services (accounting, etc.).
- Use of part-time employees.
- Using commission sales people.
- Bringing in a project manager for specific projects and splitting project profits.
- Rehiring retired people.
- Capitalizing on family capabilities (that are often free).
- Seeking help from friends.
- Covering expenses only.
- Hiring "project" people and/or independent agents that consult rather than be employed. In this case, new tax laws may still require an IRS reduction from wages.

Unfortunately these stop gap measures do not lead to "an organization"— at least, it doesn't until you have enough cash flow to *hire* an organization in the first place.

For companies that struggle through this gestation period, the period often lasts more than 9 months, unless the firm gets a break. It is common for the emerging firm to struggle through 3 to 4 years of hand-to-mouth operation before it goes under, or grows through an influx of capital generated from outside sources or internally through sales.

Emerging companies should identify those fragile decisions made during infancy that will lead to a strong puberty and adulthood. A small error at the beginning of a business can lead to delays in reaching the goals of success. It is very easy to miss your goal if you make the wrong decision at the beginning (Fig. 3-5).

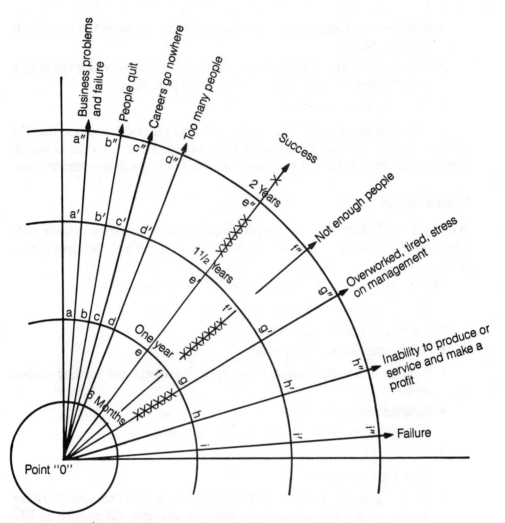

xxxxx: one path to success
The personnel and management decisions made at point "0" affect the pathline one takes to success or failure.

Fig. 3-5. Build an emerging company staff in 6 month time frames.

The personnel decision a manager makes at the zero point affects the pathline you take toward successful employment practices.

Problems begin to take shape as a company moves outward in years. At certain checkpoints (intersections), symptoms and problems can occur, and you must be able to react in order to find the road to success. You may have to make adjustments to get back on that road.

In an emerging company, funny things can happen when problems are solved because sometimes they are solved incorrectly.

In one case a plant went down due to calamity. The whole firm lent a hand in building a new building and putting equipment back into operation, bringing the firm back into full production in a matter of a few months, but this speed led to later problems. Cheapness of materials and speedy engineering left the building fragile so that a freak gale blew down a portion of the building, leaving the firm at half production again.

The point is, managers should *identify those fragile decisions* during infancy that will lead to a strong puberty and adulthood. Using mapping concepts, it is easy to illustrate that a little error at the beginning of a project or business leads to success or takes you a long way from it.

During this tenuous time of startup, when you are day-by-day finding out if you have a real business or not, there are four personnel axioms that you must follow:

1. Don't box yourself into people problems. A man or woman who needs a lot of hand-holding has no home in an emerging company.

2. Concentrate on hiring self-starters and people who can perform without guidance.

3. Hire people who know the value of an order and have a kind way to treat customers.

4. Avoid clock watchers; your people should be project and goal oriented, in accordance with a timetable.

WHO ARE THE BAD GUYS?

Even with good hiring practices, the dynamics of growth of a threshold company often lead to problem people. What makes them different in an emerging company is that they can harm you more, and more quickly; thus they need to be identified and dealt with more quickly. The typical problem people include:

The Instigator. He or she may also be called the agitator. Be careful of the instigator or agitator. They come in many forms. For example, although our society has become much more tolerant to race, creed, and color in the workplace, sex discrimination is becoming more dominant. Sex discrimination takes many forms; touching, patting, petting, jokes, comments, solicitations, and threats. Many times they are subtle and sometimes they are innocent. The instigator may file a charge if your policy on sex discrimination is too strong. She or he knows it is possible to get someone in trouble easily if your firm takes a strong stand in such matters. The instigator is not limited to discrimination, however.

The Absent Employee. A small or emerging company should be lean and hungry, and certainly cannot afford to have people absent. When hiring, explain your expectations in a firm way and be quick to separate people that don't meet company standards for being on the job. Absenteeism is often a precursor to turnover problems, so it is important to spot absenteeism in its early stages and deal with it promptly (Fig. 3-6).

Spotting It

It is easy to spot absenteeism on a time card, but sometimes time card data is not analyzed thoroughly. Salaried employees probably don't punch the clock, yet an absentee analysis for them should be included in all company absentee analysis.

You should develop your own system for spotting the absenteeism problem, however there are some clues to watch:

- In a manufacturing operation, one way is to spot production or machine downtime. This is often traced to absenteeism.
- In a service industry you usually see a drop in sales or revenues.
- Cost of sales per employee can relate to absenteeism.
- Customer complaints related to delays of any kind.
- Accounting can often spot absenteeism symptoms, for example, variances in direct labor overhead vs. budgeted figures.

Symptomatic of the absentee problem, you should watch:

- Increased shipping and expediting costs.
- Increased part time help expenses.
- Idle time.
- QC (quality control) problems.
- Sick leave and overtime payments.
- Changes in employee benefit charges (for time not worked).

Curing It

- The best cure is not to let it start in the first place. Start your company with a policy of regular attendance; if this is initiated as you begin operations, there will be no need to change the policy (with grim consequences) at a later time.
- Reward good attendance with cash bonuses or other items that are meaningful.
- Widespread absenteeism may call for outside diagnostics to employee dissatisfactions that may extend from poor morale due to lack of benefits, to drug and alcohol related problems, or to illness.
- Involve unions and supervisors in terms of tracing and counseling.

A growing company should pay particular attention to absenteeism among its long-time employees. Rapid changes in company goals might mean management styles have changed (for better or worse) and have left some old-timers behind (because they can't keep up with the changes), or left them upset.

Fig. 3-6. Absenteeism: Spot it! Cure it!.

The Dud. It is quite possible to hire a person that appears to be a bomb-shell, but the firing mechanism just doesn't work. For example, once hired, many secretaries do not know the meaning of hard work. In recent visits to large office complexes, a salesman showed us a four-page presentation consisting of a marketing program being recommended to a client. There were two pages of text and two pages of titles—a task that took the man's secretary 2 days to perform. (Why was that person hired in the first place?) By comparison, we know that an emerging company must have help that can knock out that same job in 2 hours or less.

How do you get a secretary with that talent and dedication? Be prepared to pay for someone who *has* the talent from a previous job so that you don't have to pay for the training. Prepare a specific work load that you expect to be accomplished during the first two weeks on the job. Review conditions then and don't hang onto anyone that is less than what you require.

Don't be a sucker for a pretty face when it comes to hiring someone who can't cut the mustard behind the keyboard. A good secretary is really an administrative assistant for the CEO of an emerging company. She or he works for the CEO, not the office manager.

The Angry Employee. While behavioral scientists have found that persons who habitually do not express anger tend to have higher blood pressure than persons who express anger openly, the latter can be hell to work with.

Angry or hostile people don't fit well in an emerging company. There is too much interaction among people, and the delays and lack of communication that parallel argumentative situations should not be ignored but eliminated.

Anger—and resentment, too—are like gunpowder. In little doses it can be handled, but in dynamite proportions it creates uncontrolled explosions. The latter kind of employee usually does not belong in the threshold company.

The Jealous Employee. Jealousy—and resentment—affects personal performance and productivity. These traits are two essential "musts" of the manager of a threshold company. "Coping With Jealousy In the Office," *Texas Woman Magazine,* October 1979, suggests that women are the most bloodthirsty when it comes to office jealousy; especially when they are resentful of each other.

As the manager of an emerging company, you can deal with job jealousy, whether among males or females, a little easier than in old hard-line organizational chart companies. The new firm will experience growth and new positions will open up more often, giving, for example, the person who was passed over for promotion another opportunity for advancement in a short period of time.

The Company Gossip and the Grapevine. The only way this kind of person can exist in an emerging company is by management flows—i.e., giving people something to talk about. This problem can be nipped in the bud by constantly disseminating information to employees by meaningful company newsletters *written with management input* and dealing with the problems and potentials of your employees. Honest messages directly from the CEO will squelch gossip, especially when management thinks and talks in a positive manner. Do not make management decisions on gossip or hearsay.

The Backbiter or the Second-guesser. This individual can be very disruptive to your organization, hurt morale, and detract from your supervisor's leadership effectiveness. If you can't minimize the individual's effect, you are better off without that person.

Considering those problems and problem people, there are four early-bird steps that help the manager deal with the situations that arise:

- Early warnings
- Early diagnosis
- Early remedial action
- Early dismissal

The latter becomes particularly important if cases go to arbitration. An arbitrator may have no sympathy, or better, *should* have no sympathy, for an organization that carries a problem person on the payroll for two or more years and then dismisses the person for problems that have been taking place since the first days of employment. This is particularly true at management levels where the person is constantly under review by professionals and peers and where the problem should become obvious before "tenure."

MANAGEMENT STYLES

Styles, and in some ways, capabilities, keep managers from dealing with difficult people. Certainly some people should never have been hired in the first place. This happening can be the result of a common type of weak manager—one who is *afraid* to hire good people. If your company grows, this type of manager will self-destruct. This manager will surround him or herself with marginal employees and, as the work load increases, will be unable to get the job done. The result? The manager, will become inundated with work to the point where he or she can no longer fulfill the obligation of the job. You probably have a policy of trying to promote from within, but he or she hasn't given you anything to promote. To solve the problem, you'll probably have to hire somebody over the person, let him, or her go, or do a lateral transfer. None of those options are very pleasant.

Another difficult type of employee to manage is the highly creative one. Many times these people feel you cannot mandate creativity; therefore, they'll be very reluctant to set goals and objectives. They also can become bored with their job. They typically do not possess good people skills. Be careful. If you don't insist that they follow corporate policies, you'll find yourself with a prima donna who cannot or will not function as part of a management team.

As a chief executive office (CEO) or chief operating officer (COO), you are continually encouraging teamwork. Some people just are not team players. It is important that you determine early who are team players and who are not. If you have an individual who is not a team player, it is important that you determine whether or not you can tolerate someone in his or her position of responsibility who acts alone.

Many times a non-team player is an empire builder. The longer you let it go, the higher this person will build the barrier between his or her department and the rest of the company and the broader the chasm will come that you will eventually have to breach. Be very careful of empire builders, for when it becomes necessary to make organizational changes, it will be difficult for anyone to understand how the department operates.

Fortunately, we have outgrown the period in American history of the young nonconformist, anti-establishment employees. That group is now in their 30s. The young employees now under 20 can be developed into team players and work with others much easier than in the 1970s. At the same time, many older employees might never change, and often it is a waste of energy trying to change them. What you see is what you've got. When an old-line company turns into an emerging company, some employees with years of service might not fit in the evolving organization due to lack of technical talent or other failure-to-adjust reasons. Terminating an older employee is never easy, and today it is even more complicated due to the documentation required to ensure a company is not guilty of age discrimination. Try counseling these people.

COUNSELING AND APPRAISALS

Firing is usually a last resort for most managers, but what is the first resort? It is counseling and appraisals.

If you have turnover or suspect that you have people problems, you can probably get to the cause through a morale survey. Some companies choose to refer to these as "company improvements surveys." You can probably administer and evaluate the results of this type survey yourself, but it is best to get some professional assistance when preparing the questions.

In analyzing the possible source of problems with an individual or the company as a whole, it helps to try to understand what is important to the individual employee. Many times it is such things as free time, weekends, recognition, status, children's education, religion, or even lack of a parking place, that makes up individual values. Empathy is the key.

To start, the most simplistic classification is that people are either *people-people* or *things-people*. People-people are those who enjoy supervising and working with and being a team player. They're typically marketing or manufacturing supervisors. Things-people are typically those who would prefer to work with facts. These are often accountants, engineers, machinists, et al. The latter group are often the ones who are most difficult to work with, to motivate, and to involve in goal setting. The bottom line in dealing with these individuals comes back to empathy and finding "which button turns them on."

In the small or emerging company where the motivation of the individual employee is so important, the CEO also has a dual role of being the chaplain. As the company grows, this role becomes more difficult and can be delegated to a personnel manager or to an employee assistance program.

Employee assistance programs can be quite rewarding. When you consider there is such little investment, the return on investment (ROI) is phenomenal. About every 3 years the people from the employee assistance program have a short review session with your supervisors. The supervisors are counselled on how to recognize changes in employee performance that might indicate a personal problem. The supervisor does not attempt to counsel the employee, but instead refers him to the employee assistance coordinator who is usually someone in the personnel department. This coordinator discusses the employee's problem and refers him or her to professional organizations. Problems commonly uncovered are alcohol or chemical dependency, marital, health, family, or financial. Many of these problems, of course, are covered by the employee's medical insurance and others can be helped through nonprofit service organizations.

It isn't uncommon for a manager to get a call on a Sunday, particularly at Thanksgiving or Christmas, from a family member to offer thanks for helping put his or her family back together or for solving a problem. And it isn't uncommon to receive calls to bail your employees or their progeny out of jail. These are the joys and heartaches of managing a small or emerging company—experiences too lowly for the presidents of the large multi-nationals.

The most valuable tools to the employee, then, are motivation plus counseling and assistance. These should be married to the employee appraisal (Fig. 3-7). The employee appraisal should be conducted with every salaried employee at least twice a year. You should make it as objective as possible, but leave some subjective areas for discussion. These areas could include self-improvement through continuing education such as Dale Carnegie for motivation, and engineering or scientific symposium for engineering know-how.

The appraisal should be conducted in private between the supervisor and the employee during a period when you will not be interrupted. An interesting approach (occasionally) is to give the employee the appraisal form in advance and ask them to do a self-appraisal. Sometimes you get the best results from that. There was an old adage "praise in public and criticize in private." The private appraisal is the time to talk of the employee's weaknesses.

Through the appraisal or series of appraisals, you and the employee can determine where his or her weakness lie. After a number of attempts, it is sometimes necessary to determine if you will continue to try to improve or ignore the weak area because the employee possesses some specifically high levels of strengths that can be emphasized for his or her and the company's betterment. In other words, you could both be expending a great deal of energy in attempting to improve an individual's performance in an area that can be ignored.

Fig. 3-7. Employee appraisal: An example.

EMPLOYEE PERFORMANCE EVALUATION

This Employee Performance Evaluation form has been designed to generate the following result.

1. A formal discussion between supervisor and a subordinate
2. For the purpose of discovering how the subordinate is presently performing on the job and
3. How the subordinate can improve his or her performance in the future
4. So that the subordinate, the supervisor, and Multiplex Company, Inc. as a whole will benefit.

Ideally, the supervisor and the subordinate should both review a blank copy of this evaluation form independently, making no marks on it, and then meet to complete an evaluation of the subordinate. This will encourage a joint discussion of the items on this form without the liability of any written preconceptions and give both parties the opportunity to state their views and compromise: Of course, the evaluation interview should be more than just a joint filling out of the form, there should be discussion of its implications for the future.

Evaluation Performance

Part I. - Often times the non-routines goals are weighed heavily in performance evaluations and the activities for which the job was actually justified are overlooked. In this section we wish to concentrate on the major day to day responsibilities of the job.

List five of the most important aspects of the job and then measure performance on a scale of 2 to 10 with the higher number representing the more satisfactory performance.

- We wish to identify areas where performance has been strong.

- We wish to identify areas where performance could be improved.

In Part II. - We wish to review the employee's performance level against ten basic characteristics and/or skill factors common to effective professionals and managers.

In Part III. - We wish to identify a developmental program for the employee based on the strengths and weaknesses.

Fig. 3-7. (Continued)

NAME _____ JOB TITLE_____ DATE _____

Part I. List the five major responsibilities of the job in order of importance where possible. Comment on how well these responsibilities are being performed and then place an X in the appropriate column of the rating scale with 10 representing the more satisfactory performance.

EVALUATE THE PERFORMANCE

NO.	RESPONSIBILITY	PERFORMANCE COMMENTS	RATING SCALE				
			10	8	6	4	2
1							
2							
3							
4							
5							

TOTAL POINTS PART I _____

Describe areas where you feel performance is particularly strong and a significant contribution is being made.

_____

_____

_____

Describe areas that you feel need improvement.

_____

_____

_____

Fig. 3-7. (Continued)

Part II. Below are ten basic characteristics and/or skill factors common to effective professionals and managers. Place an X in the appropriate box with 5 representing the more satisfactory performance.

FACTORS	5	4	3	2	1
1. Job knowledge - The total knowledge and information possessed with respect to the techniques and methods involved in carrying out his/her duties.					
2. Human Relations Skills - The general ability to handle problems of a people oriented nature with his/her subordinates, peers, and supervisor.					
3. Ability to Plan & Organize - The ability to organize, plan, schedule and delegate work effectively.					
4. Communication - A measure of the ability to select and pass on information and the resulting effectiveness. Both oral and written communication skills should be considered.					
5. Ability to select, direct, and develop subordinates - The ability to motivate and stimulate subordinates and recognize their capabilities and to obtain outstanding development of them.					
6. Sound Decisions - The degree of judgment used and the effectiveness of decisions made and conclusions reached.					
7. Attitude - The degree of interest demonstrated in the job and in the company, and the willingness with which work assignments, supervision, and company policies and operating procedures are accepted.					
8. Initiative and Creativity - A measure of self-starting and the facility for original thinking and innovating.					
9. Cost Consciousness - Ability to perceive cost improvements and/or control budget.					
10. Attendance - Record of attendance and punctuality since last performance.					

TOTAL POINTS POSSIBLE PART II   TOTAL POINTS RECEIVED PART II _____
TOTAL POINTS POSSIBLE PART I & II _____ TOTAL POINTS RECEIVED PART I & II _____
TOTAL POINTS RECEIVED PART I & II ÷ BY 100 OR 95 = _____ % FOR EVALUATION

Fig. 3-7. (Continued)

CONTINUING EDUCATION PROGRAM

Job performance and experience alone may not prepare you for promotion. Continuing education and personal improvement are a part of the formula for career growth.

As you finalize the semi annual evaluation with your supervisor, you should include some goals for career development. Multiplex has a procedure for educational assistance.

In order to be able to determine a person's interest in development, we will recognize career development points.

Points may be earned on the following basis:

1. 5 points per college credit hour completed.
2. 1 point for each seminar completed outside of St. Louis.
3. 1 point for each evening seminar or class attended.
4. 1/2 point for each one day seminar held in St. Louis during working hours.
5. Correspondence school may also qualify for career development points.

Guideline for the number of career development points you should attempt in a given year:

1. Non-degreed - 15 continuing education points.
2. Degreed - 10 continuing education points.
3. Graduate degree - 5 continuing education points.

Courses scheduled in previous year.

Scheduled	Completed	# Points
1.		
2.		
3.		
4.		
5.		

Courses scheduled in current year.

Scheduled	Completed	# Points
1.		
2.		
3.		
4.		
5.		

Comments: _____

Employees Signature _____ Date _____
Supervisor's Signature _____ Date _____
Rater's Signature _____ Date _____

If you have a problem employee and have worked hard with him or her to correct serious problems, you should set time limits for correction. People problems are like dead fish—they get worse with time. If you have got a significant problem with an employee and it is not getting any better, it can then have a negative effect on the remainder of the organization. They may perceive that you are ignoring the problems.

If it reaches a point where you do have to terminate someone, it is best to do it face-to-face. You make it easier on yourself if you do it late in the afternoon and continue the termination interview past the normal quitting time. That will save the individual embarrassment. Performing the distasteful task at his or her office allows you to get up and leave without lingering discussions in your office, where there is no escape. In terms of severance and/or holiday or vacation pay, you can save yourself a great deal of effort by covering these questions in personnel policies. To avoid a big morale problem, consider the problem of Christmas layoffs before the start of a new fiscal year. Officers should consider layoffs at a time when it will not create problems with remaining employees. Although companies should act quickly when layoffs are necessary, a close look at personnel requirements can take place well before the year's main holiday period.

If your company is non-union, the best way to stay so is to treat your employees fairly. Provide wages and fringe benefits that are equivalent to or better than those in your industry and area. You might also want to have a profit-sharing program. How far you go depends on how much you want to stay non-union. Emerging companies are likely targets for unionization—at least at the plant level. There are many aspects of avoiding unionization. Key facets include: pay that is comparable or above industry standards; high morale and the potential for growth; and promotion and advancements in responsibility.

If a union does organize your shop, don't think that it is the end of the world. Unions' power and influence have been on the decline for the past 20 years. There is no indication that this trend is going to reverse. Service organizations typically are not unionized and they are becomming more dominant.

In your negotiations with the union, don't agree to or sign anything that you can't live with. If you do sign it, then live up to your agreement. Just because the union takes over the representation of the people doesn't mean that you have to lose your credibility.

CHARGING PEOPLES' "PARTICIPATION" BATTERIES

The first battery that has to remain charged is your own, especially if you are the CEO or COO. To keep the current going and the work flowing, enough cannot be said about the value of a good secretary. The good secretary knows the policies and procedures of the company and can accomplish the work you assign. The *great* one also understands the mission statement of the company and what its values are, and can handle problems for you in your absence with employees, vendors, or particularly customers, thus ensuring they feel satisfied that something is going to be done. You want a mature secretary who can make decisions, but knows the limit of authority.

Over the years you are going to develop a number of loyal employees. You can't buy or hire loyalty; it takes time to develop. You'll know whose loyalty you can depend upon. Don't try to rush it. At the same time, longevity does not guarantee loyalty. Don't take people for granted.

If you've got an individual who is giving you 120 percent effort, he or she could have problems in their personal life. Divorce is common. They also might not be bright enough to complete their work during the regular work hours. In either case, do not necessarily take the amount of effort expended as a measure of competency or loyalty.

Owners of small or emerging companies often have family members as employees; this can create many different problems. For one, it creates a problem for the people who supervise them. For another, it creates a problem with promotions and morale when someone else feels that he or she is more deserving and is not a family member. One suggestion which will help you, as well as the family member, is to require him or her to work full-time for someone else for 2 years before they can work for your company. With this in mind, the individual will join your company with some experience and maturity and will gain more respect from the other employees.

Buffing up your own management style is also important. It is healthy for a company to have people who have different type personalities, approaches, and styles of management. However, it helps if styles are not philosophically different. For example, hiring a general manager of the Gestapo variety—or one who manages by dictatorship—is usually incompatible with a good, loyal, hardworking, honest, intelligent manager, who manages by persuasion and example.

Lateral transfers provide one way to save a good employee. For example, in one instance a vice president of manufacturing promoted his brother to plant superintendent. The latter individual wasn't a people-oriented type person, yet people-orientation was required for the position. The man was becoming a nervous wreck at the age of 35. Transferring him into the manufacturing engineering department solved all the problems and gave him a new impetus to advance. Indeed, emotional fitness should be watched carefully because pressures of being part of a growth industry can be quite severe. People can turn to alcohol, drugs, or be subject to depression and nonobjectivity. Threshold companies need to address the questions of emotional fitness of their employees. (This is not an area that should be assigned to an operating manager, but rather to a professional, often someone tied to the corporate health insurance program.)

In a *lateral transfer,* what you attempt to do is first find a position that the employee is capable of handling—one which won't expose him or her to becoming a victim of the Peter principle (i.e., working up to a level of incompetence). Then you embellish the position with its importance and stature. You transfer the individual into this new position with no change in salary. The employee can make the transfer without any financial burden and, at the same time, preserve ego. If the new position does not justify the salary which he or she is receiving, you might have to reduce his or her percentage of annual increase in your annual review until it is more in line with the salary range of the new position.

Finally, one of the most difficult types of employee problems is how to handle the employee who has scar tissue. This employee has gone through some very unpleasant experiences with a previous employer. The person is obviously capable or you wouldn't have hired the individual. But he or she is very restrained in approaching problems and expressing his or her opinion. You might say this person is "goosey." There might be only one solution for this type of employee. First, of course, you have to recognize the problem. Secondly, you need to give positive reinforcement and express satisfaction with his or her job to rebuild his or her confidence. Recognize that in some cases the scar tissue can be generated or created within your own shop. In these instances, if you have too many of these type people, you will find it very difficult to focus on long-range plans. The people are just too insecure to think beyond short-range.

YOUR FAMILY AND THE ORGANIZATION

While Bette Davis, the actress, may not have much in common with a growth company or an emerging industry, she has been quoted as saying that the first 10 years of your career you love it—the career—nothing else. Forget the family. The idea behind these statements is that you must devote 24 hours a day to a career. In contrast, the authors believe that the employee who puts his or her family into a freezer while they "do their thing," might easily return home one day to find a defrosted home life. Unfortunately, too many managers of growth companies go charging upward expecting the family to remain in perfect balance, and upon their return (after a decade of fast track), they expect to pick up where things left off. That's impossible.

Kids grow up and spouse's personal goals change. In retrospect, the job, the title, the salary, and the position can become inconsequential.

One answer is: Don't get married; don't pretend to have a family when you only are giving lip service to it. Or, spell out intermediate and long-range goals along with time priorities *you* believe are important. It *is* possible to have a family and a career, but you have to be explicitly honest with yourself and realize that the job is demanding, but so is family involvement and participation.

When you think about it, an emerging or growth company can provide a winning way of life for the family in many respects. To avoid the tradeoff conflict, the company *and* the individual should know what a person wants in terms of life activity—and to know when he or she wants it. Spelling out these personal viewpoints ahead of time, and letting the company know them, can (sometimes) ameliorate conflicts before they appear.

Emerging companies demand that people work hard; it is very naive to think otherwise. Also, the larger a company grows, the harder it is to look at each individual's wants and needs. *That* look is the responsibility of the individual. It is the company's job to provide a way for the individual to convey his or her thinking to the firm.

Question: Where does the real problem come?

Answer: It comes when you run into a situation where the employee has been loyal to you during the dynamic stage, yet now he or she is burned out, even to the point of a mental or physical breakdown. This incapacitation can lead to individuals becoming corporate outcasts because they no longer can perform and there was no plan on what to do when these situations arise.

4

Marketing:
What It Really Is
and How to Do It

REAL MARKETING, THE KIND THAT IS SUCCESSFUL, IS "FIGHTING IN THE trenches." It means following leads (many of them bad), one-on-one appointments with people that don't treat you particularly well (some of whom you don't really like), long hours, report writing, developing contacts, and working a hospitality suite for 10 hours while your feet ache and you are surrounded by people who are tipsy, loose-tongued, and tight enough to think they are funny. It is *very* hard work and quite unlike a business where the customer comes to you.

In addition, there is the integration of advertising and public relations with sales and business plans, sales goals (boggies), and the pressure to keep expenses down while productivity stays up and inventory stays down. There is probably no other single discipline in an emerging business that is more misunderstood than marketing. In addition, an emerging company has to add to its list of problems that many people don't know the firm, its employees, and its products, plus the company might not have a good track record.

Still, there are ways to overcome these disadvantages. One way is to turn marketing into a total system of synergistic business activity designed to plan, price, promote, and distribute products and services to active and potential customers. As such, the emerging company should initiate marketing programs that encompasse:

- Market definition
- Product planning
- Market research
- Research and development, plus manufacturing and technical service
- Competitive analysis
- Distribution
- Advertising
- Public relations
- Sales promotion
- Sales

To effectively carry the market plan to fruition, a manager must utilize all of these company activities.

Whether an emerging company is selling a service or a manufactured product, every employee is a profit center. This is true from the person on the assembly line to the salesperson in the Salinas, to the service on your copying machine. Small and emerging companies should try to have employees think that manner, with each person "marketing" his or her work to the company for a profit. Even on a production line there are customers to consider; step 2 of the line is the customer of step 1, and so on.

With this thinking, each person is definitely a part of marketing—a fact that becomes more obvious when you realize that the individual employees and not the organization are responsible for the quality of the product or service that ultimately lead to customer satisfaction.

Although R&D and marketing are responsible for development of new products and bringing them to the marketplace and a salesperson sells a service, it is the first-line employee who is responsible for repeat business. In manufacturing, this person is responsible for making the product of good quality and at a targeted cost that fits the market need. In service, he or she must perform not only the job that has to be accomplished, but also satisfy wants when the situation demands it.

MARKET DEFINITION

As a company opens its doors or as a mature company initiates a growth program, one of the most important elements of marketing is to decide precisely what business you are in. Small companies, particularly as they struggle to obtain cash, often dilute their efforts by chasing opportunities that are actually out of their main line of business.

Why do they do this? Because they see an opportunity to obtain cash—the lifeblood of business survival. Although this approach to marketing might be necessary, or might even be wise once in awhile, (to land a project that will give instant dollars and add a one-time bulge to the bottom line), nonfocused marketing is not a recommendation for the emerging industry.

Instead, the *two cardinal rules for growth* companies are:

1. Carve out a niche in the market (and then expand on it).
2. Create a product mix that includes a mixture of products with long- and short-term payouts.

PRODUCT PLANNING

In the '80s, some small companies have been growing at much higher rates than large corporations. There are two facets to this growth. First, small or emerging companies have dynamics and drive that are not present in large companies. Second, large companies, by their sheer size, cannot grow as fast on a percentage basis.

Because of size and the related overhead, small companies can get a foothold in niche markets. In fact, some firms' recent dynamic growths are related to providing products for the giants. This is true in areas as diverse as electronics to chemicals and food products to heat exchangers. When volume is low, it sometimes just doesn't pay for a large company to handle the production of some small orders. The emerging company often comes into existence tied to novel technology or services that are responsive to customer needs and wants. Thus, to maintain growth, new businesses should maintain a balance between emerging and maturing products or services, noting well their position on the bell curve associated with product life cycles.

MARKET RESEARCH

Customers' needs and wants change, however, and emerging companies should keep abreast of these changes by employing good market research. Many managers of emerging companies shy away from those words (market research) because:

- They think its expensive.
- They don't believe the results.
- They don't understand market research.
- They don't see its value.

Some of these reservations are legitimate, but anyone who feels a company can do without market research is doomed to become one of the 7 out of 10 businesses that fail after 5 years.

There are various types of marketing research (Table 4-1) that vary in price and value. Generally, if you are dealing with a reputable, small market research company with esoteric interests, you will get what you pay for. A product-market analysis, for example, might run about $14,000, depending on the information required and amount of field work. Obviously, a market research going into plants and offices to gather data would be no less expensive than your own people making sales calls. That is one reason why sales reports and relationship management are vital tools in market research

Where companies get stung with market research is in hiring big-name consultants to do work when these firms really don't have any expertise in the relevant area of interest or when the firms rely on computer models, many of which are trash. There is no substitute for logical thinking.

As an overview to economic data, productivity data, and operating rate data, managers can turn to the Department of Commerce and to the Federal Reserve System (often referred to as "The Fed"). The Fed was voted into existence by the United States government to establish monetary and credit controls on the banking industry. Since then, it has become an unusual source of market information (much of it free); this is true for other parts of the federal and state governments as well. Overall, the government is only one source of data. Regardless of the source, the important thing is knowing how, where, and when to use these sources of information, placing a value on their contents, and determining the cost of this research.

**Table 4-1. Rating Market Research Information
(Source: Weismantel International).**

Information	Relative Importance*
Company sponsored market research	9 – 10
Internal company data	6 – 7
Multiclient research and syndicated market research reports	5 – 6
Research from industry publications	5 – 6
Purchased reports & databases from market research firms	4.5 – 5.5
Government publications & tapes	4 – 5

*10 = Most Important

RESEARCH AND DEVELOPMENT, MANUFACTURING, AND TECHNICAL SERVICE

New businesses and emerging companies develop their product ideas from research or concepts of the original manager(s). Sometimes a person quits a job at a large company to pursue a new product or service which they feel offers significant advantages over what currently exists.

In some way this information came from market research or from simply recognizing this narrow focus. A growth company should push its product into the market quickly. Why?

It may take large companies—the dinosaurs—a long time to stand up; but once they do, then facilities and financial strength can carry a lot of momentum into the market. Furthermore, large companies are not always slow to act.

A smart approach, when you are an emerging company, is to fire before you aim. By being small, you can move fast and outmaneuver corporate giants. Use this advantage while a market opportunity is hot. While others are performing feasibility studies, you'll be counting profits. Act fast!

This does not imply that the emerging company does not know the location of the target. The gun may be firing at an already identified niche market that needs to be fired upon immediately, before others start shooting at it.

A small company might be surprised, however, at just how fast a large company can act (or react) when faced with competition. In the 1960s for example, General Food's (GF) Maxwell House Division learned from the trade, that a competitor was about to introduce a new coffee, something GF itself had been contemplating.

Within a matter of 3 months, Maxwell House had designed labels, produced cans, and filled and placed them on the shelf a month ahead of the competitive product. This totally stole the thunder from the opposition, placing them in an underdog position in the marketplace because supermarkets cut their first deals with GF.

This illustrates three submarketing principles:

1. Get there firstest with the mostest.
2. Keep your marketing plan out of the hands of competition and trade until you are ready to deliver your product.
3. Manufacturing can be an integral part of successful marketing (Fig. 4-1).

Considering the interfaces between R&D, manufacturing, and tech service, a company can't sell a product if the company doesn't have it in the warehouse or can't get it delivered on time. For example, a small paint company developed a novel line of 14 colors for exterior house paint and introduced the products in March—just before the painting season. Two colors (Forest Green and Bark

Strategy

☞ Was the marketing plan checked to ensure consistency with the company's overall business plan?

☞ Did the marketing business unit prepare a marketing plan? (Realize that this unit may simply be one individual.)

☞ Did you superimpose a public relations and advertising plan onto the marketing plan preceding it by 4 months and 2 months respectively?

☞ Was adequate marketing research performed as available?

☞ Did the marketing plan clearly identify specific objectives by Standard Industrial Classification (SIC) code and with target customers?

☞ Was the actual decision maker contacted? (i.e., the person who is truly responsible for placing the ads—this may not be the purchasing department.)

☞ Was a milestone chart created with specific assignments and target dates?

Sales

☞ Are sales expense for travel, advertising, and public relations consistent with the budget?

☞ Were sales promotions, customer contact, trade shows, and other activities documented for both sales and follow up?

☞ Was collateral (brochures and other sales support documents) ordered in time to be useful?

☞ Were salespersons adequately compensated?

☞ Was a lead follow-up program put in place to qualify leads and to identify which leads resulted in sales?

Other Activity

☞ Did marketing receive the necessary support from computer services, engineering, R&D, tech services, or other departments such as transportation and warehousing?

☞ Did management support marketing by actively calling on key accounts and implementing relationship management?

☞ Was there need for better communication at any level?

☞ Did sales meetings accomplish specific goals?

☞ Was there too much paperwork?

Fig. 4-1. Checklist for a marketing audit.

Brown) were not manufactured because the chemists couldn't get the formula right. It took until September to put these colors into production, and all during the painting season, dealers and customers were furious.

In this case, and others like it, sales were lost and customers dissatisfied when the new product was not available when the sales department said it would be. Unfortunately this is a common problem in emerging industries that often bring new products to the marketplace. There is a methodology, however, to ensure this doesn't happen. It involves an interaction of marketing, R&D, and manufacturing. Even if you are a dealer, distributor, retailer, or service company, you should understand the basics of manufacturing processes, lead times, and other production techniques.

Also, for continued corporate strength, R&D must be producing a mix of products that have both short- and long-term payouts.

COMPETITIVE ANALYSIS

Every company should develop an understanding of the strengths and weaknesses of the competition—especially the industry leaders. Mimic what they do right and improve upon what they do wrong. Compiling an analysis checklist helps (Fig. 4-2).

In addition, the emerging company should perform a self-analysis. Analyze what you have been doing right and build upon it; look carefully at what has worked for you in the past. Analyze where you have found new business in the past and how you got the orders. Are you targeting high-potential customers?

An emerging company should study the nature of the relationship between the number and size distribution of competitors in a market (market structure).

☞ Analyze competitor's products—strengths & weaknesses.

☞ Analyze competitor's goals.

☞ Analyze competitor's pricing strategy.

☞ Analyze competitor's markets and marketing strategies.

☞ Perform a substitution analysis.

☞ Analyze competitor's production & facility capabilities.

☞ Compare investment, operating, and maintenance costs.

☞ Perform a financial profile including cost analysis.

☞ Analyze competitor's technical and process capabilities.

☞ Perform an international competitive analysis, if applicable.

Fig. 4-2. Ten commandments of a competitive analysis checklist.

Couple this to an analysis of each competitor's performance. This tactic is of crucial importance to emerging industries and the managers responsible for evaluating their own company's competitive efforts.

The best solutions to a competitive analysis and marketing questions in general, are based on common sense. Most of the time answers are not totally new. (To date the authors have not uncovered any test to identify common sense in employees; however, a sense of humor seems to be one common denominator.)

DISTRIBUTION

Your chief marketing executive needs to be mature and experienced in supervising. He or she needs to be aware of and support your policies and programs on personnel management, evaluations, appraisals, promotions, and compensation. Also, he or she must be an expert in distribution networks.

Direct sales by your own sales staff can be expensive—especially during growth periods. For that reason, a small or emerging company might find it best to utilize dealers and distributors or even manufacturer's representatives. This is true in selling either a product or a service.

A manufacturer's rep usually works on straight commission and does not take possession of the goods. Dealers and distributors often take possession with dealers concentrating on retail or over-the-counter sales and distributors working from warehouse stock. This obviously varies from industry to industry. Some manufacturers' reps also sell and receive commissions for selling services, and the percent on services can vary from the percent on goods. Rep commissions generally vary from 5 to 25 percent depending on the item sold while distributors work at as much as 40 percent to compensate for the inventory carrying costs. You could even choose a combination of those options. A combination method of distribution has some definite advantages in reaching different types of customers by different methods of distribution. The more different methods of distribution you have, however, the more complicated your entire marketing program becomes.

There is one advantage to manufacturers' reps because they only get paid for what they sell. At the same time, their time is divided among a number of principals and they might not be committing the effort to your product line you think they are. If services and after-sales service is important to your business, you cannot get the response from a manufacturer's rep that you can from your own salaried sales force.

A dealer or distributor organization can be an effective mode of distribution since the dealer or distributor is motivated to sell a product he or she has paid for. At the same time, establishing a dealer and distributor organization is a very time-consuming process; in many cases accomplished by trial and error. For this reason, most agreements have a 30- to 90-day escape clause.

Choosing the best rep or distributor often involves talking to the purchasing agents of the best prospects or customers in a geographical area. They will usually volunteer information as to who has the best qualified sales and service available.

Many companies who set up very effective dealer and distributor organizations, 10, 15, or 20 years ago, now find themselves in a very difficult position. Some of the principals of these dealers and distributors are now very successful and affluent businesspeople. Because of the long-standing relationship with their principal, they now have exclusive territorial distribution rights. The principal finds him or herself now in a position of having a dealer and distributor who is not as responsive to the needs of the customer. This type of problem can be partially alleviated by retaining certain key accounts that the company serves on a direct sales basis and perhaps where the distributor receives a modest override from the manufacturer.

One of the most difficult problems of a combination distribution system is the series of discounts and pricing combinations that can be created. Take caution and be particularly cognizant of the conflicts that can be created as you review your company's marketing strategy. These can often be resolved with a marketing audit (see Fig. 4-2).

ADVERTISING

This topic is also covered within chapters 8 and 9, however, the subject is mainly one that ties directly to marketing.

What makes a good advertising program for a growth company? What is the best form of advertising (direct mail, magazines, catalogs, etc.)? Is cost per exposure a meaningful statistic? These are legitimate questions for a small or emerging company whose budget is small or emerging. The answers to these questions come easily from an advertising agency, but it is not unusual for agency costs to be beyond a budget. In these cases, the company should create an "in-house" agency to take advantage of advertising discounts and work with an outside consultant for the "creativity" part of ads and brochures. This technique may turn out to be the most economical until you can afford a full-fledged ad agency.

Also, the question of where and when to advertise can be answered by studying the editorial planning calendar for those magazines that reach your target audience. Ask for the magazine's "Media Kit." Also, to determine which audiences are covered by each magazine, buy a subscription to Standard Rate and Date Service (Chicago, Illinois), or to Beacon's Publicity Checker (Chicago, Illinois). How much to advertise is a budget and management decision.

As this text is designed for emerging companies, the best recommendation might be that you select a smaller agency where your account is important and where they will be responsive to your requirements. You will probably want to pick an agency that has experience with your industry. An agency with experience will know which periodicals to use and what type of advertising works best. The agency will also know how to get free publicity and public relations value. Also, consider by what mode you want to promote your products—i.e., radio, television, newspapers, magazines, direct mail, etc.—and select an agency who has expertise in this field. You can waste a great deal of money in advertising. For that reason, you need to have your budget defined, have deadlines established, and be sure that your people don't cost you more money by missing the deadlines.

PUBLIC RELATIONS

Public relations (PR) is a means of communicating with the outside world as well as internally with company employees. PR takes many forms, including news releases, bylined stories in magazines, being quoted in stories, presenting papers at trade association meetings, and other forms of external exposure such as brochures. Internally, PR takes the form of house organs, company newspapers or newsletters, and other internal PR methods. Be aware that the "grapevine" can be a real problem when it comes to internal PR, especially when the wrong messages reach employees from that route. The concept of a PR plan can be quite brief, but a good plan is integrated and completely consistent with market objectives (see chapter 8).

SALES PROMOTION

Sales promotions are another effective tool in the marketplace, especially in relating to retail sales. "You gotta have a gimmick!" These gimmicks can range from "2 for 1" discount coupons, to special "freebees," etc., for retail store shelves. If you are in an industry that deals directly to industry, little promos such as coffee mugs with your "sales pitch," ink pens, golf hats, week-at-a-glance calendars, etc., put your company name in front of the customer. One of the most unique coffee mugs we have ever seen was one that changed colors and graphics with the temperature of the coffee. Coffee drinkers (and there are many of them) think the cup is unique so they keep using it. Therefore that particular company name is always visible to the customer.

Sales promotions, however, are much more than gimmickry. It includes an integrated program that ties the promotion to a specific goal. That goal is there by design to:

- Increase sales in a certain industry or SIC (standard industrial classification) as designated by the government.
- Work off inventory that has become too high.

- Create additional exposure (by tying new-product promotion to old-product promotion).
- Introduce new products.
- Call attention to the company, a product line, an improvement, or something that the company is doing.

Sales promotions are often most successful when they are aimed like a rifle rather than when they scatter like a shotgun. For example, one company pinpointed that it wanted to reach 100 plant managers of a particular industry. To ensure the plant manager received the promotion, the company designed a special box that contained a hard hat. To get to the hat, the box had to be opened a certain way for the promotional literature to be seen. To ensure the box was considered important, the company sent it Federal Express.

This effort turned out to be one of the most successful promotions ever conceived by the company. This result was because of the promotion itself and because each of the 100 recipients were called upon within a day of receiving the package. One promotional manager believes that promotions, direct mail, and telephoning are a trinity that must be worked as a unit. Also, the manager never sends out more than 10 direct mail pieces at a time so that each can be followed up individually. Most promotional mailings often fail due to lack of follow-up.

Similar promotions fit the service industry with the most successful items being something that is useful in day-to-day business and not something that will get tossed into the garbage when the recipient gets home or back to the office.

TRADE SHOWS

Trade shows offer important and valuable marketing opportunities for an emerging company. It often pays to attend, even if you do not have a display booth. Why?

Trade shows can be the source of a great deal of marketing information. This is an opportunity to learn a great deal about your competition, and at the same time, to meet a number of your customers who might be very geographically dispersed. If you are active in your trade associations, the show is an opportunity to meet with associates who may not be either customers or competitors, but who can provide significant information on what is going on within your industry.

Many companies have hospitality suites available after the show hours. These are also good opportunities to meet with your customers, but the suites can be an expensive bust. If you don't get the right people or you get too many people in one night, you can lose the effectiveness. So many companies have hospitality suites that there are many demands on your guests' time. While you are hosting your own hospitality suite you are also deprived of the opportunity of attending other's hospitality suites; particularly those which are held by magazines and trade journals.

One way to get the people to a hospitality suite is to invite them to dinner. You can distribute invitations at the show for specific evenings, dividing your personnel up so that each one would take a different customer or group of customers to dinner that evening. If your people know to whom they're assigned for dinner, they can spend their time in the hospitality suite with those guests. Distribution of the printed and engraved invitations on the show floor is sometimes much more effective than mailing and asking for RSVPs, but both approaches can be used in concert.

Another effective approach is to have a private room in the convention center or nearby hotel where you serve a light lunch and refreshments. Typically, the food service at conventions is mediocre, expensive, and slow, yet most people are happy to sit down and relax for awhile. In many cases, the rooms are free and you are charged only for the catered food service. Again, it is advantageous to distribute invitations at your booth. Doing so also ensures that your customer or guest will visit your booth. You also want to have someone at the door welcoming the guests and asking them to register.

Most trade shows provide training and seminar sessions as well as breakfast speakers and a banquet. Seminars can be very valuable and it often pays to have some of your people participate and evaluate the quality of the sessions for future reference. The banquets can provide you with a tremendous opportunity to invite a large number of your customers to something that is unusual and possibly very special. You can buy an entire table of 8 or 12 seats and probably invite five times that many customers before you'll fill the table. That would be, at least, a large number of your customers who are pleased that they are invited. If at the last minute you don't have the table full, you can fill it with your own people. After all, they'll probably get more from a business value perspective by attending the banquet and associating with some customers as well as peers in related companies than they would by eating dinner alone.

You've probably read those paragraphs and then ran to an adding machine tape on the cost of doing all these things. Trade shows are not cheap. If you're going to have a booth at a trade show, you want to be sure that you have enough people to run the booth. Scheduling people's time in the booth will be appreciated by the staff as well as by the customer. You'll be in a position to tell a customer when the person whom he or she wants to see will be available. If you have people in your booth, have them there for one purpose only: to meet the customers and promote the company. Don't let your people sit there and organize their catalogs or do their expense accounts. Tell their spouses and friends that you're happy that they were able to come to the show, but to not take valuable space in the booth and be trapped with the people working it.

Don't commit the funds for an expensive trade show until you have first screened it by attending as an observer. Most shows allocate space and location on the basis of how many years you have attended. Many shows claim to allocate space and location on this basis, but in fact are heavily influenced by politics. If you want to make a strong showing at a trade show, then you want to improve your location and booth size, so become active in the trade association that sponsors the show.

You'll probably find that it works best if you have one person in your organization responsible entirely for the show. He or she is responsible to see that the booth is shipped in a timely fashion, invitations are printed, work is scheduled or organized, that the booth is set up early enough and in proper order, and that the booth is taken down properly, packed, and shipped. They are also responsible for the budget, hotel room reservations, transportation, catering, and ensuring the preregistration of the chief people attending the show. Remember that it is usually necessary to register to exhibit at a trade show, and make your reservations as much as 6 months in advance. Be careful of overlapping schedules.

SALES

Some large, structured companies have departments that provide all the parameters a salesperson needs to make the sales call. In growth companies, the salespeople themselves often develop their own research and planning. Coupled with the ten facets of marketing in the emerging company, there are two specific sales points that are crucial:

- Know the specific needs of each customer.
- Know exactly which person has the decision-making influence for making the purchase.

Once this ammunition is available, the salesperson is ready for a battle that includes a sales call or a major dog-and-pony show. Remember, however, that many a great sales presentation has been wasted on an individual who has no authority to make a purchase. When the correct individual is found, it would be helpful to know as much about this person as possible. You want to convince him or her of the benefits of your product or service.

The key word in selling is ''benefit.'' There must be some benefit, some reason presented to the buyer, that would induce him or her to purchase. We often think immediately of satisfying the purchaser's need through price, logistical improvements, products advantage, etc.

Don't forget that the person doing the purchasing has needs that might be divergent from those of company's. Sometimes satisfying his or her individual needs or wants can be sale productive. It cannot be overemphasized that in the purchasing agent's mind, the purchasing agent is an important person and has needs and goals also. Don't go around them unless the situation demands it.

A precursor to the sales call includes the use of role playing and simulated sales calls (Fig. 4-3). What makes sales calls different in a new company is sales resistance a customer gives vs. dealing with an established company that he or she knows.

Rarely does the buyer volunteer to purchase. After all of the time spent in the planning and execution, the salesperson must remember that his or her purpose is to leave the appointment with a purchase order. "Ask for the order" each time you make a sales call.

Whether the response to an order request is positive or negative, the sales call is not complete until the followup is made. This consists of reviewing the meeting and preferably making notes for the company or personal file. Any infor-

---

Date: September 20, 1987

The call is on Q-COMPANY.

Product they make: High-efficiency widgets.

Product you sell: Shipping containers.

In preparation you should consider:

☞ What is your company's position in containers? How does it compare to Q's needs?

☞ Do you offer advantages in price, delivery, quality, etc.?

☞ Are there import/export implications?

☞ What are Q's specifications.

☞ How does Q receive the product?

☞ Are there any expansions planned that would increase their needs?

☞ What are current market conditions?

In role planning you should:

☞ Draw up the necessary charts and graphs you will use in your presentation.

☞ Have someone portray the Q-COMPANY purchasing agent who is 35 years old and has the potential to move up in the company, is friendly, enjoys golf, hunting, fishing, and spectator sports. (Or the agent may be a 70-year-old wise guy, etc.).

☞ Have someone critique your effort.

Fig. 4-3. Role-playing a sales call: An example.

mation or literature that was promised during the sales call should be delivered as soon as possible. If an order was obtained, the salesperson should trace the order to ensure its prompt and proper delivery or that the service sold is adequately and well performed, especially if it is the first sale to a company. If no order was obtained, begin planning the strategy for the next sales call.

It takes a special personality to be a part of a company involved in dynamic growth in an emerging industry. The changes that take place often come quickly (as in electronics). Your product or service is probably unique and this fact offers some advantages. However, *"The man with something unusual to offer will always play second fiddle to the man who has nothing to offer but the art of offering it!"*

TELECOMMUNICATIONS

No book on small business would be complete without mentioning the telephone and its usefulness in developing a new business. With facsimile (FAX machine) equipment becoming more important in business, as well as telephone lines used for on-line or off-line computer networking and information retrieval or transfer, the small business must pay close attention to its telecommunications system.

Today several long distance companies vie for your business and it is beyond our technical scope to dig into these idiosyncrasies. What is important to know is just what you can expect to accomplish by using a phone, which today can be as close as the gearshift on the floor of your car. From that point of view, you can always stay in touch with your office or your customers. (Some field salesmen and saleswomen keep a hand-held computerized record of all key accounts in the glove compartment of their car for easy reference and calling from the field.)

What every small or emerging company should understand is that telemarketing is much more than putting a bunch of people in a "boiler room" and have them call everyone at dinnertime. It is a form of public relations and a cost-effective way of staying in touch with accounts that are too small to visit on a routine basis. There is a planned, effective way to rate each account for telemarketing, and these techniques are well described in a series of free booklets published by AT&T. They include:

- *Keeping Customers Satisfied.* Suggestions for building brand loyalty and expanding your customer base.
- *Expanding Your Markets.* Ideas on how to convince current customers to buy more and persuade prospects to buy.
- *Improving Your Field Sales Productivity.* Tips that can help your sales force open more doors and close more sales.
- *Capitalizing On Money Management.* Advice on putting together a cash management program that can cut costs and increase profits.

- *Making Advertising Pay Off.* Proven techniques that can make an advertising program or a promotion speak louder and work harder.

- *Automating for Productivity.* Ways to combine telecommunications and information management tools to increase profits.

- *Developing International Markets.* A variety of inbound and outbound calling services that can eliminate costly face-to-face sales calls by bringing overseas customers closer to home.

- *Terms of The Times.* A dictionary that defines today's most often used telecommunications terms in plain English, not jargon.

MARKETING OVERSEAS

Most of what has been described already pertains to doing business on a local or national scale. To do business on an international scale is many more times complicated. The amount of management time and effort necessary to do business internationally is exponentially greater than the results achieved.

Regardless of what business you are in, there is a possibility that you can be affected positively or negatively by foreign trade. To ignore this fact is to stick your head in the sand. Of the major trading powers, the United States government is probably the most naive. American businesses have been plagued by inept trade leadership for more than 28 years. American industry has been expected to be the muscle behind the United States' continually changing foreign policy. Examples of this are the wheat embargo that resulted from Soviet intervention in Poland and the embargo on the exploration of pipeline equipment that resulted from Afghanistan. The multi-billion dollar trade deficit is a national crime. Politicians talk of open trade, free trade, and fair trade while U.S. corporations and manufacturers are exploited by foreign entrepreneurs. For example, the U.S. valve industry is just a shell of what it once was because dumping (selling below their cost at home) by foreign competition put many U.S. companies out of business.

Involvement in foreign trade by the emerging company, therefore, requires that chief executive officers stay aware of threats that could affect the viability and future of their companies. If a company has a valuable product line and a competitive advantage, there is a good possibility that some foreign manufacturer will try to duplicate or improve upon the product. Involvement in exports and monitoring imports provides the chief executive officer and his or her staff with the knowledge of what foreign competitors with lower raw material and labor rates might be doing to affect the success of the business in future years. The U.S. International Trade Commission monitors all products coming in and leaving the U.S. These reports are available to U.S. businesses.

Obviously there is potential for offshore sales where a company's product has some distinct advantage over anything available in the foreign market. There is an opportunity in many cases for significantly higher profit than what might be available in the domestic market. Pricing of a company's products should be done on the basis of the value perceived by the customer and not just by its cost. One U.S. company made a product out of cold rolled steel utilizing a technology which it alone possessed. It had produced as many as 1 million of these items per month at a selling price just under $3. Very few foreign nations had a requirement for this product for more than 100,000 units per year. Foreign companies, therefore, could not justify the high initial investment to manufacture the product out of steel if the technology was available elsewhere. The alternative method of manufacturing was to manufacture the product from brass. At one point in time the equivalent item manufactured from brass was $22 on the international market. The customer was happy at any price less than $22. The U.S. company was obviously very pleased with any price over $3. So it wasn't hard to make everyone happy.

Another advantage to foreign trade is the potential of obtaining raw materials or components at a lower cost than available domestically, thus improving the company's competitive position.

Finally, a major benefit to international trade is the potential advantage for the future. If the United States is going to remain a major economic power for generations to come, the trade deficit must be ameliorated. To do this will require a strong stand and the elimination of the United States' exploitation. It will also require the government to offer some enticements for more companies to become exporters. Now is the time to investigate your potential to export, especially with dollar devaluation making U.S. goods more competitive in foreign markets.

For many years exporters enjoyed a tax advantage through Domestic International Sales Corporations (DISC) which now, for the most part, have been converted to Foreign International Sales Corporations (FISC). There is good reason to believe that similar incentives will soon be established to alleviate the detrimental effects of the foreign trade deficit on the U.S. economy.

For foreign trading partners, international trade is second nature. For emerging American companies, it can be very, very difficult. First and most importantly, it takes a tremendous commitment by top management to the time and resources necessary to develop foreign trade. Second, things take much longer to establish in international markets than they do domestically. Third, it takes a particular type of person with a love for traveling outside of the comforts and security of the United States to generate foreign trade. Fourth, it takes exponentially more time and effort to generate a dollar of foreign sales than it does domestically. Fifth, it takes much longer to make anything happen in the international market.

You must understand that your product must really be unique to be sold in many countries. The Japanese economy abounds with non-tariff trade barriers, but more importantly the Japanese people are brainwashed socially from childhood to buy Japanese products because their country needs exports to survive. Many other countries, such as Latin America, Australia, and New Zealand, have restrictions on importing any product that is manufactured within its country. Also, it is extremely difficult to import anything legally into Brazil. So, some markets are limited.

In addition, if your product requires after-sales support, you aren't going to succeed with one person, part-time or full-time, spending his or her time on international sales. You will require at least a small department. Someone must be at home to answer telexes, letters, and inquiries while the senior international marketing manager is traveling. For the company with limited resources and the potential for international sales, a starting point is to encourage as many of your middle and top management people as possible to make international sales trips. Try your best to make these sales trips enjoyable. Stay in good hotels, eat well, and pick up some of the cost of their recreation on weekends. If the employee's wife or husband enjoys travel, encourage the employee to take the spouse with her or him. A spouse could be a real asset in foreign business entertainment and in developing relationships. Let the individual pick up her (or his) air fare, and the company can handle the taxi and hotel costs. These costs are insignificant for two people over one.

In summary, whether you are marketing your product domestically or internationally, you must first determine what your method or methods of distribution will be. This question can best be answered by defining what your business is and what your market is. Don't forget to consider what after-sales support is required. Many sales are lost due to lack of follow-up—especially with potential customers—and lack of service. A company can ruin its reputation by "selling and forgetting." A company's reputation is also open to damage by its using the wrong dealer or distributor.

Don't make long-term commitments initially. Allow yourself the opportunity to make a change if you made a mistake.

5

Relationship Management: The Key to Customer Satisfaction

EMERGING COMPANIES ARE PRIMARILY SMALL BUSINESSES. THEY ARE MORE flexible than big businesses and are directed and led by opportunistic entrepreneurs.

Emerging companies have an opportunity to do something unique with, to develop, or to exploit an opportunity known as Relationship Management (RM). The following paragraphs should give you enough information to initiate an RM program and to take advantage of the potential you have in this area.

In many of the recent bestsellers, a lot has been written about niches, nichemanship, staying close to the customer, sticking to your knitting, and doing what you know best. A lot has also been written about excellence and quality. However, the key to this excellence and quality is an understanding and an implementation of relationship management.

Whether you run a restaurant, a cleaners, a repair service, a manufacturing concern, a professional consulting firm, a service company, or an advertising agency, you can create a niche or develop a unique opportunity that will distinguish you from your competition. Furthermore, for those of you who are concerned about foreign competition, it can make you impregnable.

In its simplest form, relationship management is giving your customers not only everything they need, but also everything they want. This task, however, is not as simple to enact.

There must be a total commitment to RM. Both the personality and culture of your business must be inclined to want to implement RM. You have to begin with your mission statement. Include RM in your strategic plans and operational goals as a firm commitment to excellence and a dedication to unparalleled customer service. You must have the ability to understand the customer's needs and to provide the customer with what he or she wants. The bigger your company gets, the more difficult this chore will become.

It is much harder to go into the field to find and bring in a new customer than it is to have a satisfied customer want to do business with you again. The secret is to build and maintain a working relationship to ensure customer satisfaction so those customers you have keep coming back again.

If you study your industry and your competition, you will be able to recognize or uncover those areas where you can provide the customer with a high level of service both before and after the sale. Once discovered, the first stop is to try RM on a limited clientele. It is a lot easier to provide this "tender loving care" if your company has always provided a high quality product and been sensitive to a customer's complaints. However, as your company grows, and as the number of customers increases, it becomes more difficult to continue developing and nurturing those types of relationships that you had in the beginning. The philosophy built upon listening and finding out what the customer wants and then giving what he or she wants (as opposed to what may have been available), becomes harder to do. So, it requires a plan.

RELATIONSHIP MANAGEMENT STEP ONE: Commitment

In an effort to learn how to perpetuate and duplicate an RM philosophy and its mode of operation, one firm "went to school" to study those firms who either claimed to have a relationship management program or who were trying to develop them. These include such organizations as the Mellon Bank, IBM, Citicorp, Coca-Cola, and many others. Usually there are more failures than successes. But there is a common thread that bonded those who were successful. The successful companies were those who did it *au naturel*. They were the ones whose culture was based on customer satisfaction. For the most part, they didn't teach relationship management formally; it was just a whole part of how they did business.

As P.T. Barnum said, "You can fool some of the people some of the time, but you can't fool all the people all the time." You have to start with a quality product or service. You have to make sure that the customer is really satisfied with whatever he or she paid money for. In summary, you must produce a product of quality.

You have to be ready to put your money where your mouth is. If whatever you do carries a warranty or guarantee, you should be ready to provide a better warranty or guarantee than any of your competitors.

Certainly, some of these things will cost you a little bit more money. But you might be surprised when the customer recognizes value and is usually willing to pay a little more for the satisfaction. Often a company gets an order, even when it is not the lowest bidder. What you must create is a real or perceived value from the customer's perspective. Firms implementing RM have quantitative measures of customer service, and one facet of continuing corporate goals include improving those indices.

Everyone in your company should be motivated and included in this idea of relationship management. One company doubled its warranty on equipment, having no idea what it might cost. This occurred during a recession and all employees were concerned about their jobs. When told what the company had done, it was explained that their help was needed to make sure the equipment that went out didn't come back. Everyone took the warranty promise as a personal goal. The firm adopted a slogan: "Doing What We Do Best Better." Keep in mind that RM does not have to be connected to a unique product, a warranty, or an unusual situation. Even a common product or a commodity product can be tied to RM if combined with a unique service or the will (by all employees) to be considered "the best" in the eyes of the customer.

Furthermore, RM is ideally suited for a well-defined market—particularly commodity products or services that are widely available. Here RM is ideally suited for a supplier that can offer more than just a low price.

RELATIONSHIP MANAGEMENT
STEP TWO: Quality and Service

One concept of relationship management is: RM is an ongoing interaction with a client that provides mutual benefit to both client and the supplier. The client provides adequate profits to the supplier and the supplier provides valued equipment and/or service to the client. Perhaps a better definition for relationship management is "the developing of a high level of trust and understanding with your customers and vendors." In the past 2 years, "quality" has become an integral part of RM.

You will note that profit hasn't been emphasized in these definitions. This does not minimize its importance, but instead, it implies that with RM, satisfied customers lead your firm to profitability. A good business deal is one in which both parties come away satisfied.

At IBM, relationship management is a part of the business culture. The culture was started by Mr. Watson when he founded the company, and this culture was drilled into employees. Mr. Watson believed that since their equipment was being leased, if the company was to survive and succeed, they would have to see to it that the customer was happy and the equipment never returned. Thus, through necessity, relationship management became a part of the culture of IBM. It was handed down from generation to generation and is the *modus operandi* for its doing business today. At any company, RM should be an extension of, and an impression of, corporate culture.

If quality, service, and customer satisfaction are not a part of your corporate culture, you have a long way to to in getting those return customers to help your business grow. But if you are committed to staying close to your customer, some of the ideas expressed in step three might help you develop a relationship management program.

RELATIONSHIP MANAGEMENT STEP THREE: Action

How, then, do you take the next step forward, and how do you measure your success? As already mentioned, quality and service must be a part of your company's culture. Next, you must:

- Develop a positive relationship with all customers.
- Take the necessary actions to improve these relationships.

As a start, take an inventory of the resources available within your company and determine how to utilize those resources. Who in your company has customer contact and is capable of being responsible for developing and managing relationships with individual customers? Depending on the nature of your business, or the geographical area in which you conduct your business, RM could be a job for you alone or for a number of people in your organization. The obvious measure of a successful relationship is the growth in sales with your existing customers, and your overall share of the market.

RELATIONSHIP MANAGEMENT STEP FOUR:
Manager's Responsibilities

The relationship manager's responsibilities should include the following:

- Ensuring that the customer's needs are met in terms of quality, service, or satisfaction, so that confidence in your company grows.
- If appropriate, developing organizational and not just personal relationships.
- Making sales calls and maintaining relations at different levels of your customer's organization.
- Delivering "excellence" by means of relationship teams composed of sales as well as your operational staff.

These four facets of RM employ the building of an RM team having a team leader. The success of the relationship management team will depend on high quality planning, management information systems, and team leadership.

The tool at the team leader's disposal, in addition to any personal skill, will be the marketing department's tools—(e.g., call reports)—plus the skills supplied by his or her team members in the utilization of RM techniques that extend to formal and informal client contact and even to a company's standard telephone procedure.

The more customers you have, obviously the more people you should have responsible as relationship managers. The more customers you have, the more top management people should *not* be relationship managers. That is, top management should assist the relationship managers in making customer contacts, visiting the customers, welcoming them to your place of business, assisting in contract negotiations, and providing commitments for the company's performance.

Depending upon the complexity of your business, you might need to have members of your staff who possess specific technical expertise become involved in specific portions of a relationship. For example, if your customer involves professional people—i.e., engineers, finance, legal, etc.—you probably will want to involve their counterparts from your company.

RELATIONSHIP MANAGEMENT STEP FIVE:
Building the Database

As in any type of marketing function, marketing intelligence is the key to success. Any company trying to develop a relationship management program should begin to develop a master file for each customer. In this file information is placed in a database system and it can be accessed by anyone on the relationship management team. It is a lot easier, today, to keep this information on a computer with multiple access. Even in a retail business, this database can be as simple as the names and addresses of your customers, members of their family, preferences, birthdays, and anniversaries.

When the relationship is between corporations, this file would consist of organizational charts, dossiers on the key people, and informal meetings where the team leaders would meet with members of management or the relationship management team to brief them on developments of the corporation. These meetings could be both informal as well as formal. Good information is often exchanged on the golf course, and even at Scout meetings. Team leaders would be responsible for continually updating the database.

The relationship management plan is a dynamic process. It should include all that the relationship management team leader expects from his or her various team members. Also, it should include the plans for having the relationship grow and prosper.

It is suggested that whatever type of relationship management plan you embark on, it should not be a program that calls for volumes of paper and reports which will not be read or referred to. Responsibility for documentation lies within the various departments to record what they need to carry out their functional responsibility.

It was mentioned that relationship management is dynamic. From time to time relationship management team leaders need the assistance and participation of other members of management who are not the team. An example might be the involvement of an international group because the customer is contemplating a move into international markets. Delivery of an order could be a customer's concern. At that time the production manager or warehouse supervisor might be asked to participate.

Also, if the customer's concerned about whether raw materials are available, someone from the purchasing or scheduling department might be brought into the relationship. The customer might have some specific design of technical interest, at which time the RM team would include engineers or technicians.

The structure of a relationship management team may vary from customer to customer. Also, the number of your RM team members may vary from one person (the team leader) to as many as are needed to finish the job. The relationship management team operation and function is similar to performance under a matrix organization. In a matrix organization, the team members' responsibilities remain with the specific departments. It is the intent, however, that the team members themselves will develop relationships with their counterparts in the customer's organization.

RELATIONSHIP MANAGEMENT: Fringe Benefits

A good relationship management system will foster participative management. It will also contribute to management development through participation on the teams. Staff strengths and weaknesses will be more apparent, thus assisting the CEO in his or her succession planning responsibilities. Success in RM will create recognition and foster growth in the company. The participation in relationship management will provide cross-training, and this cross-training can result in backup and relief of people who handle the stress relations with customers. Consequently, an effective relationship management program will help to deny your competitors access to your customers.

To implement RM, then, you must include it at all levels of customer communication—telephone, personal, and written.

The first contact the customer has, whether with your switchboard operator or another employee, is important. Whoever answers that phone should identify him or herself. That way, if the customer isn't treated right, you have a chance of finding out who the source was. Also, it gives the people who answer the phone a chance to have personal customer contact; it is an opportunity for these people to begin a relationship with the customers.

Telephones in business establishments should never be allowed to ring more than four times. After that, the people calling become annoyed or hang up. Someone, regardless of whose responsibility it is, should answer the telephone after the fourth ring. Phone manners are essential to good relationship management. One of the worst sins in RM is to have a temporary employee answer the telephone and claim that he or she is "just temporary," so they don't know anything. This gives the whole organization a "don't-know-anything" stigma.

For those of us who have customer contact, screening should be done only when absolutely necessary. Many of your customers will be calling long distance at their expense. To have a customer's call screened by a switchboard operator and a secretary is bad telephone manners unless you are not in the office to answer the telephone yourself. A customer who has placed the call to you with the intent of placing an order can often change his or her mind totally when faced with having to give his or her name and explaining the call prior to being "switched" to the party he or she was calling. Most people are quite put out by the "holier than thou" attitude of a switchboard operator or secretary making management decisions as to who may or may not speak to the people in the offices. Don't let all of your hard work in building a customer base be destroyed by such a simple thing as the way incoming calls are handled.

Equally important is to not leave a person hanging after a call has been answered. If the individual or secretary does not answer the phone by the fourth ring, the switchboard operator should intercept the call and ask the caller if he or she wishes to continue to wait while the operator attempts to locate the party. Today's phone-answering machines where you keep pressing buttons to leave messages or place orders (or whatever) can undermine good RM if the system annoys customers.

Top management people who are involved with customer contact probably should have a private number that their key customers know. If you are not in, the call should roll over to a competent secretary or person who can talk sensibly to a customer who needs you or to a type of phone mail or message center if the call comes in after hours.

The nature of your business may warrant that you receive a number of incoming calls from customers. Many times these customer calls should be handled by the service or sales department, but often the customer insists on talking to someone in top management. If you have this type of problem, convert the problem into an opportunity. Make the customer a source of marketing information (Fig. 5-1). Depending upon the business you are in, the questions will vary, but the central theme of relationship management is the same.

Any customer who calls you wants to talk to you. Any customer who wants to talk to you is a telemarketing opportunity. If your business is sophisticated, you might have the customer's data file on a screen or have the data cards and files, (referred to earlier), accessible. In any event, it gives you the opportunity, even if you're a retail establishment, to talk to that customer about services or

---

Questions to ask an in-calling customer:

☞   Is his or her store a franchise or company-owned operation?

☞   Who owns the franchise?

☞   How many stores do they have?

☞   How old is the equipment?

☞   Who is his or her contact at the regional office?

☞   What are the plans for new store openings in the current year?

☞   What are the plans for remodels?

☞   Who makes the decisions on remodels?

☞   Who is his or her service company?

☞   How does he or she like the company who is providing the service?

☞   Does he or she get good service on weekends or at night?

☞   Does he or she need any training?

☞   What are you doing for him or her that could be done better?

Example is a retail food franchise calling an equipment supplier.

Fig. 5-1. Using a nuisance call as a source of information.

products. If you can talk to him or her about things which are personal, that gives you an even greater opportunity to put the customer at ease.

If you use multiple levels of distribution, it would probably be best for you to have a different series of questions for each level or type of customer that may call in.

RELATIONSHIP MANAGEMENT STEP SIX:
Formality and Informality

When contacting a customer, whatever the occasion, use your strengths, be yourself, and above all, be honest. This is true whether your personality is "down home," soft-spoken, technically oriented, or sportsmanlike. Remember, we all have weaknesses but, more importantly, we all have strengths.

Personal relationships come out of one or more personal meetings or a number of phone conversations. They are often developed at shows, seminars, or technical meetings. An individual who meets you in person is more likely to open the door to you for an appointment than one who has never seen you before.

You aren't going to change; your personality is formed. You're just going to begin using more efficiently and effectively what you've got to offer. Be sure the customers know who you are and what you do.

If you are trying to build a relationship, know the *subject*. Also, develop a dossier on the key individuals at your RM accounts (Fig. 5-2).

Look upon meetings that you have with people (in your effort to build a relationship) as being two types: formal and casual. The casual meeting will be more of the opportunistic type whereas the formal meetings will produce the greatest results.

The most important objective of a formal meeting is to make it meaningful to the client. Some light talk is fine to break the ice, but too much light talk will take valuable time from both of you. Too much light talk will also give the appearance that you don't have anything meaningful to say and the client might think of you as the court jester. After the meeting has settled in and you are getting ready to get to the heart of it, make a statement as to the value you feel the client will get out of the meeting. This statement, in many cases, can be derived from "what we do best." It will also be the result of the homework you have done in terms of what the customer's needs—and wants—are. This statement also enables you to determine current interests in such areas as: quality, service, reducing, delivery, etc. Get the message across also of what you hope to accomplish in this meeting.

When you've called a formal meeting, you want to prepare, in advance, a list of particulars to accomplish. Many times it is good to have a printed agenda that

---

☞   What are his or her origins?

☞   Where did he or she live?

☞   Where did he or she go to school?

☞   How long has he or she been with that company?

☞   Is he or she married or single?

☞   What is the spouse's name?

☞   What is the spouse's occupation?

☞   Does he or she have children?

☞   How many?

☞   What sex?

☞   What are his or her hobbies?

☞   What are his or her personal values?

☞   What is his or her political leaning?

☞   What is his or her religion?

Fig. 5-2. Know your customer and know your customer's key people: A checklist.

you can distribute, but be prepared to get shot out of the water. The customer can have his or her own agenda which might not mesh with yours, but nonetheless, you'll know quickly what he or she wants to do.

Keep the meeting on meaningful subjects. If there is more than your prime contact in the room, you may find that participants will get sidetracked on minor or specific problems off of the main subject.

Determine early on in your discussions what your time restraints are.

If you anticipate that you're going to have a difficult meeting; rehearse! Don't make one person be totally responsible for the conduct of the meeting. Share the responsibility. Give the other person a chance to think and recapture his or her thoughts by picking up the ball.

If you get into a difficult situation either in a formal meeting or in a telephone discussion and the customer is bombarding or blasting you, try the following technique. When there's a pause, ask the question: "May I ask a question?" Also the words: "May I make a suggestion," is an ideal way to broach ideas that a customer might not have thought of. Probably, he or she will say "yes" or "certainly." This can derail his or her attack and make the individual say something that is affirmative at the end of a string of negatives. It many times helps to turn the meeting into a discussion, as opposed to a tirade.

When you begin a formal meeting, try to split up the seating. Try not to have all of your people on one side of the table and the customer on the other. It looks like the plaintiff versus the defendant. Sit among them. Watch their eyes. Try to avoid sitting at the end of the table, which suggests that you are in the attitude of lording over everyone.

If there is a particular contact man or woman with this client (with whom you are trying to build a stronger relationship), try to put your own contact person in a position where he or she can argue for the customer. Obviously you have to pre-arrange this in order to make concessions appear to be a result of the contact person's request.

If you are in a situation where a key decision maker joins the meeting late, ask one of his or her subordinates to review what has been covered. The results will be that the key employee looks good, the key employee knows what the executive wants to hear, and you could learn what the customer's strategy is.

If you are in an important meeting where there is negotiating, be prepared to concede on minor points, such as how long the meeting will last, when you go to lunch, etc., so then you can take a harder stand on the major points.

It sometimes is appropriate in discussions to pause and leave a prolonged period of silence. This takes skill as well as patience. It can seem awkward and you might pass the time by writing notes, but the purpose hopefully is to have the customer initiate a new theme or bring up something which is important.

If you have a difficult problem to resolve, a task force or matrix organization to solve the problem might be a good approach. The customer will be impressed with such a team effort.

When you solve a problem, do it through the proper channels within both your organization and the customer's. Don't create another problem by stepping on someone's toes.

RELATIONSHIP MANAGEMENT: Some Helpful Hints

Dress appropriately for whatever type of meeting. If you are over 40, you can begin to dress in a fashion that people become accustomed to seeing you, i.e., your dress conforms to the image they have of you. Unless casual attire is how you are perceived and accepted by the customer, it is usually not appropriate for business meetings. If the customer gives you the impression that you are going to have serious discussions, wear your sincere or your semi-sincere suit.

Conversely, in some parts of the country, some businessmen are turned off by a coat and a tie. Engineering projects in Louisiana or Arizona often demand construction attire. Also, in some parts of the South, you still can damage your credibility by sending a Yankee into the territory. Know your customer's tastes.

Casual meetings, as mentioned, are usually opportunistic. You need to be careful not to be overbearing. If the customer's spouse is present, keep an eye on the spouse. If the spouse gets off on his or her own discussions, fine, but be careful when your discussions become too businesslike that the customer's spouse doesn't become irritated. Be sure, during the course of your discussions, that you periodically involve the spouse in conversation. You want to make sure that the spouse isn't offended to the point that he or she doesn't want to have another casual meeting with you at some future date.

Casual meetings can take a number of forms. Typically these would be cocktail parties, trade shows, association meetings, golf outings, etc. At a trade show, if it is an important meeting, you might want to get off to the side and give the individual a chance to relax and avoid the distractions that can occur in the booth. On the other hand, at a cocktail party, particularly if you are one of the hosts, you don't want to get isolated. Casual meetings in most cases are a good opportunity to get to know the customer better. Also, as mentioned, it is an opportunity to get to know the spouse. Be sure you write the name down. It is also helpful in developing a relationship with a customer to get to know the secretary. A secretary can help you get that appointment when the client is unavailable.

Besides formal and casual meetings, there are also opportunities that give you a chance to begin or develop a relationship. Some of these are job change and new responsibility. If you can approach an individual at such a time and offer your assistance, it can be a great door opener. The individual is probably feeling a little insecure and may be very receptive to anyone offering a helping hand.

Getting the most out of the trade shows is covered in chapter 4. But in terms of relationship management, some additional thoughts on conduct at a hospitality suite are appropriate. People who have customer contact and are involved in your relationship management program should be required to make an appearance at your hospitality room. This is especially true if one of the customers (for whom you are responsible) should make an appearance. This often offers the possibility that your employee will meet someone that they never met in person. Employees who attend your hospitality rooms or any social function sponsored by you should make a point of introducing themselves to each customer.

If you have some type of a lunch or dinner where you invite a number of customers, you should not allow more than two employees or their spouses to sit at one table. Preferably a member of top management should greet the guest at the door.

Another opportunity to establish relationships is in old relations. This includes college, peers, friends, former employers, and those you have previously met at a trade show or elsewhere.

RM can often get quite personal—even to trying help a person in his or her personal plight. In these cases, be sympathetic and a good listener, but don't put yourself in an uncomfortable position. If you don't counsel people in your own personal life, doing it as part of RM can fail because it won't appear to be sincere. If you can talk to a fellow for thirty-five minutes about his divorce, or talk with a woman for twenty minutes about a problem she's having with her son in college, it can become a lasting way to establish a relationship. Also, lasting friendships develop when you try to help an individual find a job when he or she is out of work.

Again, tell people what you are going to do for them so that they feel they get value out of meeting with you and wouldn't be resistant to doing it again.

Relationships take time to develop. You need to find out what the customer appreciates. If they like to see you early in the morning, you might consider bringing donuts. You'll make points with the individual and the office staff. Does he or she like to go out alone without his or her spouse—or to take his or her spouse along? Don't try taking your spouse if he or she doesn't enjoy going out with your customers.

Also, if your customer is married, flowers or a personal gift at a holiday are usually appreciated. Watch for important events: births, deaths, sicknesses, hospitalization, etc. Take the appropriate action to show that you care. If you send flowers for a sickness, death, or birth, send an appropriate arrangement to the home. It will get more notice.

Be accessible. Particularly be accessible by telephone; be willing to respond and come to the customer's need.

Be honest. As Mark Twain said: "Always tell the truth and you'll have less to remember."

A simple idea that keeps your name in front of a customer and sets you apart from the competition is a simple thank-you card. A card which tells the customer how much you appreciate his or her business. Often it is a good idea to include an individual's business card with certain correspondence.

Above all, be real and don't be phony. Be yourself.

Keep your relationship on a high plane. It is preferable to not let your attempts to establish a relationship with a customer degenerate into heavy drinking, carousing, or whatever. Good RM managers normally find out that good-natured fun is good business. Clients who get involved in sordid dealings are customers that usually don't last. If you have had an experience like this, try to avoid getting into another one.

In your diagnostic analysis of the customer, a good way to understand him or her is to determine his or her personal values. In the course of this analysis, you can sometimes learn what sport the customer enjoys. In some cases, a fishing trip or golfing date can be good opportunities for informal business discussion. Tennis usually only helps to begin the relationship because there is little chance to talk, unless there is an after-the-game opportunity. Be careful that you know how important winning is if you engage in competitive sports. If these "sporting" business meetings are to take place on weekends, it is again important to include your customer's spouse or even an entire family (if you are to attend a spectator sport such as baseball or football). This really adds a plus to your side of the ledger as far as the spouse is concerned, since rather than taking away from home life, you are adding a special outing for the whole family. This is a bonus for both sides and you come out the winner instead of a loser (as you would be if you took away from your customer's family life).

It is important to recognize that some people, perhaps even you, do not build relationships easily. Don't let that be a concern; you can still be a very meaningful contributor to a relationship management program. You can be a feeder. You can be the person who meets with someone, or at least gathers the information and passes it on for someone else to work on. Also, be aware that RM works differently when outside the U.S. For example, in Germany, long-time associates often do not work on a first name basis. For you to do so in one or two visits can be a serious *faux pas*.

RELATIONSHIP MANAGEMENT STEP SEVEN:
Written Techniques

Written techniques can be as simple as greeting cards or thank-you cards—i.e., Christmas, birthday, congratulatory, and condolence. Even cards, however, have to be appropriate and sincere.

The next simplest type of written communication are the thank-you notes confirming a meeting that was held and thanking the person for the time they spent. At the same time, they hopefully open the door to an opportunity for a future meeting and discussion.

Written communication is also important in confirming a customer's order, sending an invoice, or when responding to a problem or request from a customer. Many times, when faced with these difficult types of letters to write, two or three officers of the company might want to review the letter before it goes to a customer. This informal review process emphasizes how important and permanent it is when you convey something to another person in writing. In spite of the informal review process, there is often an occasion where an ambiguity has been missed. It can be extremely difficult to retract something which has been put into writing. As the CEO or COO of your company, you should receive a copy of all correspondence that is mailed and signed by any one of your officers.

Before you write a serious letter to a customer, ask yourself if you really want to put your feelings, at that moment, in writing. Do not let proprietary information leave your offices. This information includes anything which has not been specifically created for external use—i.e., drawings, computer printouts, customer lists, etc. Most customers hold you responsible to protect their proprietary material. If in doubt, ask and ask again or do not send the material. Challenge the distribution of internal proprietary information.

All this might seem very simple and concise. The fact is that relationship management only begins after a relationship is defined. The hard, laborious work of sales calls and developing an interest by a prospective customer as part of RM deserves close attention by every marketing manager, president, and CEO.

RELATIONSHIP MANAGEMENT STEP EIGHT: Keeping Score

There are two ways to look at relationship management. One is to consider what new business can result from a good RM program. The other is to evaluate what business could be lost if a key customer dropped your product and services—particularly without your knowing about a problem. The latter problem deserves serious attention.

Can you imagine a situation where, through the grapevine, you learned that one of your key accounts was thinking of changing to a new supplier. Imagine that you called in your marketing manager, your sales team, and everyone involved with the account only to learn that everyone of them said: "Everything is OK."

Imagine that the rumor persisted and that three months later you again called upon your people to ensure that there was no problem with the account. Your staff again insisted that: "Everything is OK."

Imagine that 3 months later this key account switched suppliers with a resulting loss of millions of dollars of business, and that you learned about the dilemma from the morning newspapers, at a point in time where there was no possibility of recovering the business. The decision to drop your company as a supplier was poured in concrete.

This synopsis is a true story, and it is not an unusual one. It often happens when your customer experiences personnel changes. It happens in every industry from advertising to communication and computers to x-ray machines and filters. To get around the problem, one approach is to put your RM program out in the open where everyone—customers and employees alike—can see it.

One firm formally approaches its clients with a formal Customer Satisfaction Quotient (CSQ). Key executives on both sides sit down annually and go over a formal list of questions (Fig. 5-3). The customer "grades" the supplier, and only a passing grade of 90 is acceptable to ensure RM is working. Anything below 90 deserves serious and immediate remedial RM action.

In some cases, large companies are forcing suppliers into RM whether they want to consider it or not. Dow Chemical, for example, has taken supplier evaluation to the extreme. First, they are limiting the number of suppliers qualified to supply certain products. Second, they are eliminating manufacturers from the Approved Vendor's List (AVL) whose products do not meet minimum standards for quality, on-line operation, and mean-time-between-failure. Third, the company will drop firms from the AVL when there are repeat problems related to technical concerns or service. In addition, maintenance personnel now hold a seat on the purchasing board with veto power over products that don't work in the plant and that result in downtime.

As a consequence of these type programs in many industries, RM becomes a facet of business that must be implemented at all levels of customer interface from first echelon plant and corporate management. It implies that your firm develop detailed RM skills-assessment, self-evaluation and external-evaluation (Fig. 5-4) that sometimes receive the assistance of a third party observer or consultant who can perform the evaluation objectively.

This story probably involves the lowest level of RM that tradition tells us. It covers the case of the waitress at the Chicago Merchandise Mart who made it a point of learning the names of all the people who routinely sat at her station. She took the time to learn about the people, their families, their business, and even their birthdays—sending cards on important occasions of promotion or sympathy. Her tables were always full, proving the old adage: You do business with your friends, not your enemies. In some ways, that is what RM is all about.

Our company has adopted a *Relationship Management Program* that is meant to ensure that we are really fulfilling the needs of the firms who hire our services. The whole idea behind this is to ensure that there is a way of measuring the quality of the work we are doing. This is the best way to ensure you are satisfied. We want to fulfill your needs—and your wants and desires. The following *CSQ* questions are quite simple. (We might refine them in the future.) On an arbitrary scale of 1 to 10, we want to have a passing grade of 90 as you answer the following questions:

- Have we performed all the assignments you have given us to your satisfaction?   _____

- Do we satisfactorily understand your marketing objectives?   _____

- Are we helping you reach those objectives?   _____

- Does our work create legitimate leads for you that result in orders?   _____

- Are we technically competent to do the work you desire?   _____

- Do you believe that the cost of our services are realistic for the benefit you receive?   _____

- Do we meet deadlines in a satisfactory manner?   _____

- Does our creativity and ideas presented help you to increase profits?   _____

- Do we have the flexibility to meet your changing marketing requirements?   _____

- Are we satisfactorily presenting the correct image of your company?   _____

We would like to review these questions with you and receive comments as to how we can do a better job in helping you increase profitability, or improve other aspects of your corporate and technical goals.

To be given to customer to fill out.

This example is a CSQ used by a public relations firm with its clients.

Fig. 5-3. Gauging your Customer Satisfaction Quotient (CSQ).

Knowledge and Experience

☞ Do you know the industry and its needs?

☞ Do you know or have state-of-the-art technology?

☞ Is your product knowledge adequate?

☞ Do you understand the market and how it changes?

☞ Are you familiar with purchasing policies and pricing?

☞ Is your communication network in place for both personal and paper?

☞ Do you know the needs and wants of your customer?

Marketing Considerations

☞ Are you informed about pros and cons of competitive systems or services?

☞ Do you have the financial wherewithal to meet customer requirements?

☞ Can you sell and service all levels of customer accounts?

☞ Are your people trained and competent?

☞ Do you have a "response plan" to customer needs and wants that includes a "reaction time"?

☞ Can more than one person respond to a customer when necessary?

☞ Are simple, reliable contacts in place?

Management Characteristics

☞ Does the customer recognize your company's focus on management by objective?

☞ Does the customer interface with your standards and quality control procedures?

☞ Can your company perform favorably under stress?

☞ Are your people considered honest?

☞ Are you and your staff hardworking?

This list of questions is not meant to be all-inclusive. Each firm can develop its own list and develop a rating system (e.g., 1 to 10) for performance. This rating can be internal or external and can also be applied to individuals whom you are considering as part of an RM team.

Fig. 5-4. Relationship management skills assessment: A checklist of considerations.

6

Financial Survival: You've Got to Be Resilient and Smart

THE SURVIVAL OF THE NEW, SMALL BUSINESS IS DEPENDENT UPON IMMEDIATE and sustained cash flow; it needs profitable orders. Likewise, the survival of any emerging company is dependent upon good financial information.

Although few CEO's are from the financial discipline, he or she must have a total understanding and trust in the financial information provided. This obviously means having a good financial executive, controller, or outside accounting firm. Yet, in the case of a new business, there is often no such thing as a comptroller or financial officer and the individual responsible for overall management becomes the financial officer by necessity or by default.

GET THE REPORTS YOU NEED

There are some common financial denominators when you consider the capitalization and operating expenses of an emerging company and a small new company. Consider first the company who is in business and has reached the point of departmentalization, including one department called "Accounting."

Keep in mind that, just like engineers or any other professional, accountants have their idiosyncrasies. They are often "things people" who are very precise. An accountant, many times, will expend more effort to have his or her figures balance to the penny to determine whether the numbers that make up the total make any sense individually. If you want to see frustrated CPA's and accountants, just analyze a financial statement by way of ball park estimates and percentages.

It is not always easy to find an accountant who is creative. This does not mean one who can juggle the books to give you whatever answer you want, but rather one who can create systems and reports where none exist. Part of the reason for this attitude is because accounting is primarily a history exercise. Normally the corporate staff will need to define what is needed to run the business and then ask the accounting department to provide them data (Fig. 6-1).

What You Need	*Why You Want It*
☞ Inventory Data (raw material, work-in-progress, and finished stock)	Inventory carrying costs can reach as high as 40 percent annually. Increasing inventory turns can provide much needed cash.
☞ Monthly Actual vs. Budget Reports	A monthly tally and running total of expenses can spot where problems exist or can occur. This is a "take action" report.
☞ Sales Figures Backlog and Profitability Report	To compare vs. budget and project.
☞ Fixed and Variable Cost Report	To use as an expense control item.
☞ Cash Flow Statement and Projection (To include aged accounts receivable and purchasing requirements.)	To ensure operating funds will be there to pay sales reps, R&D expenses, and other costs.
☞ Ratios (These vary from industry to industry. The key is to utilize performance reports and performance ratios that compare planned operations with actual performance. Other important ratios include: Profitability ratios, liquidity ratios, efficiency ratios, market value ratios—important for public companies, growth ratios.)	For example, in the paint industry, the ratio of raw material cost/sales is an important figure because it indicates when one of your main expenses is getting out of line. You may have to reduce raw material costs by reformulation or raise prices to maintain profitability.
☞ Weekly Management Report	Key to controlling operations.

Fig. 6-1. Defining what you need from accounting: A checklist.

Realize that you can ask for too much information and that a *WANT* is not necessarily a *NEED*. The cost of accounting—not cost accounting—can sky-rocket if managers place too much emphasis on generating reports that are not really essential. There is a tendency to do that today because the computer can manipulate figures rather quickly.

Having criticized and pointed out the problems with accounting, it is now important to emphasize how vital this tool is for obtaining good financial informa-tion—especially in controlling operations. Here, a weekly management report can be of critical importance (Fig. 6-2). These paragraphs describe some of the information that can be calculated from the data.

1. Most companies have a fairly standard order processing system. You should, therefore, be able to project off your opening backlog what your sales are going to be during a future period.

2. Using the same logic as number 1, you can determine if you are receiving orders at a rate to satisfy or exceed a future sales budget.

3. Shipments will also indicate if you are going to satisfy the current period sales forecast and by comparing new orders (number 2), with shipments you can project a growth in your backlog.

4. Gross sales can indicate whether samples or consignment orders have been shipped by comparing it with shipment dollars.

5. Credits can give you an indication of warranty or return problems.

6. Net sales and net sales month-to-date compared to your monthly sales budget, give you an indication of how you are doing for the month and, obviously, comparing that information with last month's sales can give you an indication of how you are doing for the year.

7. Suppliers' invoices received will give you an indication if you're receiving merchandise faster than you're shipping it or anticipate shipping it. You certainly should know the percentage of your cost of sales that is mate-rial. You can therefore very easily calculate how many dollars of sales the week's receipts can generate and the same for the month's. If you are receiving material faster than incoming orders you can anticipate a grow-ing inventory and accounts payable balance.

8. If you have goals for maintaining certain levels of finished goods inventory and obtaining certain finished goods inventory turns, you can use your finished goods inventory balance to determine if you are on target for your goals.

The CEO's responsibility is to chart the course for the corporation. Accounting is an essential part of his or her support. A vital part of the total cor-porate planning consists of the financial plan. As with all other planning, it is a

WEEKLY MANAGEMENT REPORT

WEEK ENDING: _____

SALES INFORMATION

	WEEK	MONTH TO DATE
BACKLOG OPENING:	_____	
ORDERS RECEIVED:	_____	_____
SHIPMENTS:	_____	_____
BACKLOG CLOSING:	_____	
GROSS SALES:	_____	_____
LESS CREDITS:	_____	_____
NET SALES:	_____	_____
MONTHLY SALES BUDGET:		_____

SUPPLIERS INVOICES RECEIVED:	_____	_____
FINISHED GOODS INVENTORY–		
CURRENT PRODUCT LINE DATE–	_____	_____

FINANCIAL INFORMATION

CASH BALANCE:		_____		
ACCTS. PAYABLE BALANCE–TRADE		_____		
ACCTS. RECEIVABLE: MONTH OPENING	% OF TOTAL		% OF TOTAL	
30 DAYS	_____	_____	_____	_____
60 DAYS	_____	_____	_____	_____
90 DAYS	_____	_____	_____	_____
120+ DAYS	_____	_____	_____	_____
TOTAL:	_____	_____	_____	_____

SALARY PAYROLL: (GROSS $)		_____
FACTORY PAYROLL:(GROSS $)		_____
DIRECT LABOR PRODUCTS (ESTIMATED $)		_____

PERSONNEL INFORMATION

	LAST WEEK	THIS WEEK	CHANGE
HOURLY	_____	_____	_____
SALARY	_____	_____	_____
TOTAL	_____	_____	_____

HOURLY HIRES:	_____
TERMS:	_____
SALARY HIRES:	_____
TERMS:	_____

Fig. 6-2. The weekly management report.

good rule of thumb to have three periods of history for each period you want to plan forward. This means that to have a simple, one year budget or plan, you would need three years of good historical data. A new company might not have three months worth of data, but it should still have a budget—with account numbers—estimated for 12 months.

HOW TO PREPARE A BUDGET

Preparing a budget is sometimes complete guesswork, but it is surprising how a guess comes close to reality because once the numbers are on pages, they become precise goals. Although a budget is the job of business unit managers, with input from each profit center, the CEO provides input and reviews the final budget report. Budgets should not be cast in concrete but have flexibility to take advantage of unseen opportunities or react to misfortune.

Flexible budgets should be a tool for the chief executive officer or chief operating officer. Flexible budgets are those that change every time something significant happens. These normally are not distributed. Why? The CEO is supposed to provide leadership and direction to the company. Employees, seeing all the changes in the ''flexible budget,'' could perceive management as constantly vacillating, procrastinating, and changing the direction and the rules.

Your entire corporate staff will utilize to a high degree the accounting department's numbers to prepare and to repair their budgets and to modify forecasts for the chief executive. For the purpose of our discussion, we will assume that your business is rather complex, from an accounting standpoint, and that you have multiple product lines with employees doing a variety of functions. We'll also assume a broad geographical area of distribution that is highly service-oriented, or that the company has a combination of all of the above and more. In other words, there are a lot of areas where financial reporting can go wrong.

Many businesses have failed because they lacked good financial information. The CEO must have a thorough understanding and acceptance of the financial information that is generated. Many times each department head will keep his or her own set of books. A CEO should see to it that the information generated by the accounting department becomes the central database on which the entire organization functions. The problem that can occur is when a dynasty grows that really doesn't service the company.

As a matter of control, the CEO should never allow the accounting system to be changed without his or her concurrence. A simple change such as reclassifying a product can result in a serious forecasting error in future years when marketing attempts to make its projections using historical data. A new financial manager will always think he or she has a better way of doing things. Be careful that one does not destroy historic records.

Having said this, let us also emphasize that sometimes accounting can add more to the bottom line through savings of taxes, insurance, or negotiating lines of credit, than you can save in operations or maintenance. But again, the ultimate responsibility for the financial success and viability of the corporation lies in the hands of the chief executive officer. This responsibility cannot be delegated.

CHOOSING YOUR BANK

We have talked a great deal about expense management. In fact, the success of an emerging company is probably more dependent on debt management. If you don't control the balance sheet, the entrepreneur in the emerging company will be spending more time on the care and feeding of his or her banker than on doing what the entrepreneur does best, i.e., building a better enterprise.

There might not be an industry in our country today that is going through more significant changes than the banking industry. It may also surprise you that the banking industry is not nearly as sophisticated as you might perceive. Selecting the right bank—and banker—for your company is extremely important. Why? Because bank policies and individual loan officers can sink your company faster than a competitor if you need money and can't get it. For example, in 1985, Republic Bank (Texas), had a policy *not* to lend money to any restaurants—even if a certificate of deposit equal to the loan value was being put up as collateral. This certainly would not be the bank for a company expanding into the franchise food business. Furthermore, you should know and analyze the loan officer or lending committee. Some banking units take absolutely no risks and consequently can be of little financial help to a growing business.

Obviously, any emerging company can use some practical tips on how to select that bank. Here are a few.

- Investigate the bank's loan limits. Some might not be able to finance your venture without going to corresponding banks for help. This means you have to convince two or more loan committees of the viability of your loan.
- Investigate what other services it can provide, such as payroll or accounting. Customers often get preferential discounts that make these services competitive with other data processors.
- If doing business internationally, investigate the bank's ability to willingly accept payment of drafts made on foreign banks—and to do it quickly and without special charges.
- Compare banks before choosing one. Interest rates on loans, auto financing, leasing arrangements, and interest paid on non-working capital varies from bank to bank.
- Try to deal with a bank that understands the business you are in, even if the bank is not local (neighborhood).

- Know the bank's loan philosophy before starting an account. For example, one bank was given instructions from it's parent not to make loans in the food or restaurant business even if the loan was totally backed by a certificate of deposit of face value equal to the loan.
- Try not to bank out of state—at least not initially.
- Try to work with banks started by businesspeople who were not bankers. Get to know the bank board members and not the loan officers at the desk.
- If your company expects to use unusual financing or apply for Small Business Administration (SBA) loans, ensure that your bank can and will handle these transactions.
- Know who the corresponding banks are and their loan philosophy.

The best time to select a bank is when you don't have a great borrowing requirement. Then, you are in the driver's seat. The banker sees you as a source of deposit with minimal risk. You should be able to negotiate a line of credit for at least a year.

In choosing a bank, the first thing to determine is if the bank understands your business. Examine the restrictive covenants closely. They will be significantly different for different industries. A bank that is heavily involved in real estate or construction loans will have covenants far more restrictive than what a manufacturer would want to agree to.

A bank with restrictive convenants would be more inclined to ask for personal guarantees from the owners. It can get its money back faster this way than by selling an apartment house. A manufacturer, on the other hand, could offer receivables that can be readily turned into cash as his or her security.

Whatever your business, resist making personal guarantees. A bank, typically, is going to want to see periodic financial statements. Don't agree to give it any more than what it asks for or you'll be spending all your time explaining the statements. A simple balance sheet and income statement should be sufficient.

One of the things most people fail to mention to you when starting your company is obtaining *personal credit* before you take the leap into business (while you are still solvent). Invariably, a new company is cash poor and the principles involved often pour their own cash into the firm until family and personal bills begin to suffer.

It is easy to say that that kind of firm shouldn't be in existence anyway, yet it is from this kind of optimism about a company's future that successful companies emerge. Before embarking on that new venture, advice to the wise includes:

- Preparing a glowing financial statement.
- Applying for credit cards (American Express, Diner's Club, MasterCard, Visa), at many places. Have these cards as a ready reserve when cash flow begins to wane.

Obviously you could go overboard in this regard, but for those new, small companies that open its doors with cash flows of $200,000 or less, having this credit already established could turn out to be a blessing. It might be impossible to get that credit once the business is a fledgling.

In dealing with a bank, determine on the front end of your negotitations what the line of credit is based on. Typically a bank will want you to maintain a certain debt to equity ratio. If you do not provide personal guarantees, a bank typically will want to restrict dividends or changes of ownership in the stock. These type requirements should not be objectionable, particularly if your company is closely held and where dividends are a foolish double tax distribution of earnings. Personal financial considerations are quite important to an expanding company, especially when you consider the problems of underfinancing.

Do a thorough investigation of the bank's marketing approach. Look in depth at what relationship you will have with your account executive. Does the bank typically assign various accounts to its executives on a permanent basis, or is your account executive likely to be promoted out of your account classification? The emerging company wants a relationship with a bank that has stability in the account executive.

There are only two reasons to bank with a big bank. First, they provide services that you need, which a small bank cannot. Or second, you need a big bank with lending limits large enough to satisfy your borrowing demands.

After you have done that analysis, talk to some people who bank with that bank. Bankers are the most fickle people in the business community; the answers you receive can be surprising. Ask people difficult questions: How did the bank react during a business downturn? How long had they been dealing with the bank? How long have they had their current account executive? How often does the executive visit them?

Finally, don't overlook the other services that a bank can provide. Many banks provide financial seminars. It also provides personal, financial planning services, trust services for your pension and profit-sharing plans, and discount brokerage services. A bank might also be the source of statistical information for your industry.

CHOOSING A PARTNER OR VENTURE CAPITALIST

Most small or emerging companies are not in a position to go public, but it often considers partnerships or use of venture capital. One source for venture capital listings is *The Venture Capitalist*, published by Dun & Bradstreet. These listings provide a starting point for placements and potential partners for firms whose technology or service offer growth and high-return and high cash flow.

As a guideline for small businesses, (Table 6-1), executives might also want to refer to a U.S. government publication title: ''The State of Small Business: A

Table 6-1. Government Sources of Information.

Government Offices:	*Assistance Offered and How to Find It:*
Department of Commerce (DOC)	Publishes capacity and operating rate data plus statistics on business in general. It does studies on various types of businesses and industries at its Washington, D.C., offices. These are very valuable marketing research tools. DOC has field offices throughout the United States. Listed in the phone directory under U.S. government.
Internal Revenue Service (IRS)	Publishes the "Tax Guide to Small Business" and advises on tax matters that concern small businesses. It is listed under the Treasury Department in U.S. government section of the telephone directory.
Small Business Administration (SBA)	Has field offices in major U.S. cities. Publishes many aids for people going into business. Some of these are free; others are for sale. Conducts workshops regularly for people who want to start or improve their businesses. Generally the SBA has limited value unless you can identify a special program funded by SBA but run by a university or others.
State Board of Equalization or State Tax Board	Can give requirements for collecting and remitting retail sales taxes. Some states publish statistics on business based on the amount of taxes they collect and number of seller's permits they issue. Also ask the Secretary of the state for business assistance as well as state development agencies.
U.S. Government	The Superintendent of Public Documents distributes and sells all government publications. Their address is: Superintendent of Documents, U.S. Government Printing Office, Washington, D.C. 20402.

Report of the President Transmitted to Congress, 1986.'' This publication gives overviews of the various financial alternatives available to the small or emerging company. These include:

- owner financing
- informal investors
- banks
- savings institutions

- insurance companies
- finance companies
- leasing firms
- public offerings
- private placements
- Regulation D offerings
- Venture capital financing
- small business investment companies
- U.S. Small Business Administration (to include SBA-backed loans from commercial banks), state and/or local government funding
- bonds (including junk bonds)
- foreign investment

Now, a word of caution about dealing with the SBA. First, these loans (direct or SBA-backed) are difficult to get. Some suggest that minorities appear to have a better chance at loans, but even so, the agreement often makes you sign your life away. When a person has to put up everything he or she owns, including the house, a loan of this type becomes a terrible headache—especially if things don't work out.

Another problem with many new ventures is that they grow too quickly. In their haste to get the dollars needed for continued expansion, the key individuals who started or are running the company often associate themselves with shysters or people who promise cash inflow to the company, but fail to deliver after the first check. Often the result is legal action among the parties involved, and on more than one occasion, the company goes down the drain, drowned by time-consuming, non-management activities that bleed the energies of key executives while patented technologies age to the point of no value.

A commonsense rule of thumb prevails. If you are uncomfortable with a financial arrangement—don't do it. Also, while it seems obvious, there is thievery and chicanery in financing, with out-and-out thieves playing the game. Be cautious of the nebulous "Arab investor" who never can be reached, and of companies that sound impressive, but don't have phone listings. And, *never* pay up-front money to loan arrangers. Some pretty smart people were ripped off by these "fronts" as late as 1985 and 1986. Many of these "frauds" are still operating today. Also, beware of creative financing that you do not understand.

STAYING OUT OF FINANCIAL TROUBLE

Having said that about finances, also be careful of telling your bank too much about yourself or your business. Also, be careful of the background, and know the background and associations, of your account officer. There are horror stories about those who fail to investigate these facets of their bankers.

For example, some years ago one company that had grown very rapidly was in a highly leveraged position while dealing with a large bank. One afternoon the CEO went to some length explaining the outlook for his firm for the next six months and the strategy for capturing new markets. At the end of the briefing, a young banker thanked the CEO and said that he found the presentation very interesting. He added that he had often discussed the company with his father-in-law. When asked who the father-in-law was, he turned out to be a distributor for a key competitor in another city.

Loan officers at banks have become as transient as computer people were ten years ago. The most valuable asset they have to offer a new employer is their client list. If you compete on a local basis, remember that what you tell your loan officer might not be kept confidential.

OTHER BUSINESS COSTS

Insurance

It is estimated that 22 percent of the cost of products manufactured in the U.S. goes to insurance costs. In a small company, health insurance alone can reach 25 percent of the total budgetary expenses. By comparison, 42 percent of the cost of manufacturing private airplanes is in the insurance. Economically this reduces America's competitiveness in the world market, but on the smaller scale, it eats up an emerging company's working capital almost as quickly as salaries. It is no wonder that some emerging companies are operating without insurance. One misjudgement could put them out of business.

The small business and emerging company should be aware of one insurance document that is an excellent source for rating companies. It is the "Best" handbook that provides financial strengths and ratings of all insurance companies operating in the U.S.

Taxes

Pogo said: "We have met the enemy, and he is us!" The greatest threat to American industry is the federal government. Don't be naive enough to think the federal government would not pass legislation that could put you out of business. The recent tax legislation has put many real estate developers or financial planners under financial stress. Although there are some positive aspects of the tax law for small business, there are many expenses that are no longer fully deductible. The emerging company must keep a close eye on the tax laws. For example, in the case of a small defense contractor, the government withdrew the wage and price controls. As a result, the firm's manufacturing cost increased 30 percent.

On a producing basis of a million items, the company was losing 60 cents apiece. With the Army demanding that the firm continue to produce, it finally was operating with a negative equity. Fortunately, the company eventually received extraordinarily contractual relief.

The point is, tax considerations can easily turn a profitable business into one faced with bankruptcy. Because many emerging industries are tied to government spending, there should be an immediate attempt to diversify the customer base under these conditions.

Salaries and Employee Benefits

As a rule of thumb, employee benefits can run half of salary expenses. Money is important to people, but it is not always the main reason why people choose to work for a company. If you want good people, they should believe that they are receiving salaries commensurate with what they would be receiving elsewhere.

Inventory

Inventory carrying costs become a subtle drain on profits that are constantly overlooked by small or emerging companies. Realistically, depending on the business you are in, inventory carrying costs run from 20 percent to 40 percent annually. Therefore, a million dollars in inventory (whether raw materials or finished goods) can cost the company $200,000. Some firms have gone to just-in-time (JIT) deliveries to alleviate those costs. This forces the inventory backward to the suppliers, but the same thing can happen to you on finished goods. The spillover for financial savings comes in streamlined manufacturing or service techniques.

Financial Ratios and Net Worth

Return On Investment (ROI) is the usual measure of a company's profitability, although this number is not a true indication of management performance. This is especially true in today's market where corporate raiders force companies into a financial situation that make it unattractive for merger or acquisition.

If we consider a net profit/net worth ratio, which is an indication of percent return to stockholders, the average U.S. company runs at about 10 to 12 percent. The value for emerging or growth companies could reach 25 to 30 percent; however, in most cases the cash generated is reinvested to sustain growth. When the company is public, this is reflected in stock prices, which is why many managers choose to go public, especially if they have low-priced options. Staying private, however, is beginning to have certain financial advantages, especially when large cash generations end up in the owner's pocket.

FINANCING THE SMALL BUSINESS

Nobody said starting a company was easy, and a small company often is faced immediately with heavy expenses and no income. Factually, too many small companies start up without a business plan, a financial plan, and sufficient money. They have an idea of how they will generate income; however, there is a constant need for cash—especially when a firm adds employees and pays their benefits.

In this analysis, we must assume that the new company has a product or service that will sell. From that point on, the question is one of cash flow that includes debt financing—if it can obtain loans in the first place.

Under-capitalization is one of the most serious problems of any start-up business. Invariably it has to go back to the well (financiers) too often and many have to use up savings, borrow from friends, take on partners, or sell shares of stock.

This is a time when managers realize that friendly banks are great on TV commercials, but when it comes to lending money to small, starting businesses, most friendly banks are worthless. It can take as long as three years to obtain financing for a typical venture; say, in food processing. In some cases, the answer to the problem is to seek outside financial advice that will include a detailed business plan and cash flow projections.

It is not the intent of the book to act as a primer on finance, but rather to point out some of the trials, tribulations, and pitfalls you will likely encounter or consider. Some include:

- Substitute debt for equity; growth companies who do this can grow faster than competitors who do not make this substitution.

- Do not lose market share. Cash-rich companies become vulnerable when that happens.

- Watch for marginal suppliers who cannot generate the cash needed to provide good service. They are open to failure and can hurt you.

- Concentrate on the part of your business where a minor increase in efficiency will produce major increases in profitability.

- Switch from salary-system to salary-plus-bonus (based-on-company performance) to affect monthly cash flow.

- Carefully analyze true inventory carrying costs.

- Manage and control budgets to include Break Even Analysis.

- Focus your financial interest on cash flow coupled to profitability; do a yearly cash flow forecast.

- Pay close attention to timely payments, for growth companies increase their pool of accounts receivables.

- Growth implies need for cash for raw materials, people, etc. Don't be caught without money to pay taxes. Use a set-aside for payments.
- Lacking capacity means losing market share. Consider toll processing (subcontracting) if your company cannot finance expansion required.
- Know your minimum liquidity for operations and to stay in business.
- Prepare for running out of cash; growth and emerging companies often run out.

If you start small and provide a good service, you may not need as much cash as you think.

If you must make something, the efforts of establishing credit and obtaining funding are a necessary part of your venture. The key consideration is whether to use debt or equity financing. Each avenue has its strong and weak points.

The advantage of debt financing relates to tax considerations, retaining control of the company, increasing net return on equity, and avoiding shareholder dilution and fixed dollar commitments. In contrast, equity financing allows for future debt financing, enhances a firm's credit rating, provides for easier stock transfer, and enables the company to save dollar reserves.

JOINT VENTURING

Of the techniques, debt financing might offer the best entree to another financing mechanism—the joint venture. The emerging company can bring the people and technology while a new partner can bring the cash.

Joint venturing can be an excellent way to finance a new venture. If your company brings a product, technology, or marketing capability to the table, and a second company brings the cash, the marriage can be viable. Keep in mind, however, that these associations have a high mortality rate. To avoid business-divorce complications, a joint venture should be established with a time frame in mind and escape clauses spelled out.

By having a complete understand of what each party is bringing to the business and what each wants out of it, the joint venture has a better chance of success.

Companies should also clearly understand managerial philosophy and joint venture goals and direction. These should be carefully negotiated before startup.

The bottom line is that whatever financial mode proves best for your company, a detailed cost analysis is crucial—especially in high technology areas. Companies that fail to detail their up-front costs of starting a business and operating it are doomed to mediocre growth or worse. Too often, founders, enthralled with the importance of their new product or service, find that market acceptance is not as enthusiastic. Overzealous expectations and overvaluing the real worth of a company can actually inhibit investors interest. That results in a company stagnating until the owner dies and the firm is taken over by others or goes out of existence.

Finally, make-or-buy decisions can affect financial requirements. In today's competitive manufacturing industries, raw material and labor costs are receiving close scrutiny. There is considerable financial incentive to "buy" rather than "make" a product to avoid the dollar requirement for capital equipment and operating a plant.

7

Alone at the Helm: Managing the New or Emerging Company

IT IS HARD TO WEAR A DOZEN HATS AND KEEP 30 BALLS IN THE AIR. YET, managing an infinite number of projects at one time is the perplexing dilemma that faces the chief executive officer of almost any emerging company.

In addition, the perspectives of the CEO of an emerging company need to be different than those of large publicly-traded companies. This is not meant to minimize in any way the demands of the presidents and CEOs of the giants, but by necessity, and unfortunately, too much of the effort of managers in public companies has to be centered on satisfying the stockholders with earnings and dividends or on growth during current periods. As a result, there are situations where too little emphasis is devoted to plans for the future. That's also a serious hindrance to the future of the whole American economy.

Major problems for the CEO of the emerging company are:

- How to produce a profit this period, next year, and the year after that.
- How to provide the necessary immediate cash flow to make payroll and support necessary research and development efforts.
- How to finance the expansions in capital equipment and personnel increases.

These difficulties prove the old adage: "Some days you get the bear and some days the bear gets you." The successful entrepreneur or leader of an emerging company will survive all of these pressures by profession of one indisputable quality: decisiveness.

Also, for an emerging company to succeed, it needs the excitement of accomplishment and confidence in the future. Nothing can destroy this type of attitude faster than leadership procrastination. Unfortunately, the leaders of many emerging companies have few people to talk to about many of today's and tomorrow's problems. As the president of a closely held company, you might have only three people to talk to: your mother, your wife, and God. And two out of the three usually don't give answers.

MANAGERIAL RELATIONSHIPS

Confidants and Advisory Boards

So, the manager of an emerging company is often alone—sometimes simply because of the size of the company. He or she may be the single manager in the firm, especially during start-up. This can create a problem because the manager has no one with whom to bounce ideas, to brainstorm, or to simply let off steam. In those cases, a good concept is to sublease office space in a location where other companies or managers with similar interests are available for at least informal consultation.

For example, a new manufacturing firm in the electronics industry found an unexpected friend in the offices of a company that worked with materials-handling equipment under the same roof. The bonus for both parties was shared overhead and a comparison of sales opportunities at businesses where each made calls but did not compete, and most of all an opportunity for discussion of management problems and decisions.

Growing companies have this same opportunity. For example, one suggestion for the CEO of the emerging company or closely held business is to develop a confidant. This person, of course, is someone with whom you should have a very close relationship, preferably not one of a family nature. The individual obviously needs to keep your discussions confidential. Family members sometimes feel that they are not being fair to another family member by not sharing the problems. A close friend or possibly a predecessor to you and your position might make a good confidant. He or she should be someone who possesses enough wisdom and business savvy to do more than listen and thus provide you with suggestions.

It is difficult to choose a confidant. After all, how many people want to hear your problems? There are many, many successful business people, however, who are willing to provide guidance to management, preferably the president or CEO as opposed to lower management.

These people can take a role in an *advisory board*. The popularity of an *advisory board* is growing because the individuals have no fear of direct liability. The advisory board is not a legal board.

Advisory boards typically consist of three people, although in some cases advisory boards have five members. You should not choose only your close friends to be on your advisory board. It is best to choose the most qualified people that you can find. You should develop a checklist of qualities (Fig. 7-1) for an advisory board member because not every company has the same needs.

One company used an advisory board (AB) for about 8 years during an emerging growth period. When the concept was initiated, there were three major corporate problem areas: marketing, finance, and manufacturing. The AB consisted of an expert from each of these areas. They included a man who had been a corporate president of more than one company and was an excellent marketeer; a man who was the plant manager, or the equivalent of a vice president of most companies, for a very large multi-national company (he possessed manufacturing as well as international experience); and finally, the president of a bank that had no affiliations with the company. After 2 years, the firm began to rotate AB members. Each year after the second year, one member of the board retired and someone new joined the board for a three-year period.

If you elect to have a rotating type advisory board, you might also want to ask each retiring member if he or she would be willing to be available should the occasion arise where you need some specific help.

There are advisory boards where there is no schedule for meetings. Most ABs, however, meet on a quarterly basis. The meetings are usually for half a day starting with an 8:00 A.M. breakfast and continuing until 11:30 A.M. Pay for an advisory board can range from $250 to $500 per meeting per member. The pay would depend upon the size of the company. For those who attend all the meetings, one can offer a Christmas bonus equal to the payment for one meeting. Other means of compensation and its value depend on the business itself. Some

---

☞   Choose a person from an industry other than your own.

☞   Choose a person from your own industry.

☞   Have one financial expert.

☞   Choose people who will be candid.

☞   Have one executive genius; try to include someone on the cutting edge of various technologies.

☞   Choose a close personal friend who will identify with your interests.

☞   Choose influential people.

☞   Include a university professor or dean.

Fig. 7-1. Checklist for choosing an advisory board.

new businesses might have to rely on an AB of friends with no compensation whatsoever. Other larger firms pay more than $500 per meeting.

Most people have an understanding with their advisory board members that they may call upon them at any time between the regularly scheduled meetings for lunch or on the phone to briefly discuss current problems or situations. You usually do not expect to get a great deal of productivity from your advisory board for the first two or three meetings. Members have to learn your business as well as become acquainted with your people, company goals, and objectives. A portion of the meeting is usually spent covering the current and year-to-date financial results.

Consultants

Consultants can be very helpful in solving specific problems for the emerging company. Consultants also can be very expensive. Regardless of the consultant, it will take some time to become familiar with your business and to learn and understand your problems. While doing this, the consultant will also be taking the time of you and your management staff. Do not hire a consultant unless you feel you have the time to spend with the individual. Be certain that there is a clear understanding between you and the consultant of what is expected and what the maximum cost would be for his or her services. Be careful of hiring friends as consultants; both of you might lose your objectivity. Set guidelines for using a consultant. Don't choose your lawyer or CPA firm as a director, advisory director, or consultant. You are already paying them for their advice.

Consulting companies are as small as one-person firms working from a home to large, multi-faceted companies that have full-time staffs in many disciplines and use sophisticated computer modeling to obtain its results. For the most part, an emerging company should stay away from the multi-million dollar consulting firms. Their reports are usually far to general; and while their business plans look professional and well done, they cannot substitute for common sense and business acumen learned on the firing line. Many firms have used consultants because they have a well-known name and reputation, yet in the particular field in question, they really have little expertise.

The authors recommend that emerging companies use small or medium-sized consulting firms whose talents coincide exactly with your consulting needs. Also, do not hire the "firm." Hire the individual. You want to know the exact person who will work with you; you want his or her time committed firmly; and you don't want switches—unless you find that you've chosen the wrong man.

Start small. Do one small job and get to know the individual and his or her capabilities.

Spell out exactly what you expect from the consulting job, when you expect it, and what it will cost. Check to assure there are no interferences from other jobs during the time you need the consultant. Stick to a milestone chart and deadlines.

The way you use a consultant varies. Often they are used for trouble-shooting. In that case let the manager of the troubled area make the suggestion to bring in an expert; that way it will be his or her idea and there will be no fear of working with the outsider.

Consultants are also used when your own people are too tied up to handle a job (flexible staffing). The consultant can be hired-as-needed. If this happens often in a particular business or geographical area, you may want to press the individual to work on a retainer.

Autonomy vs. Control

For an emerging company where you are trying to control costs and overhead and, at the same time, are working hard yourself to set the pace and provide the leadership for the company, the authors advocate a flat organization structure. This means an organization structure (supplemented by matrixing) where there are very few management levels. In this case, several people answer directly to the CEO. Although most management books suggest the ideal number of people reporting to one person is from four to six, a flat organization in an emerging business might require that the CEO deal with as many as 14 people. When this many managers answer to you, they have to be good self-starting performers because you do not have much time to devote to any one person. The advantages of a flat organization structure is that it allows you to be close to what is going on with the employees and the customers, and gives you better control. Of course, there is the question of what you *desire* to control, or more importantly, what you *need* to control. These can be two different things and it is important to distinguish the difference in an emerging company. For example, the president of an emerging company might have to control one or more segments of the business and perhaps everything in that segment (Fig. 7-2).

A manager who controls the box (and not its contents) does not have to tell business segment employees what to do. He or she delegates the authority, thus creating conditions where people can manage themselves and hopefully reach their own potential. This kind of management is essential in an emerging business so managers are not burdened with constraints of doing what someone else should be doing.

"Be all that you can be," is a proper instruction to employees in the emerging company. To this, you as a manager in an emerging company should instill the reality that you are going to make people think for themselves. How? A simple solution is to let your subordinates know that when they bring a problem to you, you are going to ask them for their recommended solution. When you give a person authority, however, you must also give that individual the control function.

Top Managers	CEO			
Managers	1	2	3	4
Business Segments	A A A B B B C C C	A B C A B C A B C	C B A C B A C B A	C C C B B B A A A

Although the content of the boxes (business segments) do not change, what a manager does with those contents can dramatically change. In a flat organization where a CEO could have as many as 14 people under his or her control, the secret is to let each manager control what is in the box while the CEO controls the managers.

Fig. 7-2. Managers must face the question of controlling the box or what's in it.

Delegation

Another good way of coping with the decision-making process is to delegate authority. If you are going to delegate authority, then get out of the way and let the other person have a chance of doing it his or her way. If you are a successful delegator, you might find it could create another problem. That problem is you will develop some good, strong leaders who are capable of making decisions and they, as well as your subordinates, might get confused as to where their responsibility stops. There are two ways to cope with this problem. One is to develop job descriptions that are mutually agreed upon between you and your key personnel. It is not necessary that all your subordinates be privy to the details of these job descriptions, but they should be generally aware of what each of the major areas of responsibility are. The other is to eliminate job descriptions, which are constantly changing in a growth company anyway, and rely on the individual to create solutions within the matrix of the organization.

There is no greater threat to the future of an emerging company that a riff between top managers and the resulting deterioration of the subordinates confidence. It is no secret that delegating authority is a management technique that holds for any company, but there are some special considerations when your company is in a growth pattern.

Perhaps, as a spin-off of military training, managers have been taught that you can delegate the *authority*, but not the *responsibility*. The Harry S. Truman quote, "The buck stops here," indicates that the CEO is ultimately responsible for the actions of subordinates. With emerging companies, however, the buck stops at the first line managers. He or she must shoulder the responsibility of action him or herself. A person must not be so cautious that there is fear of signing a document, making a decision, or taking an action. Too many mistakes and you are out; if there are enough good decisions, then you move up! An emerging company is no place for the timid and indecisive. In an emerging company, the buck stops with the first person who handles it. We cannot overemphasize the importance of honesty.

Another way of looking at delegation is the emerging company delegates to an individual and not to a committee that is real or *ad hoc*. In large, older companies, decisions on projects often go through a series of individuals who pass general judgement on the project. They attach their "comments" to a routing slip until 3 months later, the material returns to the boss's desk. We call this the "informal committee buffer zone." The decision comes out under a gray statement with verbiage like "our management beliefs." In these cases, the boss can be classified as a moral coward.

Although this routing takes place in a big company, the emerging company should be acting with the knowledge of *who* is responsible for *what*. This means that the emerging company must be tolerant of some mistakes. Also, it must have people working for the organization who have common sense enough to know when they are acting in the Peter principle (Fig. 7-3), and not treading in someone else's area.

What does this imply? The need for standards!

☑ Things don't get done.

☑ Stacks of papers abound.

☑ You experience fear.

☑ Problems occur constantly.

☑ You don't know the answers to questions.

☑ You spend too much time at work.

☑ There is no time for planning.

☑ There is no time for creativity.

☑ Your day is full of reaction vs. constructive work toward goals.

☑ Physical and or mental problems occur.

☑ Signs of family problems show up.

☑ Profitability suffers.

☑ You begin to lose orders.

☑ Competition increases its share of the market.

☑ Accounting functions are out of control.

☑ Complaints appear.

☑ Good customers begin to pressure you.

☑ Deadlines are missed.

Don't *confuse* this with having too much to do!

Fig. 7-3. How to tell when you are acting beyond your capabilities: A checklist.

Removal of Old Ideas

The best way to avoid ideas is to avoid having old ideas turn into procedures. It is probably wrong to equate old ideas with bad ideas. The point is: Old thinking and the desire to maintain the *status quo* does not create the opportunity for change that is so vital for a growth situation.

Presidents and CEOs of emerging companies provide the following "first person" stories:

Story 1: Conflict among Peers.

"I once had a company where I was the president; my predecessor, as past president, was chairman of the board; and his predecessor had taken a position as vice president. Now on the surface this might appear to be an example of succession planning, but in reality it was an exercise in frustration. Each of us came from a different discipline. The older man was a marketeer. His successor was a financier. I was an advocate of professional management. More than once employees went to one or the other of us, in regards to decision-making, so that they got the answer they wanted. It was like children going to a parent who sympathized with a particular point of view.

"During this period, any major decision had to be a compromise. After two years of trying to put together an acceptable strategic plan, I finally hired a facilitator. This individual had an outstanding background and within four hours gained the respect of the entire corporate staff. It cost us $3,000 a day for this individual, but we molded the strategic plan for the corporation over one weekend."

Story 2: Conflict about Retirement.

"I once had this experience with an older gentleman who had announced his retirement at age 65. He then changed it to 67, stepped down as chairman at 67, but stayed with the company until he was 69. He then really wanted to continue on for an indefinite period as a consultant. The company gave him a two-year contract and then after that offered him continuing work on a project-by-project basis.

"In another case, a second gentleman had no plans of ever retiring. The company CEO and president initiated a mandatory retirement plan that required an officer, director, or manager to relinquish his responsibilities at age 65. A person could then continue on beyond that in a consultant capacity for an indefinite period of time, but the recommended period was two years. With the legal retirement age currently at 70, the plan was quasi-illegal for people who were not officers. The board of directors, of course, can ask anyone to resign at any time."

Story 3: More on Retirement

"I have run into many problems in dealing with older employees. For example, the board of directors of my company established a retirement age of 70 for the directors. Part of this is based on the difficulty some older people have in dealing with change. One suggestion people often made to me was 'never try to make a deal with a man who is over 65 years of age.' I have not always heeded this advice, and when I didn't, I failed in every instance. When an individual reaches the age of 65, his perspectives on problems in the future is significantly different than a young entrepreneurial chief executive officer. As a matter of fact, we employed one individual whose perspective would change every day.

"When I was 47 years old I tried selling a company to a New York stock exchange firm. If I had joined their board, I would have lowered the average age of the board to 72. We negotiated for almost a year and the axiom that there's a thousand reasons *NOT* to deal, but only a few reasons to make a deal, was proven to me month after month. The old stodgy attitude led to acquisition failure."

Relationships with Accounting

Sometimes words can be more important than figures, but this is hard to explain to accounting departments in large corporations.

For example, expense accounts are important in controlling costs in any company, but accounting departments can take things to an extreme. One engineer tells the story of an accounting department in New York City who called him in Houston to discuss a 25 cent addition error in an expense account tied to a phone booth call. When the accountant was confronted with the fact that the accounting department had wasted more than 25 cents in a long distance phone call to check on the error, plus the wasted time to discuss the matter, the accountant could not understand why the engineer was upset. Indeed, accounting can carry some things to an extreme.

The moral, of course, is that worrying about too many details will make you lose your business. Both good accountants and good managers appreciate this facet of operations, with the principle that emerging companies should not be bogged down with unnecessary or overzealous accounting procedures. A good guideline is: Keep only the records you need.

RESEARCH AND DEVELOPMENT (R&D) AND MANAGEMENT

The use of computers, widespread access to numerous databases, and instant communication have given worldwide access to a broad pool of scientific and technical information. The emerging company must learn to utilize these sources not only for marketing advantages, but also to maintain competitive advantages through:

- Developing new products via research and commercialization.
- Using cooperative R&D programs.
- Capitalizing on the international aspects of R&D.

These can be looked at from the standpoint of goals and methodology to reach these goals.

Product Development and Commercialization

Goals. Develop fresh approaches for integrating the new product development process into the mainstream of today's business environment.

Methodology. Utilize the full resources of a project business team to stimulate innovation and technical progress. Create open division boundaries to encourage the flow of innovation throughout the corporation. Use corporate restructuring when necessary; evaluate those factors that help or hinder effective R&D, evaluate R&D performance, and use different approaches to the R&D and new product development.

Use of Cooperative R&D Programs

Goals. To take advantage of the myriad opportunities for innovative R&D management offered by new technical partnerships, both domestically and internationally.

Methodology. Hire outsiders if necessary to show how joint activities can help your corporate research. Recognize the role of universities as managers of research. Calculate funding and organizational options for R&D collaborations. Carefully consider the problems inherent to research links between traditional competitors. Stay updated on consortia, make honest evaluations (realistic results vs. blue sky expectations). Find out if international research collaboration is feasible.

International Aspects of R&D

Goals. Exploit growing worldwide resources through technological innovation fueled by successful R&D to meet expanding international competition.

Methodology. Identify, exploit, analyze, and manage global R&D opportunities. Evaluate the rewards of technology sharing vs. the potential loss of intellectual property protection. Compare trade-offs involved in cross-licensing and joint ventures. Pinpoint key success variables in maintaining a competitive edge internationally. Study the implications of new economic linkages among both companies and countries.

Successful, fast moving companies have found ways to integrate R&D with management goals and perspectives through "innovative entrepreneuring teams." These help direct R&D into work that produces saleable products, both short-term and long-term. Each company should set its own guidelines for who should serve on these teams, but there are some typical considerations (Fig. 7-4).

☞ Must be creative

☞ Have good business training

☞ Understand the importance of marketing and how marketing works

☞ Understand Return on Investment(ROI)

☞ Have the necessary technical expertise

☞ Have an appreciation of time and timing

☞ Can work on a team

☞ Is candid and unafraid of criticism

☞ Is a self-starter

☞ Can mentally juggle a variety of complex topics

Fig. 7-4. "Innovative entrepreneuring team": A checklist of characteristics.

MANAGEMENT AND PROBLEMS

Some of the problems you will face as the manager of an emerging company are the same as for large companies (the way you solve them can be different); but some of them can be entirely different. Let's talk about these *different* problems, starting with nepotism.

Nepotism

Nepotism is an appropriate topic because of its uniqueness to small companies and its far-reaching effects. Nepotism, after all, is more of a management problem than it is a people problem. The people involved might be excellent employees and individually not a problem at all. The problem is their relationship with you or other employees.

There basically are two types of nepotism problems: the ones that you create by hiring your relatives, or relatives of employees; and the ones that you had absolutely no control of. The latter type is probably the most difficult to cope with. For example, this problem can be created by two of your employees getting married. You certainly cannot prevent them from doing so; but at the same time, how close do you want their working relations to be? What happens when two people of a six-person accounting department get married and the company policy is that two people in the same family cannot work in the same department?

Sometimes the situation is almost evolutionary. In one particular case, a company hired the older brother of a man who worked in the tool shop to become vice president of manufacturing. The older brother was very strong and before long had promoted the younger brother to plant superintendent. When the older brother left the company, the younger had a difficult time. It could only be resolved by transferring him, in this case, into the engineering department.

Take another case where a company permitted the general manager of a company to hire his son for a marketing position in the field. This goes somewhat unnoticed in a large company because there is a sales manager supervising the son, and the father very seldom sees his offspring. The problem occurred when the company promoted the general manager to vice president of marketing and the son ended up working directly for the dad. This situation can get even worse when the son marries a girl who also works in marketing.

These types of situations are never pleasant. Yet, an emerging company often is faced with them. The answer is to set a strict policy early in the life of the company. Get guidance for this policy by qualified individuals and then stick to the policy.

If your company is a small emerging organization, you will some day be a third generation company, if not already. Although few companies go beyond the third generation without incurring major family and/or management problems, every situation is different. Usually there is never a solution satisfactory to everyone. However, there are some alternatives and solutions to the family nepotism problem.

- Don't hire siblings of family members unless they have worked elsewhere for at least 2 years.
- Favor college graduates unless there are specific and obvious reasons not to do so.
- Go over details of new tax laws related to corporation, vs. subchapter S, vs. DBA (doing business as) proprietorship.
- Consider two classes of stock—(voting and non-voting)—to keep control of company with chosen heir(s).
- Do not force children into a business that they don't like or can't manage.
- With multiple family owners, do not expect business decisions to be unanimous. Plan accordingly.
- Have company prepare for effects of death of one or more family owners.

Regardless, the best way to handle a family business when it reaches a third generation is to have someone who is tough, strong, and fair, running the business. Many times the problems begin with the compensation of stockholder/employee family members. Normally, the people who are shareholders in a family-held business are not all experienced people and haven't the least idea of what good management costs.

The best suggestion to the president or the CEO of a family-held business reaching its third generation is to run the company professionally with professional managers. Don't try to be the matriarch or the paternal manager of the company.

Politics

No discussion of problems in an emerging company would be complete without a discussion of politics. Most people believe that recently the American dream has become somewhat tarnished. The prospects for the future that we leave our children are not nearly as great as the prospects that were given to us. In 10 years, the United States has gone from first in the world in standard of living to seventh. We've become a debtor nation for the first time. We've gone from a trade surplus to a $170 billion trade deficit in less than 8 years. A million manufacturing jobs are being lost per year. Companies are being expected to absorb the burden of the nation's debt to a greater extent while individual income taxes are being reduced for the poor-to-middle income workers.

If you think about that, it means that you can expect your company to be paying a greater percentage of its income to the government for taxes while you, as a successful entrepreneur, are going to be paying greater taxes for your success. With no incentive for success, the emerging company must also consider whether, if, or how it gets involved with politics.

Productivity

One of the problems that has caused a great deal of the decline in American business is the lack of productivity. People try to make the question of measuring productivity too complicated. They want to measure efficiency against standard labor rates and do time studies on their workers, but it's not that complicated. Set a corporate goal to increase productivity each year by a certain percentage. Calculate the increase in productivity on an adjusted sales figure, taking into account the inflation reported in the cost of living standards. Measure the productivity of your company by the total sales dollars per employee. Let each subordinate then devise his or her own productivity objectives for that person's department. The important thing is to continue to increase sales revenue per employee. This method does not discriminate against office, clerical, sales, janitorial, or production employees.

Another concern for managers of emerging companies is the need to implement new strategies; the greater problem is that you have to allow time to see if the strategies work.

Potentially, another way of solving or preventing a problem that—in spite of your best efforts—has avoided solution, is to allow the department where the problem exists to go over strength. This concept is discussed in other parts of this book, but it simply means allowing a department head to hire more people of a higher quality in his or her department for the specific purpose of solving a management problem once and for all. However, this includes the understanding that after he or she has been able to solve the problem, the department head is expected to get the work force back to the proper level in subsequent years. Obviously, this raises overhead and reduces profitability, but you will probably be saving money in the long run as opposed to continuing to struggle and being despondent over your inability to solve a short-term problem in other ways.

Staying with the productivity question, another facet of the business world that invariably faces managers of emerging companies is *unions*.

Some people feel that if their company becomes unionized, it's the end of the world. If you're not union and you treat your people right, give them rewards for performance, and follow some of the directions already covered, there is a very good chance that you can remain non-union. Should you become unionized, however, it is not the end of the world. Unions are losing membership each year and because of the economic strife that is developing in our country, the union's demands and strengths are weakening each year. Emerging companies must have keen negotiating strategies.

To help in strategy, it is best to hire an attorney who specializes in negotiations. However, the attorney can do little for you if you are in front of the National Labor Relations Board (NLRB) and have been paying below union scale, have poor benefits, and have bad working conditions. That is what brings unions into the plant in the first place.

If you have made a sincere attempt to ensure employee satisfaction, remember that the union negotiators themselves are in the hot seat. They must come out of a meeting with concessions, or they will have egg on their faces and lose their jobs. This fact comes out behind closed doors. Be prepared to deal with the politics of the situation as well as the financial aspects.

Finally, always consider the option of dropping the union completely and hiring new employees. This should be a well-known fact as you enter into bargaining.

The answer to avoid unionization, in short, is to pay above union scale, give union benefits and working conditions, work the people like hell, and reward the people like heaven.

Other Problems

Serious business problems are a lot like cancer. Quite often a company's reaction to problems is similar to a person's reaction to cancer. First the problem is not recognized, then there is the denial that it is true. This is followed by confusion and finally despair, or conversely, the acceptance of the problem and a plan to do something to cure the illness (Fig. 7-5).

1. Production can't keep up with demand.
2. One part of product line isn't ready when availability was announced.
3. Problems with initial models.
4. Insufficient lead time.
5. Expectations of customer not filled.
6. Reaction time to inquiries is slow.
7. Company is cash short.
8. Hurried hiring results in employment of incompetents.
9. R&D can't keep up with technology changes.
10. Inadequate staffing and support.
11. Lack of follow-up.
12. Too many priorities.
13. Licensing and/or legal complications.
14. Internal and external communication gaps.
15. Insurance costs skyrocket.
16. No time to plan.
17. Personnel strategy slips into limbo.
18. Facilities become inadequate.
19. Friction between staff.
20. Some of first-group of employees get ''left behind.''
21. Travel becomes excessive.
22. Stress begins to affect key people.
23. ''Hot'' spots develop with key customers.
24. Company outgrows its telephone system.
25. Work overloads occur in people and departments.
26. Morale slips.
27. Illness affects key executives.
28. Overwork leads to family problems.
29. Unionization raises its head.
30. Company is inundated with paperwork for itself and government.
31. Tax problems occur.
32. Hanky panky starts.
33. Peter principle is born.

Fig. 7-5. 33 possible causes of trouble in growth companies.

The authors have experienced numerous other types of problems including bribes, blackmail, deaths from accidents, fires, floods, shooting, and safety and environmental headaches. In many of these unique one-time disasters, the best solution we can offer is to get yourself an expert to help you resolve the problem. Not an employee, but an attorney, accountant, or engineer who specializes in the problem area.

Another solution is to take one of your young managers who is on the fast track and inundate him or her with the problem!

ERA OF EMERGENCE

While the Fortune 500 companies are having fun seeing who can make the largest acquisition using the most novel financing, all the while eliminating U.S. jobs instead of creating them (with Uncle Sam's blessing), the manager of the emerging company has a different lot (Table 7-1).

The dynamic atmosphere in emerging industries can easily lead to managers who give rise to the Peter principle. New companies, or growth companies, offer an excellent opportunity for young and talented people to take on responsibilities that they would never see within a large company unless they were on the fast track. It is not unusual to give a 25 year-old a national marketing position which, sometimes by trial and error, is handled in a very successful manner.

Likewise, incompetency shows up much faster as people work their way to their own level of incompetence—the Peter principle. Managers must deal with incompetence quickly and decisively. In many cases this can involve dismissal; however, the ideal situation is to deal with incompetence on the hiring end. Try to enlist the services of those who are willing to take out their own trash today, but who can handle big projects in the future.

The manager may wake up some morning to find out that some of his or her key employees can't handle the jobs they are in, or even that the manager is in over his or her head. In the first instance we have to face the question, what to do when a promotion goes bad. Here are some guidelines.

- Recognize it. (Sometimes it is the company or sometimes it is the individual who knows it first.)
- Read the Peter principle; watch for it in your organization.
- Create demotion guidelines.
- Create lateral transfer guidelines.
- Transfer the individual to a different area where his or her talent fits.

Of the people fired, 90 percent don't know the real reason; 85 percent of those improve their situation—get better jobs; and 75 percent make a career, but on a different career path. How many go back to the same company? About 7 to 10 percent go back.

Table 7-1. Company Management of Large vs. Emerging Companies.

Large	Emerging
Dual and even quadruple lines of authority with confusion	Direct communication and simple lines of authority and responsibility
Staff support, with decisions camouflaged in a committee report	One person responsible. The "buck" stops here
Lots of experts to lean on	Many times must do it yourself
Multilevels of management	Lean, fluid, few levels of management
Large number of reports and correspondence	Phone and verbal decisions
Company politics and ferocious power struggles	Quick conflicts get with the team; get with the project; resign or get fired
Must have multi-millions in sales to turn a project	Lower overhead can lead to good cash flow and profits.
Organizational lag	Quick response
Obsolete people in need of retraining	State-of-the-art people geared for automation, growth-dynamics and use of the computer.
Managers get stuck in a slot with nowhere to climb	Dynamic growth leads to various management opportunities
Hand-picked, fast-trackers get choice assignments	Less experienced people handle novel projects with freedom to make mistakes
New ideas never reach the top	Go into the president's office to talk to him or her about a concept
Profit responsibility is vague	Know responsibility of how your project affects the bottom line.
Most managers work for a salary	Possibility of quantum jumps in income via several modes.

However, the emerging company goes through its most drastic changes when it moves from a strictly paternal or dictatorial style of operations to one of professional management. Consider the firm starting out with one or two people, full of enthusiasm. (Ideally it is best to have one good order in your pocket before venturing out on your own.) Ideas about the future bounce off the walls like racket balls, some are useful and some are worthless, but they should help in the formulation of a plan.

Keep in mind that a person often experiences family resistance when starting out. In addition, there is a total loss of security compared to being employed by a large corporation. This loss is more than just an emotional feeling—it is real and spills over into everything from pensions to health insurance coverage. (In respect to the latter, it is not unusual for a two-person company to start out with health insurance costs of $600 per month.) The best advice for any fledgling business is to consult a good accountant or CPA at the very beginning of an endeavor to ensure IRS, social security, workman's compensation, franchise taxes and similar matters are handled properly. These are not problems you should try to handle yourself unless you already have the expertise. The sheer volume of paper in doing this work steals precious time from key business functions, especially marketing.

Ultimately, you do reach the point where staffing becomes essential, and professional management becomes important so a firm simply does not fly by the seat of its pants. Obviously, this growth in size and personnel creates new headaches.

DIAGNOSTICS

When problems do occur, an answer that often has more merit than firing, is retraining. Not every manager has taken basic management courses. Also, in seminars or in schools, an individual will learn the basic management functions of: *plan, organize, staff, direct,* and *control.* Real life experiences prove that some managers of small or threshold companies have never heard of these basic functions.

Some textbooks reduce the functions to four; some books consider planning as the only function because good planning assumes you do all the rest. Our book emphasizes planning and staffing; however, we cannot overlook the other functions completely. As your company grows, each of the other functions take on added importance with a special need for direct and control functions, which we call *diagnostics.*

The easiest way to be a leader in an emerging company is to lead by example. To lead by example takes a lot of hard work and sacrifice. If you want the people to be at work on time, get there 15 minutes before starting time yourself. If you want them to stay until quitting time, stay 15 minutes beyond quitting time yourself. If you want them to come back on time from lunch, don't go to lunch yourself or be sure you get back on time. If you don't want them taking liberties with their expense accounts, be sure they understand that you don't take a lot of expenses that you could take. If you're on an austerity program, don't have memberships in expensive clubs that you or your family derive 75 percent of use from. Also, adhere to the vacation policies, which carries the postscript: Everyone should take their vacation.

Speaking of policies, these can be very helpful tools in decision-making. A policy is really nothing more than a definition of how the company operates in cases where the same problem appears frequently. If you have the policy documented, it's not necessary for management to take the time to provide the answer. Policy manuals quite frequently take a long time to develop. So, in an emerging company, simply start one and add to, or change, it as the company grows! There is no need to write a grandiose policy manual up front, based on others' experiences, because most of the material will prove extraneous.

Don't confuse a *policy manual* with a *procedures manual*. A procedures manual basically tells how the problem is solved and where the policy manual provides the answers without going through the procedures. Most emerging companies do not have procedures manuals except for technical aspects of manufacturing, operations, and maintenance. Today, most of these should be put onto the computer so that historical records also can be recalled.

Computer historical data pinpoints problem areas in people and in machines, but there is the additional consideration of pinpointing, or diagnosing if you will, incompetence in your people and yourself.

To begin with, incompetence is a slippery call. Sometimes it is hard to find it; however, there are some flags attached to it. When these flags start waving, be prepared to act. The key warning signals are:

- Breakdowns in communication; individuals not understanding assignments; work doesn't get done.
- Delays in getting work done; lack of proper training; lack of proper information to do a job; improper equipment support.
- Errors in quality or workmanship.
- Costs go out of control.
- Personal problems; illness; drugs or alcohol; divorce or teenager problems.
- Lack of team spirit.

Diagnosing problems within an individual, however, might be easier than diagnosing problems you have as an organization, with your basic business plan, or with simple day-to-day operations.

Paper Flow

Tied to diagnostics, when considering operations, every emerging company should perform a diagnostic paper-flow analysis after 1 year of operation. By then a system will have evolved, and it is amazing how inefficient and time consuming the paper-flow system can be.

Paper, too much of it or too many forms and records, is the nemesis of efficiency and productivity. Any company or plant should perform a paper-flow analysis of its facility at least every 2 years. It is amazing what you will uncover.

One manufacturing firm found that its working supervisors were spending up to 30 percent of their time with paperwork that was ultimately filed and not used again, or that could be handled in a more expedient manner by using a computer or office personnel.

Many companies could drastically reduce the amount of paper they process simply by drawing a flowsheet of paper flow through various departments. By physically tracing forms and reports from their origin to a file (all copies) and drawing that flow onto paper, it is possible to:

- Eliminate unnecessary paper,
- Reduce duplication,
- Capitalize on the use of multiple copies, and
- Move some data into the computer for multiple-port access without the use of paper.

This concept has been utilized by small- to medium-sized companies to tie in production, inventory control, purchasing, and maintenance. For example, optical scanning codes are put into parts bins so that only the number of parts is punched into the records while standing in front of the bins, just like at the grocery store. This data is compared automatically to max-min data, and purchase orders are entered automatically. These quasi-paper and quasi-computer systems tie in with maintenance work orders—on one hand—and to the president's computer screen—behind his or her desk—on the other—to provide day-to-day financial, sales, and production information.

A Diagnostic Postscript

In an emerging dynamic company, many managers are preoccupied with the problems on their desks. These fires must be put out, and this often puts limits and constraints on overall performance. The conditions under which an individual operates obviously affects his or her performance.

Although the secret is to eliminate the cause of so many "fires," the manager still needs some simple tools to ensure the company keeps going in the right direction. We offer these ten questions as a daily prayer to start each business day.

1. What should I be doing today?
2. What should I be doing right now?
3. What am I doing right?
4. What am I doing wrong?
5. How can I do a better job?
6. Who can assist me in accomplishing my goals?
7. When will I reach my planned objectives?
8. Where should I place my priorities?
9. Why do these problems exist?
10. Is the work I am doing now really necessary?

Answering these questions will enable you to develop your skills and acquire the tools and techniques to make your job easier. It should also point to ways of breaking bad habits by substituting new, good ones for the old.

8

Overcoming
Barriers
to Communication

COMMUNICATIONS SEEM TO BE SUCH A SIMPLISTIC SUBJECT THAT YOU WOULD hardly feel it was worthy of a chapter in this book. But, regardless of how simplistic and fundamental it might seem, the magnitude of the communication problem never diminishes. This is particularly true in small companies that are growing because these firms often do not have a communication network in place. In the evolution of information transfer, someone or something is often omitted. If you just think a little about the amount of management time, effort, and money expended in an effort to communicate, you realize just how important it is to communicate well.

MECHANICAL AND PHYSICAL BARRIERS

How often in a day's time do you call someone only to have the secretary say: "I'm sorry, but he's in a meeting now, can I take your name and number?" You ask, "How long do you expect the meeting to last?" and the reply is "I really couldn't tell you, it just got started." This meeting, obviously, is a barrier to your communicating with the individual you are calling. After you have this experience a number of times with some individual, you begin to wonder whether the alleged meetings are actually occurring.

Similarly, the answering machine has become a barrier to personal communication. Surprisingly, it is the larger companies rather than the smaller ones that are using these devices to the extreme. They are programmed so that you have to push buttons for 2 minutes just to talk to a real person.

Meetings

Going back to the meeting, however, it is not unusual to find that the participants are lucky to get 10 minutes of productive communications out of an hour.

Males and females alike are frustrated by the number of meetings they have to attend. Comments like: "If I have to go to another meeting, I'll scream" are not uncommon. Many meetings are nonproductive besides.

Companies on the fast track are already pressing employees on both ends of the workday. Growth companies in emerging industries can ill afford to waste its people's time with unnecessary meetings. Here are some tips to avoid both.

- Move decision-making downward. Working foremen and forewomen are less likely to call meetings because meeting time is non-production time. A company whose productivity is rated in gallons per work hour wants to use each hour producing gallons, not discussions.
- Set maximum time periods for certain discussions.
- Control time-wasters (verbosity).
- Have an agenda and stick to it; have specific objectives. Do not try to cover too much.
- Do not allow interruptions.
- Hold the meeting while standing if it is expected to last 30 minutes or less.
- Teach and employ creative, active listening: ask questions, look at people while speaking.
- Eliminate conditions that let people "settle in," e.g., no smoking, no ashtrays, no refreshments. Build an aura of "Let's get things done."
- Utilize the "speed meeting." (This is a concept introduced by Bas-Tex Corporation, Houston, Texas, where people allocate a brief period—perhaps a coffee break or a time at the 5 o'clock whistle to focus on one topic, briefly, in a concentrated manner, to make a decision or inform a staff of impending problems or opportunities, provide specific information each needs to do his or her job properly, or to gather input from all for a management decision.)
- Utilize in-plant conference calls.
- Have receptionist, or another central party, control meeting rooms with space and time allocations consistent with real requirements. (One

growth company in the environmental field uses the terms "Large Fish Bowl," for a room that seats 18, and "Small Fish Bowl" for a room that seats 10.)

- Consider before-work breakfast meetings. These in-house conferences are deductible at 100 percent vs. 80 percent normal business meals.

Very few meetings held in the office can be conducted without interruption. There can be a three-minute phone call, a coffee break, a potty break, an interruption for a signature on a letter, or someone joining the meeting late. To the duration of the interruption itself, add 2 minutes for regaining the train of thought.

Once a manager suggested that the company should save all of the various minutes of meetings and categorize the subjects. Often the same problems are discussed so many times, all you would have to do is photocopy the minutes and change the date. The key to avoiding this problem is better meeting preparation. Set an itinerary for the meeting and stick to it. Remember, proper prior planning prevents poor performance.

At one critical stage in his career, a manager took over an operation that was hopelessly entangled with problems. There had been a succession of predecessors, each compounding the problem left before. Every program in the house was delinquent; that is, behind schedule and over the budget. To bring things out into the open, the manager held a one and a half hour daily meeting with six to eight people each day to try to understand the problems. This went on for over a month. Having the meetings and keeping the minutes and doing the follow-up took 20 percent of this executive's time. He normally put in a 60 hour week. After solving the main problems one by one, the meetings reverted to once a week. These weekly meetings, however, could sometimes last from three to three and a half hours, again because of the magnitude of the problems, but more importantly because of the players or participants. To avoid these drawn-out affairs, there are some simple rules to follow (Fig. 8-1).

And then, of course, there is the unscheduled meeting when one or two people will walk into your office and sit down right in the middle of your attempted analysis of a complicated report of a make-or-buy decision. The way to avoid these interruptions is to make sure you have an open door policy to employees when they really need you, and really leave the door open. Also, let it be known that when the door is closed, it means you are seeking privacy for personal or business reasons and there should be no interruptions. But by having the door open most of the time, you ensure that people know the accessibility rules.

An industrial relations manager once had his office in a building remote to the general offices of the plant. Management felt that he should be accessible to

Meeting Organizer	*Meeting Attendees*
☞ Prepare for meeting by reviewing previous minutes of last meeting. Have a monitor to quickly distribute minutes of current meeting, possibly by CRT access.	☞ Prepare for meeting. This will do a lot to minimize rehash. Don't bring up matters that have been handled unless others need to know.
☞ Draw up an agenda with time limits for discussion. Agenda should include a key speaker on a particular topic.	☞ Cover only those items that demand others' attention. If you are handling a project, simply handle it without discussing it unless input from others is required or questions arise.
☞ Type minutes in "reference" format so that attendees can refer back quickly to paragraphs and responsibilities.	☞ Highlight personal responsibilities with a felt-tip pen directly on your copy of minutes.
☞ Prior to meeting, do all follow-up requirements noted in minutes from last meeting. Simply ask for a report.	☞ Perform all follow-up tasks. Set specific objectives by adding to your calendar or to tickler file.

Fig. 8-1. A checklist of how to avoid rehashing old problems.

the people so that their manager could counsel with them and help them solve their problems. By moving him into the main office, there were constant interruptions with people coming in to see him, and he didn't like it. This was ironic, because in his case, those unannounced visits were precisely why he was put near the employees who needed him.

There are some very positive steps to make staff meetings shorter and more disciplined. They are more important when you are running two or more diversified companies. For example, a manager had eight people reporting to him in one company and six in the other. That in itself was a barrier to communication, (Fig. 8-2), because if the manager gave each person just 10 minutes of his day, it took 2 hours and 20 minutes just to talk to the staff. Span of control can be a barrier to good communications. So, although a flat organization can eliminate levels of management, it also limits your time with any one person.

In this case, the manager held a staff meeting telling everyone of his time constraints and suggested that in the future, each would have five minutes to describe the biggest problem and where he or she needed help and cooperation from other departments. This was a pretty good approach. It shortened the meetings and it worked fairly well. But it also points to a need—the need to study the participants in a meeting. Some people just don't fit into group dynamics.

Mechanical and Physical

• Telephones when busy, when answering machine answers.

• Office layout.

• Inadequate word processing pool or equipment.

• Other communication hardware that functions improperly.

• Sounds or noises as well as odors that can interfere with communication.

Personal and Personnel

• Attitudes can be barriers to communication—attitudes are like pollen, they rub off easily.

• Span of control—having too many people under you means you have less time to communicate with each, or a few people get more share than they deserve.

• Cigarette or other smoking can interfere with a person's ability to receive communication.

Mental and Emotional

• Body language—folding arms in front of you is a sign you are not listening.

• Anger or other emotions create barriers to communication.

• Personality conflicts.

Verbal and Written

• Semantics.
• Failure to listen.

Unusual and Other

• Meetings themselves can be barriers to communication. While a person is in a meeting, they are inaccessible to everyone not at the meeting.

• Sex—Some men don't place value on women's comments and vice versa.

• Poor writing.

• Mathematical, technical, or esoteric jargon that is familiar only to a few.

Fig. 8-2. Typical barriers to communication in an emerging company.

Meeting Participation

The sender of a message must present his or her material in such a way that the receiver is aware of the meaning intended by the sender.

Even when talking to a hundred people, the sender is in fact speaking to a hundred individuals, each deciphering the message in his or her own way. In a growth company, it is imperative that messages be clear and concise. In many cases, the person on the receiving end does not know you, your company, or your product. Yet, you are trying to sell it to the "listener." At any point in the "Communications Cube" (Fig. 8-3) there can be interference, but the goal is to keep the connecting links of the cube intact, and to realize that the information flow can also work in reverse.

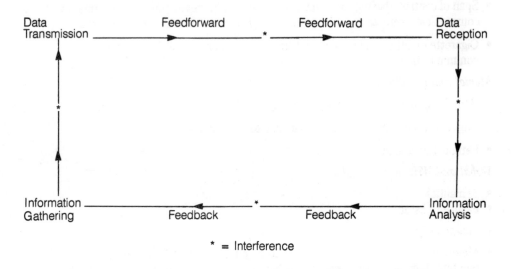

* = Interference

To keep information flowing through the Communications Cube, there are four basic rules:

1. Always consider accuracy as a goal; the information received is really what you want the person to hear or understand.

2. Consider the communication environment. Speak the same language as the recipient and you have a better chance of being understood. The language used should be that of the recipient rather than that of the sender.

3. Never make assumptions. You might well think a person knows the meaning of certain abbreviations or acronyms, but don't take it for granted.

4. Remember that communications is a two-way street. Give the recipient a chance to ask questions, or you ask them to ensure the message came through.

Fig. 8-3. The communication cube.

Every manager in an emerging company must pay close attention to meetings that are external to the company as well as internal ones. From a CEO's perspective, one meeting that deserves close attention is that of the advisory board.

One company used a three-member board that included one of the oldest friends and long-time confidants of the CEO. That board member was, by far, the poorest contributor during the actual board meeting. Yet, when the CEO gave him the time after the meeting, he would provide management with more meaningful suggestions, questions, and ideas than anyone else at the meeting. For some reason, perhaps because he didn't want to discuss at the meeting the sort of topics that previously had been discussed in confidence, he just didn't participate.

In another case, a very successful businessman was asked to participate in a roundtable that the company was forming. He frankly told the chairman that he didn't do well in groups. Some people don't. You should recognize this. In fact, if you try to impose some discipline and organization in your own staff meeting, you might run into the complication of the individual who has the most to contribute in a five-minute period often passing the opportunity to be heard.

Having learned that some employees just don't do well in meetings, in terms of participation, let's take a look at those who *do* participate.

One type of participant is the proverbial head-nodder. This is an individual who nods agreement to everything that is said, even though he or she probably doesn't understand half of what's been said.

A final point about the head nodder is particularly important in dealing with people internationally. Just because an individual nods his or her head in accord does not mean that the person—who normally speaks a different language—understands what is being said. He or she may simply be too embarrassed in front of a group to say "I don't understand."

Then, of course, there is the agitator. He or she tries to bring up as many provocative questions and topics as possible, usually to take attention off the problems in his or her own department. These individuals often have other personality flaws. In cases where there are serious agitators, a manager might attempt to change a person's attitudes, but we have found little success in this area. Most often these people end up working for another company.

The next type of meeting participant is the Emmy award winner. This individual appears to be on stage. He or she might even ask to borrow two or three minutes from the person who had nothing to say. The Emmy award winner often runs on like a broken record and can put everybody to sleep or to mind-meandering.

There are participants who actually go to sleep. (This doesn't say much for the person in control of the meeting.) This could be the result of boredom, eating or drinking too much at lunch, old age, or a combination of any of those mentioned. In any event, if you have one of these in your group and feel that participation is important, the best suggestion is to move the meeting to early in the morning. This problem can also be resolved by not having any chairs in your office and holding stand-up staff meetings—before lunch. It is amazing how this will shorten discussions.

The final meeting participant is one with a blank stare. This is the one you have to watch. First, he or she is not making any contributions; secondly, the person might be laughing at you on the inside; or thirdly, he or she might not understand what is going on. The latter is a real problem. The solution to this problem is to watch the eyes. Look at the eyes and see if the person is interested, bored, or if the eyes are even open.

The Appointments Barrier

The new small or emerging company has a unique problem. Trying to get in to see someone, particularly a person that doesn't know you or your company, involves "sales" from the very start. In many cases you have to "sell" your way even to get into a person's office. This usually starts with a telephone call. There is a right way and a wrong way to get an appointment. Also, managers should understand that not everyone has the natural knack of getting past the appointment barrier.

Many people make the call to someone who doesn't know them and begins to make excuses for the call that includes comments like: "You won't know us," or "I'm sorry for calling, but. . . ."

The positive way to make an appointment is to immediately create an image of credibility in the mind of the person that answers the phone. This can be done in a number of ways. For example, if you are talking to an R&D manager, you might begin: "Hello, Mr. Kisling, this is Guy Weismantel; I am a chemical engineer here in Kingwood, Texas, and a friend of mine recommended that I contact you." (That friend may or may not know Mr. Kisling.)

Once credibility is established, the next phase of the call deals with describing a benefit.

"The reason for the call is our company, Weismantel International, a small consulting firm concentrating on environmental matters, has developed a _____" (which you know to be of interest to Kisling's firm, or why would you be calling Kisling in the first place?)

Keep your appointment book handy and make a recommendation to be at Kisling's office because you will be in the area, but be prepared to choose another day and time that could prove to be more convenient to him.

In summary, when telephoning for an appointment:

- Plan exactly what you intend to say *before* picking up the receiver.
- State your name and company when you talk to the operator.

- When talking to the operator, and before you are connected with your prospect, ask for the correct spelling of his or her name, title, mailing address, and extension or direct-dial phone number.
- Immediately establish credibility.
- Keep your voice crisp, but don't shout, whisper, or talk in a monotone.
- Try to use the person's name occasionally during the call.
- Do not get involved in detailed discussions or arguments; save the details for the appointment.
- Never say, "May I come and see you?" Instead, pursue another tack. For example, "I will be in Baytown next week in the morning and I would like to introduce you to my. . . ."
- Always offer an alternative. For example: "Will it be more convenient?"
- Use the person's correct name and pronunciation (which the operator can give you).
- Once having obtained an appointment, you might have the opportunity to ask one or two questions to get information that will help you to prepare for the interview. For sure, ask directions if you don't know how to get there.
- If lunch is arranged, you could ask the person's secretary to set up the reservations. This does two things: it opens up the door to communication with the secretary (get his or her full name); and it helps to ensure you won't get stood up for your luncheon date, which can happen.
- Don't forget to say "thank you" and "good-bye" in a friendly manner with a "I look forward. . . ."
- Allow the person you are calling to hang up first.
- Confirm your appointment the day before. Often it is better to do this with the secretary and not the individual, who would be more prone to cancel if he or she feels pressured. That same pressure may not be there if it is a simple reminder from the secretary,
- Don't get caught in the field without confirming or you could do a lot of driving for nothing.
- Remember the average sales call costs your company $200 to make.

The Telephone Barrier

We have already touched on the telephone problem, but it deserves more attention. Why? It is often the biggest barrier in good communications. The problem starts with the busy signal. You can partially alleviate this by having telephones equipped with a beeper that tells you when you have another call. The problem with taking that second call is that you prioritize people and may end up hurting someone's feelings. For example, you couldn't delay talking to your biggest and best customer; yet you might be on the line with a potentially good customer. A more effective type of telephone is one where your secretary or switchboard operator can give you a printed message on the phone when there is someone who wants to see or talk to you.

If you can manage, apply your open door policy to the telephone. This is very important if you are are taking an active part in the marketing function of your business; then you'd better answer your telephone. People calling don't like to have their calls screened by two or three secretaries or PBX operators before they reach you. If *you* don't like it, you can be assured that the people calling you don't like it either. Hearing your voice gives a very definite opinion to the caller of your being accessible; that is an important facet of good relationship management.

Some incoming calls can be quite annoying. When you receive a call from the secretary that says "just one moment for Mr. Nelson," it tells you the Mr. Nelson feels his time is more valuable than yours, so he doesn't even place his own calls. Some managers have been known to hang up at that expression of arrogance.

We might add at this point how your *super* secretary can be a real benefit to you regarding incoming calls. If you are on a tight schedule and do not want to receive incoming calls *except* the important ones, the secretary that has a good memory for voices can screen your calls without even having to ask for names. She or he can put through the calls from the people that you wish to speak to, and simply tell all other callers that you are out of the office.

The secretary with an outstanding personality can have a calming effect on even the most irate customer. By always being gracious and a good listener, a secretary effectively screens out problems before they reach your ear. That's quite a bonus.

Time Difference. Another barrier to telephone communications is the time difference. It can be enough of a hindrance from coast to coast, but it is even more of a problem in conducting international business. The telephone has obviously become a fantastic and indispensable tool in conducting business. Although only a few emerging companies do business overseas, the growth of U.S. business in the future relies heavily on improving exports. With the U.S. having only 3 percent of the world's population, some of the greatest marketing opportunities appear outside the U.S. and, today, it is easy to talk, or facsimile anywhere in the world.

The domestic time difference problem can be helped by having people in your marketing department work different shifts. If you are in the central time zone, have someone start an hour before the office opens, go to lunch an hour before the rest, and go home an hour early. Likewise, have someone take the reverse approach, an hour later, for the west coast. If you're on the east or west coast, the answer is obviously to have a 2-hour differential in your shifts.

Another solution to the time difference problem is to make calls at home. If you're doing business with Australia, Japan, or that part of the world, this might mandate making calls on weekends to compensate for the day's difference in time. If there is a failure in communicating with your customers, you should encourage your managers to call Europe early in the morning before they leave home, and the Far East in the evening. If you use this solution, you first have to recognize the reason for a manager's tardiness at work in the morning, and you'd better provide him or her with the business telephone credit card to soften the impact on the individual's personal telephone bill.

Telex and Fax. Although one of the oldest of electronic communication devices, the telex can still be a terrific help. It can alleviate some of the time difference problems and, at the same time, provide a hard copy almost instantaneously. If you have a telex, put it in a conspicuous spot. More important today, however, is the facsimile machine. Companies, both domestic and international, are relying on these machines to transmit data quickly and inexpensively. In some cases, the purchase of a facsimile machine can be just as important as a firm's first computer (Fig. 8-4).

It is possible, if you have the proper computer configuration, to have telex or facsimile service as an accessory to your computer. The computer people will even show you the economic advantages of this accessory. The problem, however, is that the computer is often inaccessible or behind locked doors. Therefore, your important communications are conducted at the discretion of your data processing people. Stand-alone units can facilitate quick delivery.

As a postscript to telex or fax communication, where applicable, always take into consideration international trade. If a person who doesn't speak very good English tries to read your phonetic English acronyms or abbreviations, you sometimes lose the total meaning of a transmission.

"Bingo Card" Leads. A final word about the telephone relates to industrial marketing. Today, through public relations and advertising, companies receive "bingo card" leads. The telephone is the best way to classify those leads versus making $200 sales calls in person. If you get 80 leads from a news release on a new product, you must find out which are really the leads and which are literature collectors. Today, software programs are available for the personal computer that track sales leads from initial reception to order or non-order. A firm should also keep and classify these leads in "list software" for use with direct mail programs or other promotions.

1. Not all Fax machines talk a universal language. Some older machines won't talk to others. When choosing a machine, ensure that your FAX will talk to those of your key clients, customers, and suppliers.

2. Portable machines offer some advantages; however, many people who bought portable machines found that 90 percent of their use is still at the home office.

3. At one time weighing carefully the costs of leasing vs. purchase was important. The cost of facsimile machines has been significantly reduced, however, and cash flow considerations are less important, especially with FAX services now available at Kwik Kopy and similar establishments.

4. It is possible to tie in a memory phone to lower cost models of field machines. That way you don't have to pay for all the bells and whistles, but can still have the flexibility of one-button dealing.

5. Optional packages include a computer interface whereby some FAX machines work as a printer and a scanner for the computer.

6. Consider the advantages and costs of plain paper for FAX machines vs. one that uses thermal paper. Plain paper units offer certain copying advantages and paper stability.

7. Of prime importance is the speed of operation. This can be very important if document transfer includes texts or reports. Slow machines run up your cost of transmission.

8. Especially for overseas work, consider a feature that allows you to set machine for "on" during low-cost night rates. You can leave the office at 5:00 PM, turn the machine on when you leave, and find the work done when you return in the morning. Test this feature before buying. Some units promise this capability, but the machine doesn't function well when asked to perform. It is not unusual for some machines to jam up when a number of pages are being FAXed.

9. The above implies that automatic feed is important.

10. Book Mode feature of some units allows you to copy directly from magazines or books.

11. Consider technical details that include:
    a. Type (desktop vs. portable, etc.)
    b. Transmission requirements (public telephone network)
    c. Compatibility with other units (e.g., G3-G2, NA, G, MIN, FM)
    d. Document input size.
    e. Memory capabilities (± 60 pages)
    f. Document output size.
    g. Effective recording width.

Fig. 8-4. Choosing the correct Fax machine.

Fig. 8-4. (Continued)

h. Effective scanning width.

i. Paper supply (plus cutter, roll, thermal, single sheet)

j. Resolution (scanning density)

k. Resolution control

l. Image contrast control

m. Scanner type (flatbed vs. other)

n. Initial cost

o. Operating cost

p. Printing method

q. Dialing capability

r. Dimensions and weight

s. Power requirements

t. Document feed

u. Display (liquid crystal vs. other)

v. Telephone interface

w. Environmental requirements

x. Transmission speed

y. FCC regulations requirements

z. Other options: hang up alarm, delayed transmission, polling, redialing, GI compatibility)

12. Consider modems that allow for digital transfer of images directly to the computer for easy printout and format for reports utilizing desktop publishing hardware.

ADVERTISING AND PUBLIC RELATIONS

Advertising and public relations is probably one of the most important aspects of communications that an emerging company has with both its employees and the outside world. Yet, these aspects of communication and marketing are frightfully misunderstood. What makes things worse, is that the average manager thinks he or she understands advertising and public relations, yet most don't.

At one extreme, emerging companies who reach out for help in this area when the cash flow is good turn to large New York agencies that are expensive and sometimes do not have talent in the market of interest. It is not unusual, for example, for a large New York public relations agency to bill its client $150 per hour for project work. In contrast, smaller agencies with esoteric market interests can cost a lot less or work off more reasonable retainers, and often have good media contacts in specific rather than general areas.

To offer some immediate guidelines, consider the normal evolution or phases of growth in this area:

1. No advertising or public relations.
2. General manager begins to think of advertising program.
3. General manager begins to think of public relations program.
4. General manager hires advertising and public relations manager.
5. Outside agencies are hired to assist in advertising and/or public relations.
6. Advertising and public relations functions are separated, put under separate managers and/or agencies.

Phases two and three often tend to overlap, but there is an important aspect of advertising and public relations that non-experts tend to overlook. Namely, public relations (PR) should normally precede advertising by a time frame of 3 to 6 months.

Why? Many magazines and publications do not consider material for editorial use after it has been advertised, or at least consider it less than non-advertised material.

Also, many first-rate publications do consider advertising as a precursor to editorial coverage. A good story stands on its own.

Managers not schooled in advertising or public relations often have the misconception that placing an ad and getting a story in a magazine or newspaper go hand-in-hand. Some publications or special promotions do present this kind of package, but this idea of "take an ad, get a story" is considered a second-rate method of communications.

A good public relations program will be planned in coordination with an advertising program but built to get maximum exposure over the period of the marketing plan. You don't try to get all news releases and ads in one issue of a magazine. Here are some guidelines for preparing a preliminary PR program:

1. Review the specific marketing objectives spelled out in the yearly marketing plan.
2. Identify new products, new opportunities, and other materials that are suitable for editorial coverage.
3. Ask marketing managers and/or product managers to identify the specific audience they want to reach and sell to.
4. Have these managers identify which publications that audience reads, and confirm and enlarge the list of publications using Beacon's Publicity Checker (332 S. Michigan Avenue, Chicago, Illinois 60604; 1-800-621-0561 or, Illinois, 312-922-2400).

5. Request editorial calendar from these publications and identify those issues that will carry an editorial focus related to your company or product interest.

6. Prepare a public relations plan that will provide editorial material for these issues approximately two to three months prior to issue dates.

7. Identify other PR opportunities unrelated to editorial calendar, but tied to marketing plan, and create a milestone chart for PR projects.

8. Spell out verbally what PR projects will be undertaken and not the deadlines related to these.

9. *Note:* Financial PR, especially when a company is contemplating going public, is a separate plan that is strategic in nature and is superimposed on the short-range PR plans.

10. Work the plan. Milestones charts can vary in presentation to show overlap of work tasks. Program is normally built for 6-month to 12-month implementation, 12 months being common for corporate PR goals and shorter periods for special projects (Fig. 8-5).

Continuity is a key facet of advertising/PR exposure. A reader should see an ad in the January issue and perhaps a new products story in February. (The latter would have been sent to editors as early as the preceding November.) This "spread out" and continuous exposure will bring in not only leads, but also recognition.

Switching the conversation from PR to advertising, there are many aspects of advertising that lead to valuable marketing data. For example, McGraw-Hill's economics department publishes a yearly business forecast which is made available to advertisers. Their chemical engineering magazine provides a computer disk list of all processing plants of 100 employees or more for advertisers. Similar data is available from Penton and Cahners. Cahners can also tie a market program to their exposition program. Other publishing houses offer similar services.

The secret is knowing how to tie into these information and data sources. One way is to use a professional agency (Fig. 8-6) who has been through the exercise already and can save you the time and learning process of doing all the work yourself.

WRITTEN COMMUNICATION

It is astonishing how few managers are capable of writing a good business letter, a comprehensible memo, or even a simple trip report. Managers are quick to take a 3 day trip if they feel it is necessary, and spend $1,000 of the company's money, but it will take them 3 weeks, if ever, to write a trip report.

Six-Month
Public Relations Plan
for
Broadtek

To: Walter Kisling

From: Guy Weismantel

OVERVIEW

The central theme of this PR effort is speed and flexibility. Broadtek is revolutionizing the solid/liquid separation market with a new piece of equipment called SYS/SEP. The PR effort should emphasize the strong points of SYS/SEP and note that the unit is ideal for toll processing activities. Emphasis should be the target market area noted in the Broadtek Marketing Plan. A general brochure that is non-oil-patch-related must be developed.

The PR effort will initially involve:

1. New product news releases (N-1).

2. New literature news releases (N-2).

3. Service and toll processing release (N-3).

4. Personnel notices (N-4).

5. Other newsworthy events to include:

   (a). Announcement of completion of new offices and special projects (SP-1 and SP-2).

   (b). Press packets for conferences (SP-3).

   (c). Open House for editors (SP-4).

   (d). Other projects (SP-5).

6. Bylined articles when and if appropriate (BL-1).

7. Special editorial visits to uncover stories (V-1, V-2, V-3).

Fig. 8-5. Six month 1986-1987 public relations plan for Broadtek: An example.

Fig. 8-5. (Continued)

BACKGROUND

1. Weismantel International (WI) will prepare a master list of all publications that will act as a general news release mailing list for the target markets. In the area of focus, a "saturation" approach is recommended for the first four releases.

2. In addition, specific focused news stories or releases are part of the PR plan, sometimes reworking a general release from 1 above.

3. Primary PR coverage is aimed at magazines and tabloids. Local newspapers will be receiving information copies of releases and WI will try to place a story in the *Post* or the *Chronicle* about "how Broadtek copes with the new markets outside the oil patch." These are "planted" stories (PL-2 and PL-3).

PLAN

Monthly PR Review

Once every month, Weismantel International will visit Broadtek to discuss specific PR objectives for the month to include new ideas and those on the PR planning calendar. Releases will be prepared, reviewed, and released for publication.

On a quarterly basis, Broadtek will review PR plan in respect to sales objectives to include upcoming events (society meetings, VIP visits, etc.) that require PR action.

STANDARD CALENDAR

During every month, news releases and PR activities will be followed by a preplanned calendar, to include:

1. International stories
2. New market stories
3. Oil-patch stories
4. Other activity

Fig. 8-5 . (Continued)

SIX-MONTH PR PLANNING CALENDAR

	Nov. 90	Dec. 90	Jan. 91	Feb. 91	Mar. 91	Apr. 91
News Releases	N – 1	N – 2	N – 3	N – 4		
Other Activity	SP – 1	SP – 2 PL – 1	SP – 3 PL – 2	SP – 4 V – 1	SP – 5 V – 2	BL – 1 V – 3

N – 1 New Product News Releases
N – 2 New Literature News Releases
N – 3 Service and Toll Processing Release
N – 4 Personnel Notices
SP – 1 Announcement of Completion of New Offices and Special Projects
SP – 2 Announcement of Completion of New Offices and Special Projects
SP – 3 Press Packets for Conferences
SP – 4 Open House for Editors
SP – 5 Other Projects
BL – 1 By-lined Articles
V – 1 Special Editorial Visits to Uncover Stories
V – 2 Special Editorial Visits to Uncover Stories
V – 3 Special Editorial Visits to Uncover Stories
PL – 1 Stories for the *Houston Post*
PL – 2 Stories for the *Houston Chronicle*

To solve this problem, let the expense account be the trip report. Get the details you need from the expense account, and don't pay expenses until you are satisfied. Employees will soon learn that it is important to submit trip reports in a completed, timely fashion. The trip report is simply submitted with the expense report.

There are other important aspects of written communication that emerging companies should watch carefully. Creating a set of guidelines (Table 8-1) will help in time management and improve productivity.

FACE-TO-FACE COMMUNICATION

In an emerging company, despite the meeting problems already mentioned, the most effective way of communicating with an individual is the one-on-one, face-to-face communications you have with your employees.

There are two ways of conducting face-to-face communications: formal and informal. The importance of the informal communication cannot be over-empha-

☞ Personality Compatibility: Ad manager and/or sales manager must be able to work with account executive.

☞ Size Compatibility: Some companies prefer to work with agencies that are relatively the same size, i.e., small company, small agency, etc.

☞ Agency Capabilities: Will they do brochures, or do you do them yourself? Same with PR? Press conferences: Do you want them to prepare marketing plan, or just create brochures and ads?

☞ Research capabilities: Do you want them? Is a strong creative approach desired?

☞ Media Department: Do you want a strong media department to provide recommendations, or do you want to clone the pubs and shows?

☞ Cost: A big factor; some agencies want to work on a monthly fee basis. Others will work on a project basis. Generally, agencies are small business and can't wait 90 or 120 days for payment. Pub companies will either bill an agency, or bill an account and remit the fee to the agency (15 percent, generally).

For more specific details, see article in *Journal of Advertising Research*, April-May, 1984, titled: "Criteria for Advertising Agency Selection: An Objective Appraisal."

Fig. 8-6. Selecting an ad agency: A checklist (Source: Vincent Cavaseno New York City).

sized. As a recommendation, if you have two people who have difficulty communicating, perhaps you should take them to lunch, together, once in awhile. Give each of them a pair of adjoining tickets for a baseball or football game. Send them on a trip together. A trip will require them to ride along in a car as captive audiences; have breakfast and lunch and perhaps dinner together; and perhaps break down some of the personality conflicts that have resulted in their communication problems. With you not present to monitor their arguments, there could be an amelioration.

A new concept in informal discussion is to drop the lunch idea. Instead, go hit golf balls or go for a walk with an employee or a customer. People's time is so valuable; drive up to their plant in your motor home and serve them sandwiches in it. Bring a sack lunch for everyone.

Another alternative is to take people to your home for lunch. This is a way to become friends and break down barriers. It can be a positive step in relationship management. The point is, give managers *good new ideas* to save time. Too many lunches are wasted time and expensive. Have meetings during lunch hour. Then people are out eating and the phone won't ring.

Speeches

Emerging companies should foster and encourage speechmaking at all levels of management. A speech or a presentation at a society or industrial meeting is one

Table 8-1. Written Communication Guidelines for Emerging Companies.

Writing Should Focus on Results	Avoid Writing Errors	Edit	Mechanics	Tricks of the Trade
Determine goals and purpose of writing. Set priorities. Choose suitable form. Know the reader.	Remember that time can influence type of reader response. Don't use acronyms or abbreviations without explaining—even if your audience is esoteric. Put yourself in the place of the reader. Capture his or her interest to promote action you desire.	Use word processor with dictionary to catch glitches. Proofread anyway because computer passes words that are spelled correctly but don't fit (e.g., firm vs. form). Use logical pattern that remains true to writing purpose.	Choose company logo that will be remembered. This is especially good for new companies. Choose good bond paper. Use executive type.	Write more effectively in less time by stopping in the middle of a sentence. When you come back to writing you will already be started. Produce letters, memos, and reports that are a credit to you and your organization. Ensure that your message is clear and concise. Organize and outline long reports; use table of contents. Edit the work of others. Reduce complex technical jargon to an appendix.

of the best ways to reach the outside world. Done tactfully, a talk at a seminar or conference can display your wares, exhibit your company's talents in service or product, build confidence with your company and your customers, make you into an authority, and provide the basis for broader exposure through coverage or publication of your talk in magazines.

There are certain rules for speechmaking that are adequately covered in reports by Weismantel International and in various publications and organizations including Toastmasters and others.

When making a speech, be certain to understand your objective. Is it a speech about your company? Is it an occasion at which you are trying to convince someone to take specific action? There are also speeches to entertain, to motivate, or to convince. Most often, a speech is meant to inform.

Be certain to keep the speech short. People seldom complain when a speech is short, but become upset if it goes on forever. Given this, and that you have a great deal more information about the subject than your audience, limit what information you want your audience to remember, and select only two or three main points to cover.

Use good graphics, with slides being pre-tested and in order before the talk. Utilize your own projector if possible and bring an extra lightbulb. Arrive early and test the equipment before the meeting.

Also, practice your delivery and, by role playing, field questions that might be asked.

Get as much information as possible about your audience before you deliver your presentation, and try to get a list of attendees with addresses and phone numbers. Some people might want copies of your speech. Since you have written it out, you will be able to supply copies. If you promise to send copies, it is absolutely mandatory that you remember to do it. The press might also want to ask you questions so they can report on your speech. It is best to give them a copy of the written text as this helps to avoid their misquoting you.

COMMUNICATION AND SALESMANSHIP

During the boom years, when U.S. engineering design and construction firms were growth companies, the late Ralph M. Parsons told many a story about communication and salesmanship. One of his dissertations is well worth repeating today for those companies that are part of emerging industries. Parsons said:

"I remember the admonition given me by a professor at Pratt Institute and to two other boys in whom he had taken a particular interest—not because we were unusually good students, but probably because he thought we needed his advice.

"He kept us after school one beastly hot afternoon—this was before the days of air conditioning. He was sitting on a bench in the Physics lab with his sleeves rolled up, and he began with a discussion of salesmanship. He didn't say so, but SALESMANSHIP is another word for COMMUNICATING.

"A good salesman (or peddler, as I prefer to call him if he is a GOOD salesman) very carefully studies his subject to determine things he is interested in and things he would be receptive to. He then plans things that he can say or do to most effectively convey his thoughts. I use the world SUBJECT because it covers so many people—customer, prospective customers, or whomever it may be that you are trying to convince.

"A long time ago I took the Alexander Hamilton business course. There was some space devoted to preparing a prospect for a business discussion. Creating a proper atmosphere is another way of expressing it. Sometimes you talk about ball games; sometimes yachts; sometimes girls; sometimes about nothing but the business at hand. You must know your subject or be prepared to be thrown out.

"I refer to PEDDLERS with great reverence. I have great respect for them. They may be persistent, irritating, and upsetting, but without them we would all be without our jobs. They are good COMMUNICATORS with those to whom they want to COMMUNICATE. However, they do have the failing of CUTTING OFF OTHERS AT THEIR POCKETS on an inborn theory that they want to concentrate on their most productive prospect.

"A good peddler condenses his story so that the important part has maximum effect on his subject. Frequently, a peddler will horrify the engineer with what he says—possibly with dramatics or with over-simplification. However, if he is a good peddler, everything will be to the end of COMMUNICATING to his subject his thoughts in a language his subject will understand.

"I have talked with people many times on a subject foreign to their general thinking, only to find—even after continual agreement over a period of years, they have really never understood. For example, to create a routine organization chart thinking in the minds of salesmen is a very difficult task.

"A good peddler can develop business anywhere. He is of an inquiring nature, and will soon dig up a prospect and find out what he needs or wants to buy. It has always been my contention that you can drop a good peddler in the middle of a barren island and it won't be long before he has a clientele. He knows how to COMMUNICATE."

We all can learn much from a good peddler. Practicing some peddler philosophies can help each of us, particularly those of us who tend to be introverts. Whether a person is an engineer, an artist, a dirt mover, or something else, if we don't combine salesmanship with our specialty, our progress will be slow and we might not achieve the full measure of happiness from our work, nor will growth necessarily continue. In that vein, a quote from Frank Irving Fletcher, one of the best known advertising people in the country, seems appropriate. There is much to learn from his philosophy: "The man with something unusual to offer will always play second fiddle to the man who has nothing to offer, but has the art of offering it."

COMMUNICATION DRAMATICS

Communications is a two-way street between a transmitter and a receiver. Sometimes the receiver doesn't hear the message very well. Also, it is important to get his, her, or management's attention. For example, there is the story of an inventor who developed a scientific system. The inventor repeatedly tried to sell it to management, but always got a positive NO. Finally, between himself and two friends, he raised $10,000. With a certified check in hand, he again approached management and said, "Here is our $10,000. It is not much, but it is all we have. Let us spend this money *first* in the research so that we can better prove our idea, and then we will commercialize it." Management then had no alternative but to listen. The company approved the project and spent $5 million in developing the system, which became a great success.

Dramatics usually play a significant part in good communications. In that example, the inventor, through the use of dramatics (the certified check), was able to communicate to management his sincerity in what he was proposing. In a sense, money talks.

At the end of World War II, a construction firm was doing a large amount of work for a Pittsburgh company. The president of the Pittsburgh company was skeptical about completion time. The attitude was, "Your analysis tells us the job will be completed on schedule; ours tells us that it will be late. It is one opinion against another, but it's our money that's being spent."

The CEO of the construction firm went into the meeting to discuss the timetable. Prior to the appointment, however, he had secured a one thousand-dollar bill, which was no small feat in those days, as bills of that denomination were very scarce, and he put it in his pocket. As each side presented its case, the situation reached a stalemate. So the CEO got up and said, "Mr. President, here is a thousand-dollar bill. I would like to make you a bet that the job will be completed on schedule. If the job is late, the thousand dollars is yours."

The room went into an uproar. Everyone wanted to see and feel the thousand-dollar bill. Finally the president said, "As a company we won't enter into a bet, but if the job is not on schedule, our Athletic Fund will accept a donation."

The point was made; confidence ensued, and the job went forward harmoniously. The psychology of selling and of all communication is simply set forth in the Bible: "Never hide a candle under a bushel basket."

COMMUNICATING TO YOURSELF—
YOURSELF BEING THE COMPANY

In chapter 5 we learned about a company that lost a major national account after being forewarned of impending difficulties, but not being able to unearth a true analysis of its precarious position. Similarly, a company can have a precarious position internally and not know it—all for the lack of good communications. One company, for example, was within an inch of being organized by a union, but had no inkling of the problem. They found out about it when they fired the "planted" organizer for cause and were called in front of the National Labor Relations Board. For this reason, as well as those related to good management, productivity, and morale, emerging companies must not let internal communications get out of control.

One way is to rely on the grapevine—which can be pretty poor—another is to initiate a formal investigation (Fig. 8-7). There are four important aspects to this kind of communication project, which is supposed to force communications upward through the organization.

- Have the material previously prepared and reviewed.

- Disseminate the results.

- Act on those areas that require aciton.

- Assure (communicate to) employees so that they know action was taken.

Keep your door open. Let employees at *all* levels know that they are free to come to you with any comments regarding your organization and that their confidences will be kept confidential. Most importantly, let them know that: *Management Listened*!

Multiplex Company, Inc.
Salaried Employees Opinion Survey

Please read each statement carefully. After careful consideration place an "X" in the square that reflects your feeling about the statement, i.e., you strongly agree, agree somewhat, no opinion, disagree somewhat, or strongly disagree.

Be sure and give an answer that accurately reflects your attitude toward each statement. Answer each statement as you feel, it will serve no useful purpose if you are not truthful.

I am assigned to:

```
  * Manufacturing  _____
    Engineering    _____
 ** Marketing      _____
*** Administration _____
```

* You are considered to be assigned to Manufacturing if you are in: Manufacturing Management, General Supervisor, Supervisor, Manufacturing Engineering, and Production Control.

Fig. 8-7. A typical employee survey.

Fig. 8-7. (Continued)

** You are considered to be assigned to Marketing if you are in: Marketing,
Customer Service, Quality Assurance, Publications, Area Marketing Managers,
International or Technical Services.

*** You are considered to be assigned to Administration if you are in: Administration,
Accounting, Building Facilities, Personnel, Purchasing or Data Processing.

On the back of this survey you will find a suggestion form. If you have any ideas or
suggestions on how we can reduce costs or save money, please detach the form from
the survey and turn it into Personnel or Jim Wuest. You may turn the form in
unsigned.

Please return the completed survey form to Jim Wuest or Personnel.

	Strongly Agree	Somewhat Agree	No Opinion	Somewhat Disagree	Strongly Disagree
1. I always feel free to speak to anyone in top management.	___	___	___	___	___
2. Our top management tries to make Multiplex Company a good place to work.	___	___	___	___	___
3. Starting and quitting times are satisfactory.	___	___	___	___	___
4. Management tries to make this a safe place to work.	___	___	___	___	___
5. My supervisor gives praise where praise is due.	___	___	___	___	___
6. Good cooperation exists between departments.	___	___	___	___	___
7. Our insurance plan provides good coverage.	___	___	___	___	___
8. My performance is recognized by this company.	___	___	___	___	___
9. Our management keeps us informed about new plans and developments.	___	___	___	___	___
10. I would recommend employment in Multiplex to my friends.	___	___	___	___	___

Fig. 8-7. (Continued)

	Strongly Agree	Somewhat Agree	No Opinion	Somewhat Disagree	Strongly Disagree
11. My rate of pay is fair and equitable for the job I am doing.	___	___	___	___	___
12. Multiplex Company is a good place to work.	___	___	___	___	___
13. Things at Multiplex are better than they were a year ago.	___	___	___	___	___
14. Often, my supervisor doesn't keep promises.	___	___	___	___	___
15. Promotions here go to the people who deserve them.	___	___	___	___	___
16. My pay provides me with a reasonable standard of living.	___	___	___	___	___
17. My co-workers are cooperative and work well together.	___	___	___	___	___
18. Our paid time-off (including holidays, vacation, etc.) is good.	___	___	___	___	___
19. I have been well trained on all jobs to which I have been assigned.	___	___	___	___	___
20. Many times top management here does not have my interest in mind.	___	___	___	___	___
21. My abilities and skills are used by this company.	___	___	___	___	___
22. Frequently, I am sorry that I work here.	___	___	___	___	___
23. My supervisor is capable of doing his/her job.	___	___	___	___	___
24. I never become bored with my job.	___	___	___	___	___
25. Our washrooms are adequate and they are kept clean.	___	___	___	___	___

Fig. 8-7. (Continued)

	Strongly Agree	Somewhat Agree	No Opinion	Somewhat Disagree	Strongly Disagree
26. In my opinion we have benefits equal to other companies in the area.	_____	_____	_____	_____	_____
27. The longer I work here, the more I enjoy it.	_____	_____	_____	_____	_____
28. We are given little or no information about the company.	_____	_____	_____	_____	_____
29. There is not much chance for promotion.	_____	_____	_____	_____	_____
30. My supervisor generally gives me clear instructions.	_____	_____	_____	_____	_____
31. We are encouraged to make suggestions for improvements in our work.	_____	_____	_____	_____	_____
32. I am pleased to tell others where I work.	_____	_____	_____	_____	_____
33. Top management here is fair and honest with me.	_____	_____	_____	_____	_____
34. My work is pleasant—I am not pushed for more than I can do.	_____	_____	_____	_____	_____
35. My supervisor is very fair with me.	_____	_____	_____	_____	_____
36. I am worried about losing my job.	_____	_____	_____	_____	_____
37. I do not think our top management here will make any improvements for our benefits.	_____	_____	_____	_____	_____
38. Top management here is efficient.	_____	_____	_____	_____	_____
39. My supervisor always pushes me for more work than I can do.	_____	_____	_____	_____	_____
40. We are never informed about changes, even those that affect us personally.	_____	_____	_____	_____	_____

Fig. 8-7. (Continued)

	Strongly Agree	Somewhat Agree	No Opinion	Somewhat Disagree	Strongly Disagree
41. I feel that I am underpaid on my job.	___	___	___	___	___
42. Some of my co-workers think they run the company.	___	___	___	___	___
43. My supervisor is a poor organizer and does not manage his/her job well.	___	___	___	___	___
44. Consideration and attention is shown to me when I use good judgement and initiative.	___	___	___	___	___
45. Top management here is not friendly toward the employees.	___	___	___	___	___
46. In my opinion, top management here could operate the company more efficiently.	___	___	___	___	___
47. I understand the company insurance plan.	___	___	___	___	___
48. Employee benefits here are adequate.	___	___	___	___	___
49. I believe taking part in this survey is a good idea.	___	___	___	___	___
50. There is a future here for those who wish to advance.	___	___	___	___	___
51. Multiplex generally gives recognition for my cooperation and loyalty.	___	___	___	___	___
52. Too many problems exist here between co-workers.	___	___	___	___	___
53. Top management here does not supply me with the necessary equipment to do a good job.	___	___	___	___	___
54. I do not believe any good will comes from taking part in this survey.	___	___	___	___	___

Fig. 8-7. (Continued)

	Strongly Agree	Somewhat Agree	No Opinion	Somewhat Disagree	Strongly Disagree
55. I think top management here will use the results of this survey to our best interest.	_____	_____	_____	_____	_____
56. I receive good cooperation and support from:					
Accounting	_____	_____	_____	_____	_____
Data Processing	_____	_____	_____	_____	_____
Engineering	_____	_____	_____	_____	_____
Personnel	_____	_____	_____	_____	_____
Manufacturing	_____	_____	_____	_____	_____
Purchasing	_____	_____	_____	_____	_____
Marketing	_____	_____	_____	_____	_____
Administration	_____	_____	_____	_____	_____
57. My supervisor has a good attitude towards his work.	_____	_____	_____	_____	_____
58. I feel my family receives worthwhile information about Multiplex from the *News Dispenser.*	_____	_____	_____	_____	_____
59. Multiplex should have an open house for all employees, friends and vendors.	_____	_____	_____	_____	_____
60. My supervisor has a real interest in me and my progress.	_____	_____	_____	_____	_____
61. The job description for my present position clearly outlines my job functions, duty, authority, and responsibility.	_____	_____	_____	_____	_____
62. I am preparing myself for advancement to a more responsible position.	_____	_____	_____	_____	_____

SUGGESTION FORM   Date _____

If you have any ideas or suggestions on how we can reduce costs and save money, please detail below:

_____

_____

_____

_____

_____

_____

If you wish to sign, please sign here: _____

                                                         NAME

_____

9

Overcoming Barriers to Innovation and Creativity

INNOVATION AND CREATIVITY ARE SOMETIMES AT THE HEART OF AN EMERGING company. The founder or CEO usually has these qualities, although they usually don't know where they got them or how they developed these qualities. They also don't know where they are going to find more people that have innovation and creativity—the rarest of commodities. These qualities are hard to find in an interview; can't be taught in school; and, worse yet, are many times misinterpreted. Yet some facets of innovation and creativity act as common denominators in recognizing the qualities when they exist within a company or individual.

Creative people have an active right hemisphere of the brain which is artistic-oriented and sensitive rather than mechanical and intellectual, as in the brain's left hemisphere. Innovative and creative people often act subconsciously, tend to be eccentric, take risks, and have unusual work habits. Researchers have come up with models for the creativity process, which from an emerging company's viewpoint, become important in three ways.

1. Is the creative person a suitable person to become a manager?
2. Can the company afford to suffer the expenses of hiring a person strictly for his or her creativity?
3. Where do creative people best fit into a growth company?

The answer to all three questions is: "It depends."

1. In respect to management, some creative people are so focused on a project that they simply think about that project alone—without interferences or disturbances. These people might not fit well into a matrix organization, but would be great at solving an esoteric technical problem.

2. As for "paying" for creativity, most firms don't have that kind of department—except for ad agencies. An employee is expected to function in a job slot. A firm cannot afford to be without creative people, strategically, if it is to maintain industry leadership.

3. As for their fit into the company, creative people who are extroverts fit well into sales. Introvert people fit into strategic positions, such as R&D. A company is lucky enough to hire the creative person who is also practical—it should call him or her: Manager!

BUILDING THE BARRIER

Another common denominator among small business managers and managers of emerging companies is *they don't have time to think*. If there is one single recommendation that can be made regarding initiating and maintaining an innovative and creative mind it is: Set aside quiet time, at least once a week, for meditative thought. Set aside more time than once a week if you can.

In some cases, that "quiet time" is a long highway drive between cities—not between rush appointments within a city. It can also be a half-hour walk or early morning solitude. A recent study of the sleeping habits of chief executive officers indicates that they get 7 hours of sleep. The average CEO retires at about 10:45 P.M. and rises at 5:40 A.M. They often keep a pencil and pad by their bed to write down an idea if wakened in the middle of the night with an idea or a dream that provides the solution to a problem.

For younger people with "emerging families," the quiet time is hard to find. Parents get kids off to school; they themselves get ready for work; and there is a morning madhouse syndrome.

To alleviate that problem, choose a time where, if possible, you can reach the alpha state of meditation, or at least a relaxing time with your spouse after the young ones are in bed and an evening calm prevails. Meditation does not necessitate that you climb a mountain to see the guru; only that you allow a period of quiet time in order to activate those places in the brain that normally lie dormant. Often it is best in the morning.

The problem with evening thinking-and-listening time is you are usually exhausted by then; the bed beckons and your mind has slowed to a snail's pace.

It is better to choose a time when the mind is alert to response, acts and interacts with itself, asking questions, poking at ideas with a stick, being your own devil's advocate, and looking at an idea or a problem from north, south, east and west.

Choose a time where innovation and creativity are possible or at least plausible. Choose a time when you can come up with ideas.

Ideas often tie into a manager's perception of the future. The secret is to take advantage of that perception. Knowing something in advance doesn't help a person in business unless he or she can put that knowledge to work for themselves in some beneficial way. For example, when the price of gasoline was in the 30 cent-per-gallon range, some people forecasted that the price would be $1.00 within 18 months. That prediction came true, but it helped them not at all.

So, what's an idea worth? Nothing! Not unless you can turn it into something meaningful. That is where innovation and creativity step into play.

To begin with, how many times have you said, "I wish I had thought of that?" or, "I thought of that four years ago." Yet, someone else has taken the idea you had and put it into practice—hopefully at a profit. It was Mark Twain who said that unfortunately, every time he recognized an opportunity, someone else had already thought of it. This leads to two important facets of an emerging company.

- Make your idea a reality before someone else does.
- Know how to turn your idea into reality.

Also keep in mind that there are times to say "no" to an idea. Sometimes it doesn't pay to spend innovative and creative time with an idea that is not going to make a profit for the company. So the first question is: When should a person "turn on" his or her innovative-creative system (ICS) and apply it to an idea? (Fig. 9-1). Then, when should they turn it off?

KILLING AN IDEA, OR AT LEAST
PUTTING IT ON THE BACK BURNER

The first reason to kill an idea or put it into limbo is because no one really has the time to follow it up. (This assumes, of course, that money is there to follow up the idea to begin with.) It is not unusual for an emerging company to find itself "people short." During a growth phase, most individuals are hard-pressed to fulfill all their work obligations because they are wearing many hats. It is not unusual for an engineer, for example, to be in charge of construction for a new manufacturing complex, while at the same time maintaining responsibility for purchasing, production, and quality control. Yes! production and quality control, despite the conflicting interest.

Asking this person to take on a new project can be totally unfair to the individual—and his family. A simple solution involves giving this person additional help, an assistant, for example; hiring a new person; or hiring an outside consultant to handle the project. These invariably involve the question of cash flow—how to pay the new salaries—because small businesses and emerging companies are invariably cash hungry and cash poor.

In an emerging company:

- There are organizational and personal barriers to creativity.

- There are physical and mental barriers to creativity.

- There are external and internal barriers. These latter are elaborated further.

External

- Matrixed into those just mentioned, specific barriers include: size of company; time; and physical (geographical) location. For example, firms near government-operated research centers or universities can tap into the creativity of these staffs or professors. This is one way to turn on creativity.

- Have staff interface with others through society work; institute membership.

- Initiate technology transfer with both U.S. government and state agencies.

Internal

- Hire a creative leader; establish priorities; stick to them.

- Provide an atmosphere for creativity through morale and physical facilities.

- Do not inundate creative people with too many projects.

- Initiate a company policy that enhances and rewards creative thinking.

- Provide means and financing for continuing education.

- Provide forums for interfacing all corporate departments with emphasis on quarterly reports or meetings devoted specifically to innovation needs and scientific or other developments (R&D; financial; marketing, or sales; engineering; customers; vendors).

- Publish an internal house organ dealing with advanced technology. (Dow Chemical does this and the document is held quite secret, but is quite successful and well received by technical staff.) Improve technical communications.

Fig. 9-1. How to turn on your innovative/creative system.

How do you recognize when an idea is getting short-sheeted? The danger sign for this scenario is when you hear any of the following:

- "We'll come back to it later."
- "We don't have enough time."
- "This isn't the right time for it."
- "We haven't time for detail."
- "Let's think about it some more."

That's the time for management to look for a way to follow up by using a university, an outside R&D facility, or someone.

THE TEAM CONCEPT

Generally, innovation and creativity is an individual effort (Fig. 9-2) which is hard to measure. However, observation shows that a key trait of the innovative and creative individual is that he or she has a good sense of humor. Looking at that trait alone will not always lead you to the right person for a project, so one approach to idea follow-up is to choose a team—and let a leader evolve from the team.

Score Yourself: 0 for none
               5 for mediocre
          10 for excellent

- Has a good sense of humor   _____

- Is able to bring things into existence   _____

- Lots of ideas   _____

- Has eccentricities   _____

- When young, had apparent learning disabilities on the one hand, or high IQ on the other.   _____

- Appreciates and is comfortable with the abstract   _____

- Great concentration or meditation capabilities   _____

- Can get to the heart of a problem quickly   _____

- Loves experimentation   _____

- Pays heed to vague and intuitive feelings and technical or social subtleties   _____

- Uses divergent rather then esoteric thinking   _____

- Enjoys concepts and conceptual thinking   _____

- Comfortable with complexity   _____

- Willing to take risks   _____

- Enjoys art, writing, and music   _____

                                      Total: _____

Creative Genius	145–150
Imaginative	130–144
Innovative & Creative	115–129
Original & Resourceful	100–114
On the Road to Creativity	Below 100
Needs Creative Growth	Below 75

Fig. 9-2. A personal creative capability quotient.

Forming the team in a small business might be different from a firm that can be dubbed an emerging company. In a small business, there might not be enough people to form a team. That is the time to turn to an advisory board or to associates who can help the team captain. You can also turn for help by using advanced technology centers, universities, or government agencies. (See *Scientific American*, May 1983.)

On the other hand, it is not unrealistic for an emerging company to have goals of becoming a $2 billion organization within a decade and for the company to have a staff of very qualified personnel available to the corporation for new venture analysis. One type of innovation and creativity involves a new venture programs group staffed with a carefully selected in-house entrepreneurial team. The key player is a vice president of new ventures. He or she is in charge of choosing the new venture teams (NVTs) from existing personnel. These NVTs are given certain guidelines and fiscal constraints on the front end and quantum compensation opportunities upon project success. The team becomes a profit center within itself with the company venture management coming from the NVT itself.

How many emerging companies can afford this luxury? Not many! However, managers of emerging companies can benefit by emulating the concept on a small-scale or a makeshift format.

Still, companies should not choose this route to new ventures with half-hearted commitment. Such a program demands strict quidelines and orientation for the members to commit the extra effort—beyond their daily jobs and routine—to make a new venture fly. As for the choice of a leader, choose the person who can relate to the technology and has the vision to extrapolate technology into markets.

CHOOSING THE NEW VENTURE IDEA

Small businesses do very little research and development (R&D), yet emerging industries often come up with ideas and products that the marketing department then is supposed to sell. Pennzoil Corporation, who most would agree is a very successful marketing company, uses a different approach. That company's R&D is initiated by market demands. In effect, it follows the old Henry J. Kaiser approach of, "Find a need and fill it." This can be initiated by creating a wish list for a typical project or by a formal "technology scanning system" that is both internal and external to the company.

External monitoring is necessary because corporate executives often become complacent with pet technologies that can be on the downslope of the product life-cycle bell curve (Fig. 9-3). An indicator of this type of complacency is when you hear things like:

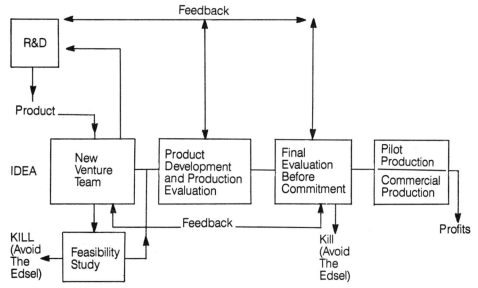

Fig. 9-3. From bright idea to reality.

- "We're making a profit."
- "We can't hold up production for that."
- "It leaves me cold."
- "It is not practical."
- "It doesn't fit in with our plans."
- "We're not ready for it yet."
- "Our business is different."

This is not to say that you should ignore opportunities for mature products. This topic is covered in greater detail in chapter 10.

Remember that in *technology scanning*, it is just as important to identify "NO FIT" projects and kill them as it is to identify those that have opportunities. Weismantel and Kisling use the phrase: "ATE, Projects—Avoid The Edsel, Projects.

If R&D comes up with an ATE project, most companies let the project die. It is better to focus on whether the technology fits the product mix and goals of another company. Sell it!

Too often projects lie dormant in one company's files while it could be making royalty monies if in the hands of another firm. Maybe it's in the files because someone said, "That's been tried before." Or maybe they said: "We can't pay for the tools." Maybe this one; this is the clincher, "They won't hold still for that." Of course, maybe there was the wise manager who had it filed because he or she said, "We don't do it that way in our plant." The manager might have also said, "It's been done that way for fifteen years, why change?"

Finally, emerging firms should consider having a consultant's input as to whether the company is choosing the right product or product mix to ensure that its innovation and creativity teams are finding projects leading to growth and opportunity. Any outside view should be looked upon as a welcome critique of company products and marketing goals (Fig. 9-4).

FROM CONCEPT TO REALITY

It often can take as long as four years to implement a new product strategy; that's all the more reason for putting a strategic plan on paper and beginning to implement it with an associated "grading system," ensuring your success.

The process begins by determining company sales goals, preparing the proper product mix, and identifying the type and location of the customers you hope to attract.

But it doesn't have to be this way. To understand the "short path" you can again turn to a Henry J. Kaiser example. During World War II, he, Ralph Parsons, and several other executives involved with the war effort met in Room 2500 in the Waldorf Astoria in New York. He was interested in magnesium and had laid out a program to manufacture the product on a very quick timetable. One man who was present brought up a whole series of reasons why it should be done another way. He wanted a pilot plant research program. That was too slow for Kaiser, because he knew magnesium was essential to the war effort.

Henry took Ralph Parsons aside and said, "Ralph, this is war and we must

---

☞ Compare outside evaluations with in-house judgments.

☞ Utilize outside critique-consultants openly and candidly with cooperation of in-house, high-level creativity team.

☞ Formulate criteria for evaluation.

☞ With client data in hand, ask consultant to screen material through an evaluation group of his or her staff and/or knowledgeable associates, without revealing company name, to get candid response.

☞ Ideas from evaluation group (as many as 100) should be summarized and presented to management.

☞ Management reduces ideas, suggestions, and comments to a reasonable level six to ten to compare for possible action.

☞ Specific ideas are relegated to market research projects.

☞ On basis of market research, go/no-go decisions regarding a product or market are made to ATE (Avoid The Edsel).

Fig. 9-4. Innovative and creativity critique: A checklist.

do things differently. I don't want that man on this project. I don't want CAN'T-DOERS! I want men who will strive to find ways and means of making the plan work. If we fail, we will have used our best efforts to succeed—we will have discharged our obligation to our government and our people.''

The man who was making the objections to Kaiser's effort was a good engineer, but he missed seeing management's objective. He had proposed an orthodox, logical plan for one set of conditions. However, it didn't fit the needs of management.

History shows that the project, as originally contemplated by Kaiser, had its problems; however, it wound up by making a magnesium slurry for fire bombs at great profit. It also formed the basis of a great chemical industry.

There is a whole list of roadblock quotations that inhibit innovation and creativity. They include:

- ''We're over the budget now.''
- ''We can't help it, it's policy.''
- ''It costs too much.''
- ''Let someone else try it first.''
- ''Cost is not important, just get it out the back door.''
- ''It's too late now, the contract is going to end.''
- ''I know it won't work.''
- ''That's Joe's job, not mine.''

In conclusion, while there might not be hard and fast rules for measuring innovation and creativity, there are certain facets and principles of innovation and creativity that make them clear and certain personnel and mechanical barriers that lead to innovation and creativity failure.

Keep in mind that ideas are not profits. Almost every company president will attest that there is no dearth of ideas. Any brainstorming session will create more ideas than you can possibly follow up. To ensure that innovative and creative ideas lead to profits, there are 10 steps that should become company policy:

1. Have specific strategic goals. Communicate these to everyone in the organization so that each person knows them by memory.
2. Focus R&D efforts to meet those goals.
3. Employ a known methodology to follow ideas.
4. Empower certain employees with the authority and the responsibility for new ventures.
5. Provide ample time for creative, innovative thinking.
6. Provide adequate compensation for ideas that lead to profits as well as good ideas that fail.
7. Learn from short-term successes as well as short-term failures.

8. Be flexible and subject to change.

9. Rely on vision and intuition using marketing research as a backup.

10. Know the importance of timing. Study demand and supply side technologies and identify where they converge.

A survey was recently conducted of a thousand Fortune companies. Of the thousand, 506 responded. Of that, 75 percent of the respondents were CEOs. Of that group, the single factor that encourages innovation in a company is top management commitment. The factors that discourage innovation are the desire to keep the *status quo*, fear of failure, red tape, lack of funds, and inadequate return on investment. An emerging company cannot be satisfied with the *status quo*. The emerging company wouldn't be where it is and emerging if it was afraid of failure.

In the latter part of the Fortune survey, there was a series of questions on the importance of establishing an entrepreneurial environment within the U.S. corporations. Of the respondents, 88% felt that it was important to create this environment in America; 84% felt their companies should do it. But only 50% felt that their company would do it. The reason is simply that large corporations, publicly held, are driven for short-term results. They need to satisfy the institutional investors. This is the area and the reason why there are such great opportunities for the small emerging company in America today.

In summary, today's emerging companies must be innovative and creative to survive. As Ralph Waldo Emerson said, ''If a man can write a better book, preach a better sermon, or make a better mousetrap than his neighbor, though he builds his house in the woods, the world will make a beaten path to his door.''

THE COST OF CREATIVITY

Today, however, you have to be able to build not only a better mousetrap, but also have the entrepreneurial (Fig. 9-5) and marketing wherewithal to come up with good ideas when threatened by competition at home and abroad. This challenge is filled with distractions and interruptions, including the greatest barrier to ongoing innovation and creativity—namely, growth itself.

Growth is costly. Flexibility is lost; response time is lengthened. And as a company grows, managers are more distracted by mundane tasks, simple accounting, complex accounting, and other business facets that a large company assigns to departments. More importantly, there are hidden expenses that don't appear on the balance sheet. This fact is best served by example.

One of the most famous growth companies in recent years has a policy that emphasizes creativity. The point of this policy is not to limit idea-flow or conceptual thinking in any way. To attain this, the company has no incoming physical exam, no drug testing policy, and no rules or constraints that make up many

- Do you react well when your company or products are threatened by new technology? _____

- Are you able to find opportunity when looking at problems? _____

- Do you continually redefine goals and have the flexibility to reach them? _____

- Are you outgoing and marketing oriented? _____

- Are you a trend spotter? _____

- Are you fair and unbiased when working with others? _____

- Can you act technically and/or managerially without prejudices, biases, or preconceived assumptions? _____

- Are you persistent and resourceful? _____

- Are you respected by your peers and employees and do you receive and act on feedback you get from them? _____

- Are you creative and innovative, full of ideas, but will honestly consider ideas and suggestions from your subordinates? _____

How To Score:

If you rate yourself high in a category, give yourself 10 points. Poorer ratings deserve lower scores. If you score under 20, you need to bone up on some skills needed for a managing and emerging company!

Fig. 9-5. Managing innovation and creativity.

firms' standard operating procedures. Yet, the company does have an income statement that any manager would envy.

What else does the company have?

- Thievery which is rampant and almost totally accepted by the employees.

- Employees that take "growth" for granted—just like the oil companies did in the boom days of the 1970s.

- Communication that is bad to nonexistent.

- Cooperation that is strictly a back-burner proposition because everyone is so busy peddling their own project.

- Lack of coordination.

- Lots of waste that is costing a fortune.

- A terrible drug abuse problem. (Which is probably one reason for the thievery.)

- An employed population that is extremely spoiled.

All this because people are so busy turning out widgets and making money that good business practices have been placed on the back burner.

Ironically, the company thinks its communication is great; it has an open-door policy right to the president—although employees generally don't use it—and believes that the corporation is doing everything right.

The moral is: Emerging and growth companies are doing a lot of things wrong, but are succeeding in spite of themselves—particularly because of their position on the product life-cycle bell curve.

10

Turnarounds: How to Get a Growing Company Out of Trouble

YOU CAN'T BUILD AN EMERGING COMPANY WITHOUT SOME DISAPPOINTMENT. Business cycles mean ups and downs. Every silver lining has a cloud.

CONTINGENCY PLANNING
People with growth plans seldom consider reversals. Any plan for new activities or change will have some adverse logical consequences. The secret to continuing successes is to anticipate these problems and to plan for them. The following are simple steps of contingency planning.

1. List all the potential problems and establish what impact they could have on your company.
2. Rate the potential problems on a scale of 1 to 10 for seriousness.
3. Rate the probability that any of these problems might occur.
4. Multiply the probability in step 3 by the seriousness in step 4.
5. Establish plans for the highest product established through step 4.
6. Identify trigger points and list the indicators of these trigger points. A trigger point is a business event that, upon occurrence, causes a manager to take action. It could be the loss of a major customer, voluntary or involuntary termination of a key employee, inflation, or increase in loan rates. For example, a manufacturer is concerned about his plant being

organized by a union. He calculates the seriousness of this problem to be an 8 on a scale of 10. The product of the probability and the seriousness is 6 × 8, or 48. A trigger point would be the appearance of a union organizer at his gate.

7. Establish an action plan that includes timing, responsibility, and cost to be taken, should you reach these trigger points.

Problems come from a variety of sources, both internal and external. Errors in judgement, economic recessions, bank complications, supplier relations, customer relations, service obligations, and warranty obligations are all examples. The manager must identify the external factors affecting the company. You must ask how your business performs in relation to others. Does your business lead or lag the economic indicators, and which indicators apply to your business?

There are assorted types of economic recessions. Primary ones are recessions with inflation, recessions with shortages, or a combination of the two. Someone in your company needs to be responsible for tracking the factors that affect your success. Sometimes a good source of information is a competitor. Recession will affect competitors. A manager should know how the competition can be expected to react. Prices could be cut; consequently, you might need to operate on lower margins.

An example of a poorly planned reaction is one of a company that manufactured strategic components needed for our armed forces in Viet Nam. The company operated under firm fixed-price contracts. President Nixon withdrew the price controls and the cost of raw materials skyrocketed. Soon the company was shipping everything at a loss. There was no control over what President Nixon did, but the firm probably should have anticipated and planned for the eventuality.

Another company operated six steel-fabricating plants in various locations along the Gulf of Mexico. They became heavily involved in offshore oil equipment. Although the firm had anticipated a potential downturn in the oil industry and felt it could weather a 3 year slump, oil prices remained depressed for far longer. When last visited, the company had closed five of its six plants.

It is possible to turn adversity into advantage. Planning for growth is exciting but planning for contractions is unpleasant and usually put off. Contingency planning can provide the CEO with the opportunity of motivating his or her people to do some of the things that needed to be done but were put off.

During recessions, better people are often available in the job market. There also can be an incentive for higher productivity to set new standards for productivity. If you have the money to take advantage of the opportunity, material and equipment might be available at lower prices. It also might be possible to negotiate long-term supply contracts. Suppliers also might tolerate longer terms and smaller quantity deliveries, which help you to reduce your inventory.

Sometimes, if you can anticipate early enough, you can introduce new products that stimulate new sales in the face of traditional sales, thus dampening the recession effect on your business.

In regards to marketing, sometimes related companies might be for sale or better marketing and distribution channels might open up. So, you see, contingency planning can replace crisis planning. Other steps that will help in contingency planning is to calculate how to get out of a situation before you get into it. Become a risk assessor and not a risk taker. Thwart the deal before you get into it.

SOME FACETS OF TURNAROUNDS

Often, the analogy for the staff of an emerging company is a group of teenagers going to their first dance. They feel they are all grown up and know what to expect, but when they get to the ball, they stand around and do nothing.

True, not all firms nor all new ventures are that way. There are hosts of examples where some rather naive Arthur Murrays have made grand successes because when they got to the ball, they got out there and quickly learned the dance steps to success. Turnaround situations often force you onto the dance floor, and even though you are new at the techniques, you have to dance before the night—and your company—is lost. Just what steps are important to the new or emerging company during turnarounds?

Harness Financial Power

When things look the darkest, it is sometimes amazing just how much power is still around you when you look for it. There might be need for financial wizardry—perhaps in the form of outside advice—that involves: factoring, flooring, refinancing, special sales deals, and other financial facets that ameliorate cash flow.

There is an old axiom that if a man with cash meets a man with experience, they might change places and roles. The secret to successfully weathering a business downturn is to maintain positive cash flow. It can also, in sustained recessions, represent the secret to survival. We will discuss some of the specific steps that you can take to preserve this positive cash flow.

The key to preserving this cash flow and engineering this turnaround is leadership. The best type of leadership is by example. Take action and be decisive!

The survival strategist acts immediately—cutting expenses, eliminating low margin products, reducing inventory. He or she weeds out marginally productive employees, and negotitates extended supplier credit as well as bank credit. If necessary, the survival strategist institutes receivable financing as well as equipment leasing. If appropriate, he or she investigates alternative, less expensive energy sources.

If the suppliers get restless, you pay the little ones first. This reduces the number of people who are badgering you.

If you really get into trouble, get a professional. The points of this text are not intended to save every company on the verge of bankruptcy. For a more expanded and in-depth discussion, the book *Turnaround* by Marvin A. Davis, from Contemporary Publishing, is well worth reading.

There is one point to observe in dealing with your bank. Don't give it a detailed personal net worth statement with which it can hang you. Don't give away personal guarantees if you can avoid it. If you do have to make a personal guarantee, make it limited, joint, and severable. The bank must liquidate the assets before it calls on you for funds.

Consider Your Product Mix

During a turnaround, you must closely scrutinize the business the company is in and the business the company should be in. These are not necessarily the same.

Turnaround focus might involve product expansion and introduction but usually involves retrenchment to concentrate on high profit centers with focus on a:

- clearly defined product line.
- clearly defined market.
- clearly defined objective.

Here, short-term objectives are crucial to have and to meet.

In looking at your product line, can you narrow it? This will help reduce inventory. Will it help your sales to loosen credit if the economy in general is faltering? Do you increase sales through discounts or lowering prices? Do incentives work in your industry? Can you increase the number of outlets where your products are sold, particularly if it means taking them from inventory and getting them out where the customer will see them? Does direct selling to the end user provide any opportunity?

Pricing

Pricing is another area that you must explore during a turnaround. Often it is most difficult to analyze and the results of price changes will not be as quick as the other turnaround steps that may be taken. In addition, a decision made in haste in pricing can have long lasting and negative effects on the future of your business.

When looking at your pricing, look at it in terms of the value perceived by the customer. Don't always base your price on cost. Can the customer receive the same value elsewhere for a competitive price? If you have items which are of a proprietary design, price it higher because it cannot be obtained anywhere else. This is particularly true of esoteric services.

Payroll and Staff Reduction

During turnarounds, a payroll analysis will help you discover other areas where you are losing cash for services that could be performed internally without losing people. Remember, positive cash flow is the lifeblood for keeping the company going and making the turnaround. In contrast, especially in times of a depressed economy, farming out certain jobs might result in tremendous cost savings. In 1986 and 1987, for example, the Gulf Coast economy suffered severely. Fabricators took jobs almost for the price of steel to preserve their own cash flow and keep employees. In these and other cases, outright reductions in work force become inevitable. By 1989, the shops were full again and margins were back to normal.

This leads to probably the most emotional part of any turnaround. In these cases, the CEO must make reductions in force. Look at personnel reductions, and reductions in force (RIFs) as the steps needed to preserve the viability and strength for the ultimate security of the remaining employees and their dependents.

Again, act decisively and quickly. Reductions in the indirect labor force are the key. There will be many feasible arguments within yourself and from your supervisors for saving an individual. However, the program for reductions in force must be universal; no excuses.

Don't take your supervisor's or your own recommendations without evaluating the long-term effects. Also be careful that you consider what the reductions will do to the overall age of the work force. Normally you save the people with the longest seniority, but these are also the oldest employees. You might find yourself, in the long-term, without any succession program. A staff reduction can often be avoided if there is a long-term plan for job security for current employees (Fig. 10-1).

Physically, do the severances with as little disruption as possible to the organization. Communicate the reasons to the employee being terminated. Later, you must communicate the effects and the results to the remaining employees.

One company set out a plan that when sales collapsed the firm would lay off so many employees each Friday until sales regained. This turned out to be a mistake. Layoffs lasted for five or six Fridays and the remaining employees became paranoid about facing the reality of a Friday. If you communicate well and properly with your remaining employees, you can minimize the negative morale effect.

You want to offer the employees being laid off letters of reference and perhaps even out-placement services. You also can offer to help them prepare their resumés. We hope you never will have to face the problems of a complete plant closing. This can be extremely difficult and there is new federal legislation controlling the responsibilities of the employer in a plant closing.

1. Use liberal relocation policies.

2. Train and retrain current employees.

3. Transfer employees between departments and divisions.

4. Bring contracted work back to plant.

5. Use hiring freezes.

6. Set up early retirement.

7. Limit student hiring.

8. Use other voluntary efforts—take vacations. Encourage sabbaticals.

9. Encourage leaves of absence.

10. Change job levels.

11. Reduce temporary and overtime help.

Fig. 10-1. Steps to ensure job security of current employees.

The nature of your business might have light fluctuations in the number of people required. This type of planning is extremely crucial. You might be able to smooth out some of the peaks and valleys by subcontracting both within and without. That is, you might find suppliers to whom you can give work during high production requirement periods and you could bring some subcontracted work in when you're slow. It is good to smooth out these peaks in some fashion since hiring new people will reduce your productivity and, in manufacturing situations, increase the potential for accidents.

Don't overlook the possibility of using overtime to gain additional production, both in the direct and the indirect areas. Again, preserving the job security of everyone is better than hiring excess people and ultimately facing a layoff. You also can hire temporaries to balance the work load. When you consider the cost of overtime and temporaries, keep in mind the social benefits that you save in terms of insurance cost, holiday pay, vacations, and medical insurance. These savings might well offset any premium you are paying.

Another possibility is to offer early retirement. You also can ask employees to take a portion of their vacation early. This has worked fairly effectively in the past. Another technique is lending out employees between divisions—if you have divisions.

When laying off hourly employees, you will probably have to go by seniority if you have a union. If you do, analyze where your problem employees are. If possible, go below that level and get rid of some of the marginal or problem employees.

Gaining Control of Inventory

Two aspects of inventory become important; your own, and your supplier's. In 1981, a manufacturing company had a dramatic decline in sales because of technical problems with a product line. This company had not had a losing year since 1972. It had grown very rapidly and, as a result, was highly leveraged. Most of this debt was the result of financing inventory where turns were less than two to one. The next highest level of debt was in receivable financing. Everything owned was in hock. When the sales dropped, the banks became very, very nervous. Reductions in the work force occurred early on, and then the company took on the inventory problem. The receivables were fairly guaranteed, so money would be forthcoming. The company was on a calendar fiscal year; their technical problems began in February, which was seasonally the lowest part of the sales year. Fortunately, the problems were resolved by mid-May. By this time, however, the company was deeply committed to the inventory reduction program. They ended the year in December with a $9,000 profit and a million dollar reduction in debt.

A good inventory reduction program can come from the simple procedure of controlling what you're purchasing. If you purchased from requisitions, tell your purchasing manager not to buy anything without your initials on the requisition. This will be a laborious process. They will tell you that if you don't get the paper work back in time, they won't be able to get the material in on time to sustain production. But your suppliers are probably by now telling you that if you don't pay them, they're not going to ship anyway.

Have your accounting department prepare a simple weekly report that gives the new orders that have come in, what has been shipped during the week, and what the receipts were of materials. It's probably not difficult for you to calculate what percentage of your sales is material. You can then easily compare the receipts against the material that was shipped in sales to determine whether you're buying less than you're using (Fig. 6-2).

Also, have your accounting department give you an aging of the receivables on this weekly report to see if they are working the receivables as hard as they can for cash. One last item on this one-page management report is a list of employees. Then you can see if you are losing people through attrition. Obviously by now, if the company is in trouble, you have to put on a hiring freeze.

You want to get the total company committed to improving your level of turns. The first thing you have to do is to *make sure all of your employees understand how to calculate inventory turns*. Inventory turns, simply defined, is your annual cost of sales divided by your average inventory.

Many factors affect inventory turns and it is improper to arbitrarily establish what your turns should be. Get some statistics from your banker. Get some numbers from people you know in similar businesses. Ask your trade organizations what turns are common for your industry. Ask your competitors what their turns are.

If you are a manufacturer, one of the factors you might examine in determining how you can improve your turns are your product structures. It is usually difficult to expeditiously change your product structures, but your manufacturing engineers can help here.

Another area to examine is the customer service level. Explore with your marketing people if it is necessary to retain component parts for service as long as you do. Also find out if you can get blanket orders from your customers or if it is necessary to ship equipment or orders as rapidly as you do. In other words, does anybody really care or appreciate the level of service you are providing? If your company's really in trouble, however, you should look at a goal of at least six inventory turns per year.

If you are going to reduce your inventory, you first of all need to have some system of control. If you don't have that type of system, or a perpetual inventory that's 90 percent accurate, and if you don't do cycle accounting, or have your inventory secured, you had better start immediately, along with your production procedures. Without a good inventory control system, you will have a lot of work ahead of you, but at the same time there's definitely greater potential for savings. Inventory carrying cost can reach 40 percent of product value in some industries.

If you don't have procedures, you'll have difficulty accomplishing anything by analyzing your records. The records have to be accurate. Start by analyzing raw materials. Cross check the effectiveness of your labor saving and inventory reduction program. Begin signing *all* checks, including payroll as well as suppliers. In doing this, you will discover other areas where you are losing cash for services, utilities, etc. Remember, positive cash flow is the lifeblood for keeping the company going and making the turnaround.

One last area that we will explore is steps in marketing that can aid in the turnaround. For example: Are there less expensive networks for distribution? Could you go with manufacturer's reps, that is, instead of salaried salespeople? Or go direct instead of through distributors? Can you offer parts discounts that will increase both cash flow and reduce inventory?

Put your managers on the road selling. This means engineers, manufacturing people, anybody who knows your product line and can do a good job representing you. It could be the salvation of their job.

Again, use caution. A mistake made in this area could have negative effects on sales and on the future of your company. Be careful to think these strategies out carefully.

The best approach to preventing a need for implementing difficult turnaround strategies is contingency planning. But as has happened to many managers—sometimes more than they care to remember—if you find yourself in need of a turnaround, the steps mentioned will help do the trick.

THE CEO AND TURNAROUNDS

Before we go any further, let's discuss the responsibilities and the role of the CEO during these tough times.

The CEO has responsibilities to the shareholders—whether a private or a public company—the employees, his or her management team, the suppliers, the customers, and the community. Many times these responsibilities are in conflict with one another.

Remember, however, that a recession or slow-down combined with good leadership provides the CEO with the time to motivate his or her people to do those things that have been considered before but never implemented. This is the time for personal commitment. Smaller companies are more flexible and can adjust quicker.

As the stress builds, maintain your own personal agenda. Maintain your outside activities. Try to get lots of exercise. Rest your mind from the extreme focus on the problems. Put in long hours at the office but try to leave your problems there when you go home. Solve the problems one at a time. Have patience, and as you look at the almost insurmountable collection of problems, analyze them from the state of whether they will be important 10 years from now.

Plan to spend 50 to 60 hours a week at the office while you are managing the turnaround. Do your work at the office. To maintain your sanity, as mentioned, try to leave your problems at the office.

Each day put on your chaplain's outfit early in the morning and again in the evening. Leave your door open. You might find employees dropping in with both their personal problems and solutions to yours. You will probably find that after awhile your employees will be working longer hours voluntarily. If they don't all get on the team, you might want to ask their supervisor to give them a little kick.

Set the example by planning to work some Saturdays. Make sure that after awhile you are not alone.

STAFF AND MIDDLE MANAGERS DURING TURNAROUND

During the past 25 years, we have heard of many cases where middle managers in new or emerging companies have taken a realistic view of the business situation, gone to the CEO and said, "You can't afford me!" Some stories continue with the CEO's response, "I can't afford *not* to have you during this time."

During such cash crunches, one way to keep *m*anagement *a*nd *w*omanagement (MAW) is to reshape compensation from salary into profit-sharing. There is no magic success formula for this type of compensation; however, middle MAW with faith in the turnaround might view short-term, smaller monthly remuneration as a small price to pay for quantum increases in pay from increased profits.

In some cases, outright layoffs and rehiring as consultants or independent contractors are reasonable. New tax laws might still require withholding, despite the employment status change. The real saving is in benefits. Here, there are some interesting possibilities.

TRICKS OF THE (TURNAROUND) TRADE

The discussion so far has had a major focus on emerging businesses and their turnarounds. But this doesn't mean that the dog should not learn some of the old turnaround tricks. One or a combination of the following ideas might lead you to turnaround success.

Acquire a Company. While acquiring a company at this stage is unusual, it can happen. Just when you are about ready to bounce payroll checks might not seem like a time ripe for acquisition. However, the right candidate might not only enhance your borrowing power to purchase the new company and obtain operating cash, but also might give you a desired new product mix to enhance cash flow.

Look for a Joint Venture. Looking for a joint venture might be to line up a new marketing channel to handle your products, and thus an immediate need to fill the pipeline, or to produce a group of products under one roof instead of two.

Seek Aid from Outside. State and local governments—especially in depressed areas—can lend a hand in various ways. Examples include: a Gulf Coast alliance set up in Texas in the mid 1980s to help small businesses experiencing difficulty. This is an SBA funded program. Sometimes SBA help is mired in slowness and bureaucracy; what the U.S. Small Business Administration can't do is help you get orders.

Government Business. What SBA can't do, General Services Administration (GSA) and other U.S. government and state agencies can. There are secrets in doing business with the government, and you should especially watch for small business set-aside projects.

Hire a Retiree. Turnarounds are ripe situations for hiring retired but experienced businessmen or women, some of whom have gone through turnaround experiences themselves. Retirees often will jump at turnaround situations because it is a "project" situation that has a definite endpoint.

Get Help from the Unions. If unionized, the AFL/CIO can be either a help or a hindrance. However, there are cases where pay and benefit cuts were exchanged for stock. The advantage here is that the union shows faith in the turnaround because the stock carries benefits only if the turnaround succeeds. This is usually a desperate action.

Get Customer Help. Get help from customers, create new sales and marketing packages, particularly by focusing on customers with whom you have good relationships. Strike deals that enhance cash flow. Keep in mind the time-value of money. Focus on relationship management. Also, get help from suppliers.

Sell and Leaseback Assets. Fund the good assets, not the bad. Cash flow is the only thing that counts in a turnaround. Funding projects or assets that can turn an immediate ROI deserve favorable attention.

Increase Export Sales. Developing export sales takes a long time. Increasing export sales would be a contingency plan taken well in advance of problems to diversify your market.

Increase Public Relations (PR) Activity. More PR, such as a news release and story placement campaign, can create leads for both new and old products if handled correctly.

Utilize Bill Consolidation. Utilize bill consolidation by transferring short-term debt into long-term debt based on an acceptable, strategic business plan.

Diversify and/or License New Technology. Expansion of new technology offers an immediate potential for new products without waiting for R&D projects to be completed. It allows compatible diversification without capital commitment if newly licensed products or technology can be brought in from off-shore.

Integrate or Spin off Certain Business. Integrating or spinning off certain business saves overhead and/or provides additional working capital for core business ventures.

Increase Sales Representatives Commissions. Increasing sales commissions might be tied to increased prices of products, but it is a good way to make sales reps work harder. This can be particularly true if the company uses distributors. However, concentrate on boosting sales and lowering the cost of production.

Lower Current Overhead and Production Costs. Check costs carefully. A 1 percent drop in raw material costs could be 10 times more effective to cash flow than a 15 percent drop in utility costs.

Hit the Competition at the Weak Points. Hit competition at week points. These points can be anything from service to quality. Be better than your competition!

Create New Alliances. New alliances can be with new customers or old. For example, if a company has its own widget plant, and also buys widgets from you, consider buying and/or operating the customer's widget plant for him or her. (National Can has done this quite effectively.)

Motivate Employees. Develop that team spirit, that sense of urgency, with your employees. Create challenges.

Increase Candid Communication. People must not be afraid to speak out to identify problems and potential cost savings on the factory floor or in the field. Let employees participate handsomely in savings realized.

Get Rid of Problem Accounts. Some accounts have constant problems because they don't treat your product correctly, are slow to pay, etc. Dump accounts that are not profitable. Some companies buy the low mark-up items from you and give your competition the gravy. Don't let this happen.

Create Inter-Division Cooperation. Some firms have divisions that don't talk to one another or don't have a sister division on the "favored supplier" list. Get to the bottom of such problems so that your own bottom line increases. Have cooperation.

Shuffle Employees. Move employees around. New management is sometimes crucial in turnarounds. Old-line managers can't do some things due to entrenched work practices and friendships with other employees.

Eliminate Unnecessary Management Tiers. Eliminate unnecessary management tiers. Flat management puts more people reporting to the CEO, but things happen quicker. It is easier to create a sense of urgency and reduce procrastination.

Study the Bell Curve. Product life cycles take on a graphic bell curve. Understand what can be done to place your product or service on the growth cycle of the curve. Geriatric industries can turn into emerging industries with the right kind of technical input. Don't be afraid to dump old products if they are unprofitable.

Use Turnaround Innovations. Don't develop tunnel vision in your turnaround. You might not be able to see the curves. Be willing to do things differently. The answer might be a financial restructuring, an ESOP, S Corporation, partnership, or another novel idea.

FROM TURNAROUND TO GROWTH

As you consult with your lawyers and accountants, remember that they are just that. For example, the CEO of a major defense contractor said, "I once had a CPA firm whose managing partner advised us that it was time to liquidate the company and save whatever we could. Instead, the CEO implemented some of the policies covered in this chapter, saved the company, and ultimately sold it for an eight figure amount which was 2.2 times its net worth.'' A better source of advice than lawyers and accountants, who aren't businesspeople, is a creditable advisory board who are businesspeople.

To avoid making errors in judgement that cause downturn, avoid making deals where you are uncomfortable from the start. Don't do the deal if you don't like the people. Also, don't be paranoid about saving taxes if a transaction is completed. And always, before you get into a project, ask yourself how you would get out of it. If you are going to go into a deal that has risks, confirm your understanding of the terms after each step of the negotiations.

Considering the many facets of turnarounds, it boils down to one goal: Making a sick company healthy and profitable. In the case of *emerging industries*, the sick company can be: one that is just starting up; an old company that by design or necessity is moving into a growth market; an emerging company that has gotten itself into trouble; a company or division that has just been acquired; a leveraged buyout (LBO); or some other conglomeration. Obviously, a turnaround effort implies that there is something left to salvage that can be turned around by better:

- management
- marketing or merchandising
- cash flow
- products
- planning
- production facilities and/or services
- technology
- better almost everything

You could reason that a turnaround company, by definition, has to be—or become—an emerging company or it certainly will go to its corporate death. The question for the turnaround candidate is: How do you become part of an emerging industry? The answer: There are many ways! (Fig. 10-2).

Overall turnaround planning is good for every company. It might seem unorthodox for a brand new company to have a turnaround plan in place as you open your doors for business; however, that aspect of planning could be a company's salvation.

It is not unusual for a new company's first year's business plan to start going awry during the first 6 months of operations. This happens more often when the firm is tied to one major product or service and, for some reason, orders do not materialize.

A rule of thumb for starting a business is to have at least one major order in your pocket before startup. A corollary is: Have enough cash in the bank to keep the company in business for a year until the cash flow—from the order in your pocket at startup—begins to materialize. A third rule—perhaps it should be first—is to establish as much personal credit as possible before embarking in your new venture. Yes! Six credit card accounts can be okay.

But, returning to the new venture that reaches a 6 month checkpoint and finds that orders have not materialized, that is the time to resurrect a contingency plan.

Part one of that plan is based on the belief that "you do business with your friends!" Think about it! You don't find it easy to get orders from someone who doesn't like you, doesn't trust you, and who might be seeing you for the first time. However, a firm or person who knows you and your talent, your integrity, and your capabilities, is likely to help you out. If these were not your company's first sales calls, they certainly should be your first turnaround calls, and what you offer them might not be the product or service you offered when you opened your doors. Why? You are implementing a contingency plan.

---

1. Do Detailed Diagnostics.

Have an outsider analyze your strong and weak points. Just as you analyze a client's needs and wants, have someone analyze you. Don't do this yourself! Have the person go through your business plan; pick at problems; and push the opportunities and extrapolate into possible ventures or products you don't see. Use someone's formula within your industry.

2. Identify Niches.

Mature markets are not necessarily dead markets. Identify niches that are growth markets while focusing on cost-reducing strategies. Add new innovation to the existing product line by working closely to identify key customer needs and wants.

3. Expand Business Overseas.

The U.S. has only 3% of the world's population; therefore, many people are still open to U.S. technology. Unfortunately, most U.S. companies don't know how to—no—don't know the first thing about marketing overseas. Think globally, but sell using local strategies and people.

4. Capitalize on Company Strengths.

Assess current capabilities and exploit them. Consider new markets using a different set of manufacturing representatives; use strengths to reach these markets.

Fig. 10-2. 30 ways to turn a mature company into a growth company.

Fig. 10-2. (Continued)

5. *Capitalize on Company Facilities.*

   Many firms are under-utilizing their manufacturing facilities—e.g., a pump manufacturer that is operating only one shift yet has excellent machining capabilities, can also do work in aerospace, defense, and other areas. (Toll process.)

6. *Co-venture into Related Area.*

   Co-partnering is a growing strategic alternative. They are often created due to weaknesses of both partners who, acting together, have synergistic marketing or other strengths.

7. *Utilize New Marketing Strategies.*

   Make products for customers that are currently making the product themselves. Use innovative ways to reach new customers. Have sales managers assist on
   territorial planning and in implementing the plan.

8. *Hire a Turnaround Manager or Do a Turnaround Yourself.*

   There are many tricks to the trade that need thorough analysis. A study of turnaround successes (e.g., National Can, Business Week, *September 15, 1986, page 132 ff; and Enichem Chemical Week, December 17, 1986, page 62 ff) will help.*

9. *Look for New Innovative Products or Processors.*

   There are a number of ways to glean this information from close use of Lockheed's Information Data Bank, to meticulous use of U.S. government technology transfer documents, to monitoring certain publications and newsletters.

10. *Increase R&D Effort.*

    Find a need and fill it. Utilize sales representatives and the marketing department to identify needs. Focus R&D on commercialization of products.

11. *Consider Acquisitions or Mergers.*

    Appoint a new venture team to investigate acquisitions and mergers. Pay close attention to companies with old owners. Pay attention to obituaries and contact key account firms in the area, plus major bank's acquisition officers.

12. *Consider Spin-offs, Segregation, and Restructuring.*

    Make five companies out of one. Smaller companies offer greater flexibility and versatility to act. Restructuring could give reason to dump expensive union contracts.

Fig. 10-2. (Continued)

13. Expand into Services of Your Own Low Tech Products.

If you sell valves, begin to service and rebuild your own valves; if you sell heat exchangers, provide replacement bundles. Key in on good accounts and offer them your expertise in a way it will benefit both parties.

14. Consider New Technology, New Materials.

Materials technology is running wild; especially ceramics. Figure out a way to make a "better mousetrap." Contact your customers to fill their wants and needs.

15. Sell Systems rather than Companies.

A firm selling a metering pump might also sell a dispensing system that is modular, complete with piping and networking. The markup and profit on the system can be much better than a simple pump itself.

16. Sell Projects rather than Equipment.

Typically, a manufacturer's rep or distributor makes between 10 percent to 40 percent on an order. If, for example, an aerator manufacturer sells a totally installed sewage treatment system rather than just the aerators, the project can add much more to the firm's bottom line.

17. Import Technology.

European technology, in some cases, is way ahead of the U.S., ditto for Japan. License technology or become a U.S. distributor of novel equipment or services.

18. Hire Marketing Research Team to Analyze Old and Emerging Markets.

Your company could have a great opportunity but not know it. Compressor or blower manufacturers should be looking at lasers; old line chemical companies should be looking at electronics chemicals, and on and on.

19. Exchange Pay and Benefits Cuts for Stock.

This exchange can be considered with all levels of management including unions. It is hard to implement, but worth investigating.

20. Modernize.

Initiate speedy and efficient use of new technology based on creative financing that meets cash flow requirements.

21. Strike at Hot Markets.

Industries such as defense use leading edge technology. Aerospace is another area that is "hot" today. Identify the market of "next year" and go for it.

Fig. 10-2. (Continued)

22. *Initiate Relationship Management.*

   Use relationship management to get more business from existing customers. Increase "market share" from those clients by closely satisfying "wants" and "needs."

23. *Hire New Management.*

   Some firms' ideas are totally geriatric. The only hope for growth is for new people with new ideas to take the company out of the ice age. With mature industries, the trend is to hire marketeers.

24. *Make Creativity Changes.*

   Change ad agencies, PR agencies, and perhaps even bankers. Look for people that can help you differently than in past history.

25. *Analyze Why Companies Fail.*

   Analyze why, then don't make the same mistake. Usually failure has many facets from poor leadership to lack of integrity.

26. *Institute Strict Financial Controls.*

   Although controls do not identify the problems, it does help to hold down costs. Line item budgeting also helps to reduce costs.

27. *Reorganize to Eliminate Bureaucracy.*

   What managers of most failing companies don't realize is that their market has changed and they didn't change with it, and that they had grown in size during growth years, but did not pour down when the market stopped growing.

28. *Analyze Competitors.*

   Once analyzed, hit competitors at their weak points.

   (a). Analysis of competitor's goals.

   (b). Analysis of competitor's markets and marketing strategies.

   (c). Analysis of competitor's pricing strategies.

   (d). Substitution analysis.

   (e). Site facility analysis.

   (f). Analysis of investment and operating costs.

   (g). Analysis of competitor's financial profiles.

   (h). Analysis of product.

   (i). Analysis of competitors' technological capabilities.

   (j). International competitive analysis.

Fig. 10-2. (Continued)

29. Eliminate "Me Too" Products or Toll Process Them.

There are over 100 manufacturers of butterfly valves in the United States. Most of the products are "me too." If your company is loaded with "me too's," consider dropping the lines to concentrate on markup items or keep them in line, but have one of the other manufacturers make your label.

30. Initiate Delphi Planning.

Delphi Planning has been forgotten recently but is an excellent way to focus on future markets. Original work on Delphi was initiated at Rand and UCLA in Los Angeles. In its simplest form, you might consider Delphi Planning as a way to consolidate logical conclusion from random sampling. For example, someone might ask: "What will communications be like in the year 2020?" Answers from people in all walks of life would begin to show a pattern of repetition and organization, and in many ways, Delphia provides a unique way to glimpse the future based on individuals' concepts. A study of precise Delphi methodology is worthy of management attention in an emerging industry, if only to ensure that your company does not get left behind.

11

Cashing Out: Selling the Company and Other Options

SMALL COMPANIES OR EMERGING BUSINESSES UNDERGO DISTINCT TRANSITIONS which, in some ways, resemble a product life-cycle curve. Four of the most common periods experienced (Fig. 11-1) are: startup; elliptical (or sinusoidal) growth phase 1; static conditions; and, elliptical growth phase 2, or decline. Very specific things that are management related happen in these periods. More importantly, however, the *Sale* of the business or its *Acquisition* or *Merger* (SAM) can take place anywhere along the curve. These are illustrated by SAM Points 1, 2, 3, 4, 5 and 5'. Just where on the curve SAM takes place has a lot to do with how much money the founders or managers of a business put in their pockets at the conclusion of negotiations. Good strategic planning can actually identify a SAM point to maximize a person's (or group's) individual profitability, with tax laws greatly influencing the options available at any particular moment.

Hostility is a key word at the SAM point, even in friendly takeovers. Two distinct factions—polar in nature—exist. One management group will prevail after SAM. Warranted or unwarranted changes will occur in both companies involved in the transaction. Thus, "cashing out," or the SAM point, can be viewed from the position of the buyer and of the seller. Separate, but not considered an important point in this chapter, is the facet of going public.

Keep in mind that some negotiations do not lead to a SAM point. The inability to sell out is a fact of life that small firms can experience because many founding owners far overvalue their company and its potential. It is not unusual for

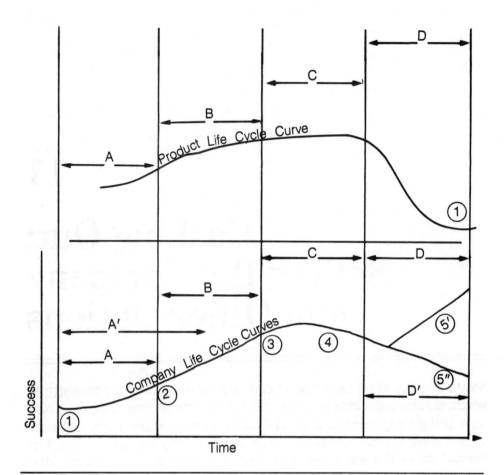

Notes:

A and/or A' A time period of individual leadership and entrepreneurial spirit with limited growth because managerial principles are not fully applied. Some managers are able to move further up the expansion curve (A') than others (A).

B Strong growth influenced by influx of new management and application of managerial principles in area of marketing, operations, and financial controls.

C Limited growth and some stagnation as capabilities and/or products peak. Need for new products and/or new goals appear.

D and/or D' Depending on success of implementation of growth principles, company proceeds on upward trend (D) or decline (D').

Fig. 11-1. Successful company life cycles.

such an owner to die, only to have an unsuspecting widow face a SAM point where, dealing from weakness, she sells out for ten cents on the dollar.

When should you determine your company's best SAM point? Here are a few suggestions:

- Before you are dead.
- When company has had three or more good years.
- When outlook is for more good years.
- When at that point in time where owner approaches retirement.
- When at a point of favorable tax implications.
- When not selling from a position of weakness.

There is no ideal SAM point if the owner does not want to sell!

With this introduction, let's tackle SAM—remembering that the best deal is one that's good for both parties. Some readers might be reading this section from the perspective of learning how to carry out an acquisition and increase the growth of their company. Others might be reading it from the perspective of how to sell their company. Regardless, whether you are a buyer or a seller, you will be a better negotiator if you have empathy for your adversary in the negotiations.

CASHING OUT

One of the primary goals of this chapter is to convince you of the tremendous amount of information you need to know about selling, acquiring, or merging a business. It is *no* place for amateurs, and it is a *must* place for confidentiality.

Confidentiality is important because the longer it is known that a company is for sale, the lower the price. Also, when employees find out a company is for sale, it shakes their confidence and security leading to a real potential for personnel turnover.

We suggest that you do some serious studying (Fig. 11-2). There are some good seminars offered by people who are in the business. You can actually go to school to take classes on the subject, a close review of books on the subject is a must.

---

1. Dun & Bradstreet (New York, NY)

2. Robert Morris (St. Louis, MO)

3. Charles Kline (Fairfield, NJ)

4. Standard & Poors (New York, NY)
   Investment Management Services (Denver, CO)

5. Weismantel International (Kingwood, TX)

Fig. 11-2. Sources of statistical data in various industries.

Naiveté in SAM negotiations can lead to many problems, especially when an ameteur sells to an amateur without professional assistance. They usually both end up in court. Get accounting and legal expertise. Also, select a lawyer who has expertise in mergers and acquisitions. Remember, there is a good possibility that after the sale, both a CPA and an attorney will lose a client. That doesn't give them very much incentive to encourage the pursuit of a sale.

You can consider the following three rules of thumb for starters:

1. SAM will take between 300 and 400 hours of negotiations. This is CEO time that must be allocated just to reach the SAM point.

2. Enter into negotiations with the idea that a good deal is a good deal for both buyer and seller. On that basis, you have a better chance of walking away from the table with everyone satisfied.

3. Whether selling, acquiring, or merging, be very careful of obligations under union pension arrangements. You might sell your business and find yourself personally liable for the obligations of the pension fund.

Reasons to Sell

There can be many reasons to sell out. Buyers can come from many sources; opposites seem to attract. Someone totally unfamiliar with your business can be a good candidate, but whoever it is, a buyer is looking to the future (Fig. 11-3).

One Dozen Reasons Why Businesses Sell Out

1. No heir to the throne
2. Age
3. Desire to become liquid
4. Estate planning requirements
5. Changes in family situation
6. Health
7. Age
8. Need for a change to avoid boredom
9. Lack of operating capital
10. Need for growth capital
11. New business interests
12. Other factors

Fig. 11-3. One dozen reasons why businesses sell out.

Small companies are interested in cost. Big companies are interested in revenues and profits.

Most industries have representative organizations, societies, and technical and market organizations that share common problems and values. It is not unusual to know your competitors and rub shoulders with them at national or local trade shows or technical meetings—and even to learn if some company is in trouble or doing well.

Members of trade associations know about, and pinpoint, owners who are geriatric with no successor among his or her progeny. The industry usually fingers this company as a buyout candidate.

In these cases, broaching the subject of buyout has two facets. One, the owner might be approachable and flattered; two, he or she might feel insulted at your thinking they would consider giving up their business. The latter case requires a tactful approach to the topic of buyout. It can be a casual comment at a dinner party or a banquet table that indicates an interest in the company should the owner ever think of hanging it up or cashing out.

Good companies are hard to find and so are legitimate buyers. When there appears to be the potential for a match-up, one or the other or both parties should initiate a letter of intent. Although letters of intent are non-binding, it expresses the sincerity of the parties. This in turn can trigger the next sequence of events, which might be deeper discussions or perhaps even an agreement that, although the interest is there, the timing is not right.

Common sources of buyers are competitors, suppliers, employees, venture capitalists, public companies, and even blind ads. The most potentially dangerous negotiations are with competitors. They learn the business and the strategies and then leave the seller holding the bag. If a competitor expresses interest, a seller should withhold confidential information until they reach a point of earnest money.

Unless a seller feels very confident that the employees have a source of capital and the necessary business acumen, it is extremely risky trying to sell to employees. Employees can have a difficult time financing a buyout, despite the large number of leveraged buyouts (LBOs) that have taken place recently.

A seller might be approached by an employee group if it leaks out that he or she is considering selling. An owner of a business, knowing managerial capabilities, can almost evaluate LBO potential based on the knowledge of the strengths of the LBO managers. They will ask you for extension after extension and concession after concession. The focus will be on buying the business and not on running the business during the negotiations. Company performance will slip and if the seller doesn't grant the concessions and extensions, the employees will become unhappy with the seller, thereby further affecting performance.

A legitimate buyer of a business has a lot in his or her favor if the buyer's banker has already given tacit support to expansion and if he or she can show

how the integration of the two companies results in a broadening of the product line and perpetuation of the seller's business. This latter aspect of a buyout can become quite important. Many owners want assurances of business continuity with their customer base or simply for the ego satisfaction of what they started will continue.

Companies serious about purchasing or merging normally have an acquisition plan. It can be something well defined on paper and known by all key executives of the firm. Informal plans might simply be the knowledge that a CEO will always look at a potential buyout candidate because, "It never hurts to talk." (A hint for firms operating in an acquisition mode is to include a box item about acquisition potential on the call report forms used for internal marketing consideration.)

There is an axiom that "once a business is advertised for sale (even if a blind P.O. box in the *Wall Street Journal*), it isn't worth pursuing." Although that adage is not totally true, the thinking behind the statement is. Good deals are gobbled up long before they reach the newspaper. This is not to say newspaper ads should be ignored; some leads are genuine (Fig. 11-4). Yet anyone who has contacted business exchanges, finders, or brokers, realizes that 90 percent of those listings are trash; the point being that buyers go through a lot of chaff before they get to real wheat (Fig. 11-5). Obviously then, acquisition-minded companies approach any prospect with a great deal of skepticism. (This evaluation experience often puts the buyer in the driver's seat in terms of knowing how to handle negotiations.)

Fig. 11-4. Typical answers from a *Wall Street Journal* ad.

January 19, 19___

Dear Mr. Weismantel:

This letter is in reference to your response on a Wall Street Journal advertisement regarding a food processor and distributor which we are representing for sale.

The sale consists of two plants, rolling stock, and farms. The plants are now operating as two independent units even though the stockholders have interests in both plants.

The companies process primarily fryers and fowel for the retail and institutional market. The marketing area consists of Oregon, Washington, Western Idaho, and Northern California. They produce approximately 60 per cent of the local market and approximately 35 per cent of the total market.

Fig. 11-4. (Continued)

Sales for previous years have been approximately $15 million per year. The sales for plant #1 are approximately $6.3 million for an eight month period ending December 1, 1972 with a net profit of $284,200.00 for the same. Plant #2 has sales of approximately $5.2 million for an eight month period ending December 1, 1972 with a net profit of $234,800.00 for the same. (Net profit before corporate income tax.)

There is a total of 225 employees. The plants are completely unionized. The plant's production can be increased approximately 20 per cent without any additional equipment investment or shift additions.

Management will remain for a specified time even though retirement of some of the stockholders is the basis for selling. The sales price is $2,090,000.00 with negotiable terms. A stock transfer will be considered from a stable company, however, a small amount of cash will have to be generated for one of the stockholders.

January 19, 1973
G.E. Weismantel

We are also representing a large berry and fruit processing firm which distributes nationally with an established brand name. They are completely dominant in several types of fruit. The sales volume is approximately $2.5 million per year. The company can support an increase of approximately 20 per cent in volume without any additional investment in facilities. Financial statements are not completed as yet, however, profit for 1972 is believed to be above $100,000.00. Sales price is $600,000.00 plus inventory which includes all prime commercial property, equipment, and rolling stock.

If you have any further interest in an acquisition of this nature, please give me a call. Additional information will be given to qualified interested individuals or companies. It would be appreciated that any discussion pertaining to these sales be kept confidential.

Thank you.

Sincerely,

Check Sheet: For Sale, Acquisition, or Merger [SAM] to Screen Potential Candidates

Name _____

Company Name _____

Address _____

City, State, Zip _____

Telephone _____

Objectives:

A. SAM Objectives: _____

_____

_____

_____

_____

B. Key Area of Interest: _____

_____

_____

C. Companies Involved:

Industry _____		Finance _____	
Banks _____		Life Ins _____	
Outside U.S. _____		Railroads _____	
Airlines _____		Utilities _____	

D. Government Agencies Involved:

EPA _____	IRS _____	
OSHA _____	Other _____	

Screening Information Required:

A. Analysis to be Performed: Once __ Monthly __   Quarterly __   Semi-Annually __

B. Review of Time Periods: _____

C. Additional Reports Required: _____

D. Other Data: _____

Fig. 11-5. Checksheet for sale, acquisition or merger (SAM) to screen potential candidates.

Fig. 11-5. (Continued)

SAM Filter:

A. Company Size:

_____   Do not wish to use this screen

If screen is invoked, answer one or more of these questions:

_____   Total Assets

_____   Total Sales

_____   Total Net Income

Specify:

Greater than $_____

Less than $_____

For Time Period:

_____   Latest Fiscal Year

_____   Recent 3 Year Average

_____   Recent 5 Year Average

_____   Each of Recent _____ Years

_____   Other (specify): _____

_____

_____

B. Company Market Value:

_____   Do not wish to use this screen

If screen is invoked, please answer following questions:

Specify $_____

Greater than $_____

Less than $_____

Fig. 11-5. (Continued)

For Time Period:

_____ Current

_____ Recent Fiscal Year

_____ Recent 3 Year Average

_____ Recent 5 Year Average

_____ Each of Recent _____ Years

_____ Other (specify) _____

_____

_____

C. Capitalization

_____ Do not wish to use this screen.

If screen is invoked, please answer following questions:

Specify Percent:

Greater than _____%

Less than _____%

For Time Period:

_____ Recent Fiscal Year

_____ Recent 3 Year Average

_____ Recent 5 Year Average

_____ Each of Recent _____ Years

Other (specify): _____

_____

_____

D. Capital Efficiency:

_____ Do not wish to use this screen

If screen is invoked, please answer the following questions:

Specify:

_____ Return on Common Equity (before and/or after

taxes).

Fig. 11-5. (Continued)

_____ Return on Total Invested Capital (before and/or after taxes).

For Time Period:

_____ Latest Fiscal Year

_____ Recent 3 Year Average

_____ Recent 5 Year Average

_____ Each of Recent _____ Years

_____ Other (specify): _____

_____

_____

E. Asset Turnover:

_____ Do not wish to use this screen

If screen is invoked, please answer following questions:

Specify:

_____ Sales Per $ Invested Capital

_____ Sales Per $ Gross Plant

Screen:

Specify $:

Greater than $ _____

Less than $ _____

For Time Period:

_____ Latest Fiscal Year

_____ Recent 3 Year Average

_____ Recent 5 Year Average

_____ Each of Recent _____ Years

_____ Other (specify) _____

_____

Fig. 11-5. (Continued)

F. Profit Margins:

_____   Do not wish to use this screen

If screen is invoked, please answer following questions

Specify:

_____   Operating Profit Margin before Depreciation

_____   Pretax Margin

_____   After Tax Margin

Screen:

Specify percent:

Greater than   _____%

Less than   _____%

For Time period:

_____   Latest Fiscal Year

_____   Recent 3 Year Average

_____   Recent 5 Year Average

_____   Each of Recent _____ Years

_____   Other (specify): _____

G. Stability of Growth (Total Sales, Total Profit, Earning Per Share [EPS], etc.)

_____   Do not wish to use this screen

If screen is invoked, choose basis (EPS, etc.) and answer the following questions:

Specify percent:

Greater than   _____%

Less than   _____%

or

At Least   _____   Years of Increase in Past 10 Years

Fig. 11-5. (Continued)

For Time Period:

_____ Last 10 Years

_____ Each of Last _____ Years

_____ Other (specify): _____

_____

H. Growth In Sales:

_____ Do not wish to use this screen

If screen is invoked, please answer following questions:

Specify percent:

Greater than _____%

Less than _____%

I. Earnings per Share [EPS] Data:

_____ Do not wish to use this screen

If screen is invoked, please answer following questions:

Select:

_____ 10 Year Log Linear Growth EPS

_____ 5 Year Log Linear Growth EPA

Specify percent:

Greater than _____%

Less than _____%

J. Book Value vs. Price:

_____ Do not wish to use this screen

If screen is invoked, please answer following questions:

Specify ratio [multiple]:

Greater than _____x

Less than _____x

Fig. 11-5. (Continued)

For Time Period:

_____ Current

_____ Latest Fiscal Year

_____ Recent 3 Year Average

_____ Recent 5 Year Average

_____ Other (specify): _____

_____

K. Price to Selected Assets [see Chapter 6]:

_____ Do not wish to use this screen

If screen is invoked, please answer following questions:

Select:

_____ Price to Working Capital

_____ Price to Cash

_____ Price to Net Current Assets

Select and Specify Ratio [multiple]:

Greater than _____x

Less than _____x

For Time Period:

_____ Current

_____ Latest Fiscal Year

_____ Recent 3 Year Average

_____ Recent 5 Year Average

_____ Other (specify): _____

_____

L. Price/Earnings Ratio:

_____ Do not wish to use this screen

If screen is invoked, please answer following questions:

Fig. 11-5. (Continued)

Specify multiple:

Greater than _____x

Less than _____x

For Time Period:

_____ Current

_____ Latest Fiscal Year

_____ Recent 3 Year Average

_____ Recent 5 Year Average

_____ Other (specify): _____

M. Additional Information Required (Specify):

_____

_____

_____

_____

_____

Common practice among firms interested in a SAM is to work through their banks, CPAs, lawyers, and private consultants who act as finders and are active in the SIC area of interest. When using banks as a source, both the acquisition officer and the trust department are points of contact.

Matchmaking is becoming a big business for large banks in the money centers. Similarly, small banks assist their key accounts in selling, acquisitions, merger, divestiture, and spin-offs. The role of a bank varies from a nonfee basis to placement of additional banking business as compensation. Companies interested in acquisition and mergers should develop a list of acquisition officers at key banks.

In addition, SAM data is available from investment bankers, brokerage firms, industrial research organizations, trade journals (including direct contact with editors), governmental agencies, and industry associations—and from selling companies themselves. The point of this discussion is that a potential seller should understand where a potential buyer gets SAM leads. With the lead in hand, it is important to understand the acquisition thought process (Fig. 11-6).

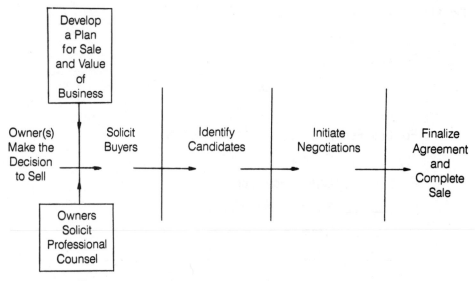

Fig. 11-6. Phases of business buyout (Negotiation Milestones).

Selling an emerging business involves preparation; preparation involves a sales effort through presentation of company records and potential. The presentation should be a restatement or recasting of the past 5 years' financials to include earnings, P/E ratios, and ROI. It should include a projection forward for 5 years. When profits are discussed, it's operating profits. When talking about earnings, it's after-tax earnings. In the presentation, look for off-balance sheet assets such as proprietary software, patents, etc. This can also include proprietary service organizations or unique strategies, potential opportunities to profit from a niche in the marketplace, distribution channels, the sale of real estate, or a profitable service function. Statistical data from recognized sources are important in a presentation. Banks can help, and consult Dun & Bradstreet databases and similar services also.

When selling, acquiring, or merging a business, the most important ratios are:

- Return on assets
- Percent of net worth to fixed assets
- Profit margins
- Accounts receivable aging
- Raw materials cost as percent of sales
- Inventory turns (as defined by cost of sales divided by average inventory).

If you are not familiar with these terms and their use in business, you should refer to some standard textbooks to bone up.

Each page in a presentation should be sequentially numbered so material cannot be added or deleted without becoming apparent. An asking price can be from 20 to 30 percent above the evaluation. A seller should not make verbal claims as to what the buyer can do with the business. The buyer will reach that deduction. Eighty percent of all deals do not work out the way the buyer had envisioned. A good presentation will present the business to the buyer in such a way that the buyer sees it's easier for him or her to make the business grow through acquisition than to make the *buyers* own business grow.

The Negotiations

The seller should work off of the presentation that he or she has prepared. The seller should not distribute any more financial information than that to start.

Don't be disappointed if you are not a participant in the negotiations from the beginning. Many times the professional lawyer or broker will lay the ground-work. Never negotiate alone. If you are the only representative from the company, then bring your lawyer. If you bring your lawyer, however, the other party probably will want their lawyer and the negotiations will take on a more formal air.

In the negotiations, don't take an adversary role. Intersperse your people into the group. Watch the expressions on people's faces during the negotiations. Don't stick one person with the total responsibility for negotiating. Dress appropriately to the conservative side. Let the other party think they are smarter.

Be organized in your method of evaluating alternative proposals. Use present value tables to analyze proposals (Table 11-1). The discount rate is the anticipated prime rate. The value of the business is adjusted to the net plus discount.

Although there are many reasons for a buyer to make acquisitions or mergers, the compelling force behind the effort is financial. This is true even if an objective may be to:

- Obtain management.
- Purchase a working organization.
- Get immediate sales and marketing help.
- Enhance growth potential.
- Purchase on-line operations (to make things or deliver services).
- Create cash flow or obtain working capital.
- Relate to other reasons such as geography, technology, market share, eliminating competition.

The buying firm will expect to look at certain financial records. Also, the buyer will expect the selling firm to be prepared to provide information beyond

Table 11-1. Present Value Tables.

Present value tables are important to the sale of a business because buyers often want to purchase a business by using deferred payment. Through the present value table you can calculate the equivalent value of the offer compared to dollars received today.

Using these tables, $100,000 paid at the 1 year anniversary of signing at a prime discount rate of 9 percent is only worth $91,700, if it were paid on signing.

On the second $100,000, it would only be worth $84,200 vs. receiving $100,000 up front.

Percentages

Year	1	2	3	4	5	6	7	8	9	10	11	12	13	14	15	16
1	0.990	0.980	0.971	0.962	0.952	0.943	0.935	0.926	0.917	0.909	0.901	0.893	0.885	0.877	0.870	0.862
2	0.980	0.961	0.943	0.925	0.907	0.890	0.873	0.857	0.842	0.826	0.812	0.797	0.783	0.769	0.756	0.743
3	0.971	0.942	0.915	0.889	0.864	0.840	0.816	0.794	0.772	0.751	0.731	0.712	0.693	0.675	0.658	0.641
4	0.961	0.924	0.888	0.855	0.823	0.792	0.763	0.735	0.708	0.683	0.659	0.636	0.613	0.592	0.572	0.552
5	0.951	0.906	0.863	0.822	0.784	0.747	0.713	0.681	0.650	0.621	0.593	0.567	0.543	0.519	0.497	0.476
6	0.942	0.888	0.837	0.790	0.746	0.705	0.666	0.630	0.596	0.564	0.535	0.507	0.480	0.456	0.432	0.410
7	0.933	0.871	0.813	0.760	0.711	0.665	0.623	0.583	0.547	0.513	0.482	0.452	0.425	0.400	0.376	0.354
8	0.923	0.853	0.789	0.731	0.677	0.627	0.582	0.540	0.502	0.467	0.434	0.404	0.376	0.351	0.327	0.305
9	0.914	0.837	0.766	0.703	0.645	0.592	0.544	0.500	0.460	0.424	0.391	0.361	0.333	0.308	0.284	0.263
10	0.905	0.820	0.744	0.676	0.614	0.558	0.508	0.463	0.422	0.386	0.352	0.322	0.295	0.270	0.247	0.227

Note: These percentages have been rounded to the nearest .001

what is included in the presentation. It is not unusual for a buyer to ask for examination of the owner's tax returns as well as audited corporate tax information. An inability to provide key financial data can easily squelch a deal before it gets through step 3 of the acquisition process. It is easy to classify these factors of SAM as simple ''due diligence,'' but someone must spell out exactly what ''due diligence'' means. When talking to your attorney, there are over 100 legal facets that must be considered. They fall generally into such categories as:

- stock considerations
- warranties
- litigation
- seller and buyer obligations
- patents
- indemnification
- covenants
- contracts
- fees
- schedules and transfer dates
- skills
- conditions for termination
- resolution of disputes
- work contracts
- technical agreements
- backlogs
- noncompetitive terms

The point here is that selling a business is not always easy, and the seller must realize what is involved via ''due diligence.''

First, you should construct a road map and checklist involving all the major aspects that affect the transaction: employment, insurance, financing—to name a few (Fig. 11-7).

The acquiring company understanding the financial thinking demands the same sophisticated financial understanding by the company being purchased. Just as in the selling of a business, this includes an understanding of certain financial ratios as well as the value placed on them in evaluating certain aspects of the business.

The point being made for the small or emerging company is that there *are* acquisition expectations in these areas and you must be familiar with various types of value. They are:

- Actual cash value
- Book value
- Depreciated value

- Fair market value
- Liquidation value
- Original value or cost
- Replacement value
- Reproduction value
- Subject value
- Tax basis value

This understanding is important for tax considerations and dollar basis of the acquisition, particularly if considerable manufacturing hardware and inventory is involved. Unless you are from the financial side of business, you might need some "hand holding" to optimize the use of value in your transaction.

Reduce everything to writing. Take copious notes. Confirm and reconfirm. Before breaking up a negotiating meeting, set a date for the next meeting. Confirm the date and the time later and before the meeting. Distribute the minutes of the previous meetings. Some managers consider using a milestone chart to identify target dates for accomplishing tasks; however, most negotiations are not that regimented.

Don't do any drinking during the negotiation sessions or at lunch or at dinner breaks. Be prepared to concede on the small points such as time and location of meetings so that you can win on important negotiations.

SECTION 1: PRODUCTION

1. Sources of ideas for new products to be fully and continuously developed.

   a. Research and development staffs?
   b. Production and operating staffs?
   c. Independent inventors?
   d. Research and engineering consultants?
   e. Competitor's activities?
   f. Non-competitive activities of other companies?
   g. Scientific and technical societies?
   h. Technical and trade publications?

2. Preliminary feasibility studies.

   a. Is there any engineering or production reason why the new product should not be considered?
   b. Is there any reason from sales, management, or company viewpoints against its consideration?
   c. Is the proposed process likely to prove practicable?
   d. If not, are there other processes to be considered?

Fig. 11-7. Weismantel International's due diligence checklist.

Fig. 11-7. (Continued)

    e. What additional research would be required? What would it cost?

    f. What prospective process development is necessary? Cost?

    g. Would any unusual production problems be involved?

        (1). To obtain desired quality?

        (2). To promote safety?

        (3). To correlate with present products?

    h. Are any unusual legal or patent problems likely to be involved?

    i. Are raw materials readily available?

    j. What are the best preliminary estimates of maximum and minimum:

        (1). Production costs?

        (2). Distribution costs?

        (3). Profit margins?

3. Management and financial appraisal—preliminary and final.

    a. Which of the following purposes will be served by this new product?

        (1). Complete company's present line of products?

        (2). Fill gap in existing market?

        (3). Round out present seasonal markets?

        (4). Expand sales in present markets?

        (5). Do better job than present products?

        (6). Anticipate changing consumer needs?

        (7). Enter a new market?

        (8). Fill idle time of plant or equipment?

        (9). Substitute for products of declining demand?

        (10). Increase reputation of manufacturer?

        (11). Stimulate attention to company by new customers?

    b. Before project is finally approved, the following financial questions must be answered:

        (1). Is new capital required?

        (2). If so, will its cost be reasonable?

        (3). Has adequate anticipated balance sheet been prepared?

        (4). Does expected sales realization show adequate profit margin?

        (5). Can rapid depreciation and obsolescence items be allowed?

        (6). Does new product plant fit general financial program of company?

        (7). Will new plans be unduly burdensome on management?

        (8). What is prospective stockholder attitude?

        (9). Does prospective profit warrant risk under most adverse circumstances anticipated?

4. Legal and patent problems.

    a. Do trade or company agreements interfere with proposed plans?

    b. Do any local, state, or national laws preclude proposed designs or operating plans?

    c. Is sales of product legally unrestricted in all markets to be reached?

    d. Can needed new laws be secured with reasonable promptness?

    e. Have all label, marketing, and merchandising laws been considered?

Fig. 11-7. (Continued)

    f. Are patent rights of company adequate to prevent infringement suits?

    g. What patent protection does company have to prevent competition?

    h. What new patents could be obtained by company? By competitors?

    i. Can proposed customers legally use produce as contemplated?

    j. What public safety precautions are needed in merchandising or ultimate customer use?

    k. Have industrial safety and workmen's compensation laws been adequately considered?

5. *Raw material problems.*

    a. What new materials are required?

    b. Are adequate supplies ensured? For how long?

    c. Are sources of raw material dependable?

    d. What is the prospective geographic source or deliver point?

    e. What raw materials inventory must be maintained?

    f. What substitutes can be used if raw material supply is interrupted?

    g. What will effect of substitution be on cost? On quality of product?

    h. Can tariff changes affect raw material supply or cost?

    i. Do prospective competitors control part of raw material supply? Or can company gain monopoly?

    j. What transportation problems or costs affect raw material price at processing plant?

    k. What special storage facilities will be required?

6. *Research and development.*

    a. Is process flowsheet for new product established?

    b. How long will completion of general process flowsheet require?

    c. What experimental laboratory research is needed?

        (1). To determine yields? Cost?

        (2). To improve processes? Cost?

    d. Can standard unit equipment be used?

    e. Are designs for new or modified unit equipment available?

    f. Will new materials for equipment construction be necessary?

    g. Can equipment constructed of requisite materials be quickly had? At what cost?

    h. Do present small-scale tests ensure large-scale operation?

    i. What unusual plant design problems are expected?

    j. What special employee safety precautions are needed?

    k. Are unusual depreciation and obsolescence factors anticipated?

7. *Design and construction.*

    a. Is wholly new plant necessary?

    b. What determines new plant location—transportation, labor, power, etc.?

    c. Can new product be made at some present plant?

    d. Is additional land necessary?

    e. Does ideal ground plan fit into present operations?

Fig. 11-7. (Continued)

    f. What new buildings are necessary?

    g. Is it possible to install necessary shipping and other factors?

    h. Will new facilities interfere with present operation?

    i. Are process and equipment recommendations from development department feasible for construction?

    j. What will completion of detailed plans and specifications cost?

    k. What is preliminary estimate of new capital required?

    l. What rates of obsolescence and depreciation are anticipated on buildings? On equipment?

    m. Can adequate safety provisions be made?

    n. Are any unusual or difficult construction problems involved?

8. Production and operation problems.

    a. Can present operating executives manage new enterprise?

    b. What new subordinate executives will be required?

    c. Will new type of operating experience or skill be required?

        (1). Of executive staff?

        (2). Of supervisors and workers?

    d. Are proposed plans and specifications satisfactory to operating executives?

    e. Are all operating hazards adequately provided for?

    f. How many additional employees will be needed for each class?

    g. Are adequate labor reserves available at proposed point of production?

    h. Are unusual labor troubles anticipated?

    i. Can additional labor be found if production is increased?

    j. What is effect of wage rate on cost of production?

    k. Can new product be coordinated seasonally with present plant activities?

    l. Are adequate provisions made for employee safety?

    m. Will nuisances to neighbors be created? Can they be controlled?

    n. Will plant operation be sufficiently flexible for adjustment to unexpected heavy demands?

    o. Can shut-downs be arranged where necessary during low demand seasons?

    p. Can repairs and maintenance be provided without interrupting plant operations?

    q. Are estimates of plant capacity reasonable?

    r. Are spare parts and repair materials available?

9. Packaging and shipping.

    a. What packages will be used for new product?

    b. Can standard packages be purchased?

    c. Must packages be of special material to resist damage by product?

    d. Are needed package sizes known?

    e. Can proposed packages be shipped legally by all desired transportation agencies?

    f. Will package damage in transit be serious?

    g. Have legal labels been devised?

    h. What are dealers and consumers desires as to package—size, shape, etc.?

    i. Will packages be returned for credit?

Fig. 11-7. (Continued)

    j. What will reconditioning of packages cost?

    k. Are packaging machines or devices available?

    l. What is the cost of package ready for shipment?

    m. Will new product depreciate during storage? Will depreciation be less in bulk or in packages?

    n. Will variety of packages required necessitate storage in bulk? Or can storage be in ready-to-ship containers?

    o. What precautions are necessary for storage in bulk or in containers?

    p. What space is required for storage of containers—new, returned, reclaimed?

    q. Are adequate mechanical handling facilities provided for packaging and handling into and out of storage?

    r. Are special loading facilities required for shipping?

SECTION II: MARKETING

1. Sources of ideas for new products—to be fully and continuously developed.

    a. Sales development and promotion staffs?

    b. Sales and customer services staffs?

    c. Wholesale and retail distributors?

    d. Marketing and other consultants?

    e. Competitor's activities?

    f. Noncompetitive activities of other companies?

    g. Trade association activities?

    h. Trade literature of consuming industries?

2. Preliminary market appraisal.

    a. What industries will use the new product?

    b. How large is each consuming industry?

    c. How much of the new product will each use?

    d. Where and what are these industries now buying?

    e. Where are these consuming industries located?

        (1). Are they localized in certain areas?

        (2). Are they widely distributed geographically?

    f. Which industries show positive growth projection?

    g. Which industries show negative growth projection?

    h. What is best estimate of potential market?

3. Management and financial appraisal.

    a. Is ownership of new product established?

    b. Is it adequately protected by trade-mark?

    c. Is manufacturer adequately protected by patents?

    d. Do latter infringe any existing patents?

    e. Are all claims to royalties or other indemnities provided for?

    f. Do any agreements limit size of market?

    g. Do any agreements limit sales or advertising effort?

Fig. 11-7. (Continued)

    h. Have all transportation problems and transportation costs been foreseen?
    i. What are estimated local, state, and federal taxes?
    j. What local, state, and national laws cover manufacturing?
    k. Has legal department made adequate study of:
        (1). Employee compensation?
        (2). Possible damage suits against manufacturer?
        (3). Labor and sanitary laws?
    l. To what extent do any or all of these effect:
        (1). Cost of manufacture?
        (2). Cost of selling?
        (3). Cost to consumer?

4. *Customers' buying habits.*

    a. Who in customer organization places order for new products?
    b. Does he or she buy on own judgment or upon recommendation of others?
    c. Who else is involved in the buying decision?
    d. Should each of these be called on?
    e. What relative weight will the purchasing group give to:
        (1). Price factors?
        (2). Quality of products?
        (3). Safety in storage and handling?
        (4). Service rendered by manufacturer?
        (5). Dependability of source of supply?
    f. Does location of present source of supply offer competitive advantage?
    g. Is the market for new product subject to seasonal fluctuation?
    h. What are the market practices on discount allowances, credits, etc.?

5. *Distribution channels.*

    a. Is the market for new product subject to wide fluctuation?
    b. Is any part of the fluctuation regional?
    c. Is any part of the market stable in its demands?
    d. Is the stable market regional or national?
    e. What type of distribution organization will be used?
        (1). Manufacturers—sales branches?
        (2). Manufacturers—regional sales forces?
        (3). Home office sales force selling to all consumers?
        (4). Wholesalers and jobbers?
        (5). Manufacturer's agents?
        (6). Combinations of above?
    f. Will the new product go into the export field?
    g. How will sales abroad be handled?
    h. Will any channel of distribution be new to the company?
    i. Will selling methods fit buying habits of the market?
    j. Will selling methods fit into company's sales organization?

Fig. 11-7. (Continued)

6. Studies of competition.

   a. Who will be your competitors on new product?
   b. What is the standing of each in the market?
   c. What is the reputation of each in the market?
      (1). Quality of product?
      (2). Market dominance?
      (3). Character of merchandise?
      (4). Dependability?
      (5). Service?
      (6). Progressiveness?
   d. Will new product invite keener competition on present lines?
   e. Will new product compete with those of any customer?
   f. What in general will be effect of competitive activity on:
      (1). Pricing?
      (2). Discounts and allowances?
      (3). Service?
      (4). Sales methods and organizations?
      (5). Selling costs?

7. Pricing and credit policies.

   a. What will be the general price policy on new product?
   b. Does this fit into buying habits of markets?
   c. How does it compare with competitors policies?
   d. What will be the schedule of discounts and allowances?
   e. Do these fit into present buying habits of the markets?
   f. Will new credit facilities be needed by the manufacturer?
   g. How much working capital will be tied up in credit?
   h. Will the credit method require enlarged credit department?
   i. Will present collection policy fit new product?
   j. What is estimated cost of credit and collection per unit sale?
   k. Does general price policy create higher selling cost?
   l. Does general price policy create other sales handicaps?

8. Sales and servicing organization.

   a. Will special sales department be needed for new product?
   b. Will technically trained sales reps be required?
   c. Can company's present sales reps handle new product?
   d. Will new product affect selling of regular line?
   e. Will sales reps be needed for missionary and educational work?
   f. What effect will sales organization changes have on:
      (1). Sales costs?
      (2). Price of new product to customer?
      (3). Company profits?
   g. What will be basis of sales reps' compensation?
   h. Who will aid sales reps with research and territorial analysis?

Fig. 11-7. (Continued)

    i. Will new product need consultant or other sales service in use?

    j. Will customer need special equipment for its use?

    k. If so, who will supply?

    l. If consultant service is rendered, will customer pay for it?

    m. If not, how will service cost be absorbed?

    n. Must service people have engineering training?

    o. Will special engineering research be done to solve customers problems?

    p. Will plant engineers be available for outside consultation?

    q. Can advertising be used to aid sales service?

    r. How will service department costs be allocated?

    s. How will they affect sales costs?

9. Sales promotion.

    a. Will new products require special sales promotion set-up?

    b. Will new advertising section or department be needed?

    c. What type of advertising should be used for introductory campaign?

    d. Will present advertising be related to new products?

    e. Who will decide on media?

    f. What will be the basis of sales promotion appeal?

    g. Will technical publicity be required?

    h. Will conventions, displays and expositions be used?

    i. How will budget sales promotion program for new product?

        (1). Fixed amount as capital charge?

        (2). Arbitrary percentage of sales expectancy?

        (3). Fixed amount to be charged to first year's sales?

    j. What will be effect of sales promotion expense on sales costs?

    k. What sales promotional work is done by competitors?

    l. Will your sales promotion program create retaliatory advertising by competitors?

    m. Will it offend any part of your present market?

10. Due diligence report preparation.

    Note: Not every industrial organization is equipped to analyze the exact sequence of successive steps outlined above. This list is offered as a reliable guide in due diligence. The value of this group of basic questions depends on:

1. The thoroughness with which every person in the organization cooperates in providing the answers for those items for which he or she is responsible.

2. The extent to which all answers are free from prejudice and can be verified by audit.

3. Other factors that include detailed investigation of personal and financial conditions of all key managers and directors.

If you're in a situation where a key decision maker joins the meeting late, ask one of his or her subordinates to review what has transpired. This will give you an opportunity to hear what is important to that party. It also gives the subordinate an opportunity to look good in his or her boss's eyes, possibly helping you in your future negotiations with the subordinate.

Be candid in your negotiations; tell everything that needs to be known, otherwise red flags will go up, unraveling the negotiations.

The biggest deal killer for the seller is lack of documentation. Remember that the buyer is not a mirror image of the seller. He or she doesn't know the business like the seller.

Determine early on if the other party is genuine. A seller should not be bashful about asking them to describe their purpose, background, or financial resources. Protracted negotiations endanger the confidentiality, not to mention distract from your everyday business. Genuine buyers will be very up front and candid.

The Contract

Somewhere during the course of the negotiations, you will have to determine whether the deal is going to be stock or assets. Of all deals, 70 to 80 percent are assets only.

A seller should try to take cash. Most deals, over 80 percent, are cash or equivalent. Be careful of deferred payments. A seller should try to be sure that the buyer is going to be in business; you do not want to experience after-sale problems coming back to haunt you.

If a seller takes stock, get a guarantee or a downside protection. Be careful under the new tax laws of depreciation recapture and its effect on capital gains. You will need your CPA in this area. Carefully negotiate to include the value of goodwill.

Goodwill can become a complicating factor during the sale of a business. Goodwill makes a company attractive in terms of its ability to do business with its current customer base, but it also extends to non-competition agreements, company trade names and products, management, labor relations, and other facets of an organization. Technically speaking, goodwill is the premium you pay over book. After purchase, the new owner can't depreciate goodwill. This is a topic that requires the close scrutiny of your CPA and attorney in light of tax laws at the time of sale acquisition or merger (SAM).

It is not unusual for a buyer to ask that the seller provide some warranties as to the qualities of receivables and inventory. These should not be significant, i.e., more than 1 or 2 percent of a large deal or 5 percent of a small deal. It depends on how clean the balance sheet is. Warranties should not extend beyond 1 year. Typically, the warranty simply will say that the seller must reimburse the buyer for any receivable that is not collected within a year after the sale.

Employment contracts are a matter of choice. Try to keep the employment contract simple. Be sure that the employment contract states where the place of employment is and what the employee's job is. In a noncompete contract, something of value should be exchanged in return for the agreement not to compete. Noncompete contracts are only enforceable if the time and geographical restrictions are reasonable, i.e., 3 to 5 years within the market area.

If the seller structures the contract properly, the buyer will pay for all the accounting and legal fees. At the conclusion of the negotiations, both parties will sign an explicit letter of intent. Then they will enter into a due diligence period which can last from 45 to 60 days. It is during this time that the buyer has the opportunity to:

- Examine the receivables.
- Examine the inventory.
- Check any legal actions.
- Talk with the people.
- Examine the books.

In retrospect, there will be a chain of events that normally follow the time of the decision to sell to consummation of the deal (see Fig. 11-6). Throughout the negotiations, the seller should not pretend to be a CPA, unless he or she is one. If a company has tax loss carry forwards, it will become apparent in the presentations. Almost always there are accounting and tax aspects that you must consider. So even if it is a "one-man-shop" looking to buy another "one-man-shop," seek good accounting services.

For public companies whose data is computerized and carried in the Standard and Poors (S&P), Dun's Data Bank, or elsewhere, obtaining financial information involves simple scanning and printout of desired figures and ratios. In 1975 when a small, highly technical, emerging company in the process industries was purchased by an acquisition-minded parent, all but the final analysis was carried out by the computer at S&P. Although not all the same basic questions asked of the computer for public companies are asked during the purchase of a private, small, or emerging business, some of the considerations are the same. Also, the acquisition odds—the probability of a successful SAM—are still rather high (Fig. 11-8).

The goals, of course, will be to make the best deal possible at the lowest possible cost. The best alternatives are those that lead to "everyone wins" agreement. This often involves the subtleties of value agreements and tax considerations for both parties—although you don't try to solve the other's tax problem and appraisal assistance. Conditions change depending on what the ultimate SAM is:

Steps

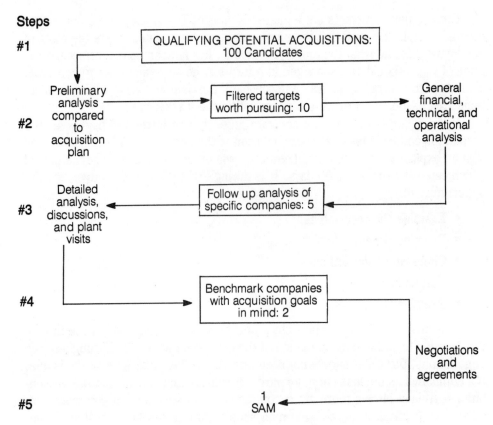

Fig. 11-8. Acquisition odds and milestones.

- Cash for assets.
- Cash for stock.
- Stock for assets.
- Stock for stock.

Detailed analysis as to the ultimate choice of transaction goes beyond the goals of this chapter.

After the Sale

Thirty to sixty days after the sale, the euphoria will begin to subside and the attitude about the sale will begin to change. The seller will realize that things will never be the same. He or she will realize he or she needs something to do and look to another career. Sometimes the need to work is fulfilled by a work contract with the surviving organization (Fig. 11-9). As mentioned, 80 percent of the sales don't work out as expected for the buyer and the seller might get fired.

Employment Agreement

Agreement made as of the first day of March 1989 by and between Weismantel International Corporation, A Texas Corporation (Weismantel), Modern Utilities, Incorporated, a Missouri Corporation (Modern) and J. Walter Kisling, Jr. (Employee).

Witness:

Whereas, employee is an executive of Modern, and

Whereas simultaneously with the execution here of Weismantel is purchasing all of the outstanding securities of Modern, and

Whereas, Modern desires to assure itself of the benefit of employee services, knowledge, and experience for a period of time and for a period of time thereafter to assure itself that the employee will not compete with Modern, Weismantel, or its subsidiaries and

Whereas employee is willing to enter into an agreement to that end upon the terms and conditions herein set forth.

NOW THEREFORE in consideration of the premises and mutual covenants herein contained, the parties do hereby agree as follows:

1. Modern shall employ employee and employee shall serve Modern in an executive capacity at the employee's location on the effective date hereof.
2. The employee shall devote such time as may be agreed to from time to time by employee and the board of directors of Modern to the affairs of Modern, recognizing that employee is also involved in other activities which take approximately half of his working time.
   a. Be subject to the direction of, be responsible to, perform all such executive duties as such shall be assigned by him by the board of directors of Modern.
   b. Comply with the procedures, principles and policies established by Weismantel for executives of Weismantel and their subsidiaries.
3. Term of employee's employment under this agreement shall be from the date hereof until February 28th, 1990 notwithstanding such term the employment contemplated by this agreement shall terminate forthwith
   a. In the event the employee (i) refuses, fails, or unjustifiably neglects to perform his duties as an executive of Modern or such other reasonable duties as may be assigned to him by the board of directors of Modern, (ii) engage in illegal contact materials detrimental to the interests of Modern, (iii) commits any material act of dishonesty, (iv) improperly discloses material confidential information of Modern, (v) acts in any way that has the direct substantial or adverse effect on the business or reputation of Modern or Weismantel.
   b. Upon employee's death.
   c. At Modern's option at the end of any consecutive period of 180 days of work during which employee shall be unable by reason of physical or mental disability to perform his duties hereunder with reasonable efficiency and neither employee nor his personal representative shall be entitled to any compensation under paragraph 4 hereof for any period subsequent to the date of such termination.

Fig. 11-9. A work contract: An example.

Fig. 11-9. (Continued)

4. Modern shall pay or cause to be paid to employee during the period of his employment hereunder a salary at a rate of at least $50,000 per year payable in equal monthly installments and may but shall not be required to grant in addition incentive compensation from time to time.

5. Employee shall be entitled during the period that he is employed hereunder to participate in all regular employee benefit plans of Modern and Weismantel including, but not limited to, such executive perquisites as employee may be enjoying on the effective date hereof. For purposes of determining eligibility under Weismantel general instructions service with Modern prior to its acquisition by Weismantel shall be deemed employee service with Weismantel.

6. During the period of his employment and for a period of two years thereafter (but in no event for less than four years from the date hereof in the event of early termination of this employment hereunder for whatever cause) employee shall not directly or indirectly (as principle agent or consultant) (i) compete within the United States or Canada with Weismantel or Modern or any of their subsidiaries in the manufacture, sale, or distribution of any product which is manufactured or in the process of development at any time during the term of this agreement by Modern or Weismantel or any of their subsidiaries or in the manufacture, sale, or distribution of any related product using similar technology or skills or which serves the same type of customer to which Modern and Weismantel or any of their subsidiaries now sell their products and/or services or (ii) have any beneficial ownership interest in any corporation (other than 5 percent or less of the capital stock of a corporation, the stock of which is listed or admitted to trading on a national securities exchange or other over the counter), partnership, firm, association, or business which a customer or supplier of Weismantel or Modern or any of their subsidiaries or which competes with the United States or Canada with Modern or Weismantel or any of the subsidiaries in the manufacture, sale, or distribution of any product which is manufactured or in the process of development at any time during the term of this agreement by Modern or Weismantel or any of their subsidiaries or in manufacture, sale, or distribution of any related product using similar technology or skills which serves the same type of customer to which Modern and Weismantel or any of their subsidiaries now sell their products and/or services. All information possessed by employee relative to Modern or Weismantel's activities of a secret or confidential nature including without limitation list of customers, names of accounts, contractual information, pricing information, cost of equipment and processes, trade secrets, confidential manufacturing processes, and other like information shall be the exclusive property of Modern or Weismantel. Employee shall not during the term of this agreement employment by Modern or thereafter (i) disclose to others or use for the benefit of others any such information so long as such information is treated as confidential by Modern or Weismantel (ii) attempt to induce any employee of Modern or Weismantel to leave its employ. All trade secrets, inventions, and procedures developed by employee or in the development of which employee participates during the employment by Modern whether or not patentable shall be

Fig. 11-9. (Continued)

the exclusive property of Modern. Modern and Weismantel and employee agrees at no expense to Modern or Weismantel to execute such patent application agreements and other documents as may be necessary to secure to Modern and Weismantel any patents which may be obtainable with respect to such trade secrets and inventions and procedures and all rights and benefits provided thereby.

7. Employee shall not have any right to anticipate, alienate, assign, or encumber in any way of the rights under this agreement and any agreement to do so shall be void.

8. This agreement and the employment contemplated by it shall be fully assignable by Modern and shall inure to the benefits of and be binding upon Modern and its successors and assigns.

9. Weismantel hereby guarantees the performance of the obligations of Modern hereunder.

10. The agreement shall be executed one or more counterparts and all such counterparts shall constitute one in the same agreement.

IN WITNESS WHEREOF Weismantel has caused this agreement to be executed ————————by duly authorized officer and employee has hereunto set his hand as of the day and year first above written.

For the seller, the important thing to making the adjustment is to have something to do that is more challenging than clipping coupons. Your spouse isn't going to want you working around the house. You will soon find out that you are looking for new activity. You will see the old company's personality or culture changing, and you might not be popular with the employees any more.

None of us who have built businesses are from modest egos. The seller will begin to question him or herself as to whether the deal was good or just lucky. The seller will wonder if it can be done again. And, don't be surprised if the seller gravitates back to his or her old industry after trying other things.

In the city of St. Louis, there is a group called Cashed Out Presidents (COPS). This group of executives have many of the same problems. COPS meet quarterly and the requirement is that you had to sell your business for at least a million dollars. Also, it had to be the sale of a going concern, not a liquidation or bankruptcy. In COPS, people share the same perspectives. The primary purpose of the group is to advise people who are interested in selling or have sold their business. There are 26 members. About half of them show up for any one meeting. COPS has been helpful to the members as they make the SAM transition, each benefiting from the others' experiences.

The buyer has his or her work cut out also. Following are some hypothetical approaches.

Concept #1. After acquiring a company, let it remain fairly autonomous for 2 or 3 years. This helps reduce any fears among employees that the buyer will turn the acquired company upside-down. Management of the acquired company often rebels. They can't understand close bookkeeping, 5 year projections, and business efficiency. They might employ a task force team to tutor the managers as to how good business practices make a company run a lot smoother. The employees soon discover that business can be fun.

Some people are worried when a big company acquires them. They picture the company as a big wolf that's going to come in and gobble them up. The buyer should provide some assurances to key employees.

An acquisition can have little or no effect on technical people. For the capable ones, in general, it's an advantage. When a person is working for a small company owned by one or two individuals, the purse strings are very tight. These companies are paternalistic hierarchies. When the president gives someone a raise, he or she knows that the money is coming out of the mouths of the president's family.

If an acquisition is handled properly, very few people will get worried about their jobs. Properly means that the acquisition must be kept quiet until just before it's transacted. Then the acquiring company should make a presentation to its new employees stressing that they have gained many new benefits, that there will be no drastic changes in their present operations, and that, in general, it's business as usual.

Concept #2. Some companies try to acquire well-organized companies. Those companies make the transition much easier. However, if the company doing the buying is high pressure and highly efficient, and the company bought is low pressure, then there will be problems. Obviously the low pressure company is going to have to make some changes.

Strategically, some people are better off after the acquisition. There are two reasons for this. First, there is better opportunities with a bigger company with more places to go. For example, an engineer who headed a small company is now head of research; it was a nice jump in salary and responsibility. Secondly, a big company provides securities such as insurance and profit-sharing that small firms find difficult to afford.

This might not do much for the employee who does not work for a bigger company, so any acquisition must adapt to personnel changeover. Before an acquisition, it is essential to identify which key people are important both in the acquiring company and in the company being acquired.

All this says is there should be synergism. That's common sense! Yet, it is pitiful how many sales, acquisitions and mergers go bad for lack of common sense.

Concept #3. Most people buy a business because they think they can run it better and that it will increase sales and profits. The marriage does not always work, however, and recognizing that fact can take some weighty, and not necessarily profitable, decisions that call for divorce.

Many companies that are acquired are put together with bailing wire and short of technical know-how. Know how to handle the problems that can result.

Small companies that are acquired are so often busy *doing* that they don't know *what* they are doing. The acquisition manager's job is to go into a company that is considered for acquisition or just acquired, observe what is happening, and make recommendations for ways to improve efficiency or to bring policies into line with the new parent. Everything suggested to a company is to convince them to change.

We find that a stop at an acquired company brings out a welcome mat, but it's usually not to hear your suggestions. Occasionally they are antagonistic. There is a theory that a person who is helped, resents that help. Nobody likes to be made a debtor. As a result, acquisitions involve a lot of hand holding or of just being available if needed.

It takes some convincing to get the acquired personnel to improve. Impress upon them that they are now part of a new partnership and that anything they do reflects on the total company.

Although you learn something with each company acquired, each time you run into some of the same problems and you might feel yourself on the same old treadmill again. You yourself can experience burnout because it usually takes from 18 to 24 months to make it fully integrated.

People don't like to change. Yet the acquisition brings about a sudden change in relationships. It's just like getting married and making a go of it. Once you get married, you find that the one you thought was self-sufficient turns out not to be. Well, you have to change the rules and adjust.

To be fair, it is not just the companies acquired that create the problems. Sometimes the parent company creates problems. So, sometimes the acquisition officer ends up having to convince the staff that the acquiring company are the ones that have to change. It is easy to get caught in the middle.

Acquisitions can be brutal and, from the seller's point of view, that is one reason why selling out should be done as much as possible when the seller is dealing from a position of strength. The buyer gets the better deal when he or she has the seller over the barrel.

In Conclusion. From these overviews, you can conclude that there are many unsuccessful acquisitions, and that the failure can often be traced to personnel problems. It helps to identify these before the SAM actually takes place, even if it leads to no agreement.

In summary, SAM errors can take place by the buyer making errors in consolidation plans or anticipating problems that eventually occur, or by the seller leaving too much on the table by being unaware of some financial facet.

The latter is more understandable because a small company is usually headed by one strong entrepreneur. Selling his or her company is a traumatic experience that requires the delicate empathy of a psychologist, with the virtue of patience being as important as faith, and optimism that the deal can be put together in the first place.

As already mentioned, timing the SAM point is crucial for maximizing the profit to the seller. Widows selling businesses where they have had no involvement leaves little in the way of bargaining power. When you reach that point, the business might end up being a fire sale. Then simple clauses that place acceptance or purchase of inventory completely in the hands of the buyer can lead to dramatic reductions in the seller's bottom line.

Obviously, the shrewd buyer will minimize inventory purchase costs, leaving the seller holding stock that can be hard to move—because the seller is out of business—or that the buyer will pick up at 10 cents on the dollar. When a purchaser has the seller over the barrel, the scars of the negotiations are never forgotten.

A buyer will often negotiate when the seller is experiencing a period of weakness. This can happen during a period of unprofitability of a void in leadership. That in itself, however, is no reason to buy a company. After all, what really makes your company attractive is its profits, potential for more profits, and ability to generate cash. Obviously profits, or profit potential, is viewed differently by every suitor, depending on factors like:

- Facilities compatibility.
- Existing and future product lines.
- Complementary product mix.
- Proprietary positions.
- Operations expertise.
- Management expertise.

In judging the company under consideration, dividend history might not be as important as earnings history. (Dividends are often emitted by emerging businesses as they plow cash back into the business in the form of assets and working capital.)

Eventually, payment can be reduced to some form of ROI with the seller indemnifying the buyer with respect to undisclosed liabilities and other factors.

The "cleaner" approach, of course, is to simply buy assets and avoid the indemnification question completely due to the complications that can arise. Another minus for the seller is the lack of a ready market for stock of a closed corporation.

Tips and Checkpoints

As mentioned, what can be very important for one buyer of a business actually can be a deterrent for another buyer. But, there are some points everyone will agree on. These include:

Growth Is Important. After the acquisition, business is expected to continue on an even keel or experience growth in total sales and profitability. Realistic growth numbers are important. For example, a seller that arbitrarily shows a sales increase from $100,000 to $500,000 without backup information could hardly expect a purchaser to base an acquisition price on the larger number.

Keep Existing Business. Keeping existing business can be an important facet in an acquisition. For instance, a manufacturer's rep might want to sell the firm but can't guarantee that the ''principles'' will remain with the new owners due to 90-day cancellation clauses in the rep or distributor agreements.

High Liquidity and Cash Flow Is Desirable. Buyer firms abhor large inventories as well as high values of fixed assets—particularly if those assets are not operating at 90 percent capacity or better.

New Hardware or Process Technology. A firm that has low-cost production advantages over the competition gets an A+ in the acquisition derby.

Stable Labor Relations. Stable labor relations can make or break a SAM. An ideal situation is a non-union shop whose wages are above union scale and whose productivity, as measured by industry norms, is higher than the average by a large degree.

General Criteria. Overall, a buyer's shopping list starts with the simple listing of industry, geographical, and sales volume criteria (Fig. 11-10). To this you add input from the seller's side which includes the legal form of the company (proprietorship, corporation, partnership, other), fiscal data, historical data, and other reasons for wanting to sell (Fig. 11-11). Finally, you must address the question of price.

CASHING OUT OPTIONS

The authors have put a great deal of emphasis thus far on selling your business. However, there are other cashing out options which you can consider. These include partial redemptions; going public; or Employee Stock Option Plans (ESOPs), to mention a few.

Partial Redemption

Most emerging companies would not have the capital or the borrowing power to redeem a significant part of its common stock and still remain viable. A partial

The following information is presented for those who are interested in acquiring a manufacturing business and would like to be notified of opportunities that arise.

Check: In the Following Area

☐ Apparel
☐ Chemical
☐ Drug & Cosmetics
☐ Electrical
☐ Explosives & Ammunition
☐ Fats & Oils
☐ Fertilizer & Agricultural
☐ Foods & Beverages
☐ Furniture
☐ Instruments and/or Process Control
☐ Lime & Cement
☐ Machinery
☐ Man-made Fibers & Textiles
☐ Metals or Metal Products
☐ Paints, Varnish & Lacquer
☐ Petroleum Company
☐ Pigments & Dyes
☐ Plastics
☐ Pulp & Paper, Lumber
☐ Rubber or Elastomerics
☐ Soap, Glycerine, Cleaning
☐ Stone, Clay, Glass

Check: In These Geographical Areas:

☐ Northeast
☐ Northwest
☐ Midwest
☐ Rocky Mountains
☐ South
☐ Southwest
☐ West

Check: With a Minimum Sales of:

$_____

Check: On the Following Basis[es]:

☐ Businesses with a history of earnings, with a minimum pretax tax net profit of:

$_____

☐ Turn around situations
☐ Start-up Situations
☐ Other Criteria:_____

Check: Form[s] of Purchase

☐ Stock [enclose annual report]
☐ Cash, within
☐ Other
$_____

Check: Management Status

☐ Retain Management
☐ Bring Management
☐ Other

Other Criteria: _____

_____

Please attach your calling card or show here the name to whom and address where correspondence should be sent: _____

_____

_____

Fig. 11-10. A buyer's shopping list.

WEISMANTEL
INTERNATIONAL

P.O. BOX 6269
KINGWOOD, TEXAS 77325
713-359-1894

Type of Business: _____   REFERENCE NO. _____

Product(s): _____   Location: _____

Legal Form: _____   Years in Business: _____

Financial Summary:

Fiscal Year Ending: 19____   19____   19____   19____   19____

Sales (Historical):   _____   _____   _____   _____   _____

Sales (Forecast):   _____   _____   _____   _____   _____

Net after Taxes: _____   _____   _____   _____   _____

Source of Financial Data _____

Physical Plant _____

_____

Management Status _____

Brief History _____

Reason for Sale _____

Asking Price _____

Other Information _____

Fig. 11-11. A Seller's ad listing.

redemption, however, although not as attractive as under the old tax law, can still be advantageous for the cashing-out shareholder as well as the succeeding shareholders.

Stock redemptions are not as attractive under the new tax law because capital gains are now taxed as ordinary income. Even so, do not permanently discount the potential of a partial redemption for tax reasons. Capital gains exclusion has occurred before and has been reinstated and might well be reinstated once again.

Furthermore, a partial redemption need not be all in cash. It can be cash and notes. The notes can bear an interest rate consistent with current rates. The interest, therefore, can provide income to the redeeming shareholder. Understand, however, that the principle on the notes is paid for by the company with after-tax dollars.

There can be a number of reasons and conditions for partial redemptions. These include retirement income for the shareholder, support for a widowed spouse, working capital for an entrepreneuring young shareholder, funds for a college education, and others.

It is generally accepted that the shares held as a minority interest in a closely held corporation are worth less than they would be in the total sale of a corporation. Although there is no guarantee, a number of redemptions of the company's stock could have a bearing on the establishment of the value for succeeding shareholders' estates.

If buy and sell agreements are properly executed, stock can also be redeemed for purposes of settling the estate. As with any type of cashing out, you should consult your attorney and tax consultant for guidance in a redemption.

Let's take into consideration the effect of the succeeding shareholders after a redemption. First of all, the redeemed stock will go into the treasury of a company. Subsequently, there will be fewer shares outstanding and the percentage of ownership of each succeeding stockholder will increase proportionately. If the stock is redeemed at book value, there will be no change in the book value of the succeeding shareholders. If it is bought for less than book, their proportionate value will increase and if it is bought for more than book, their value will decrease.

The tax code currently provides for a corporation to reorganize the structure of its equity. Many companies have taken advantage of this by converting the common stock of the senior or retiring owner into preferred stock. Preferred stock typically pays an attractive dividend that provides the individual with income. The preferred stock value remains the same and does not change with the fortunes of the company. Therefore, the value of the individual's estate is fixed. The common stock can remain in the control of the people managing the company.

Another form of reorganization is to create two classes of common stock: voting and nonvoting. The voting would typically be in the hands of those who manage the business while the nonvoting would be controlled by those not active in the business. All of the common stockholders share in the growth of the company.

Another form of capitalization is in what is sometimes called phantom stock. Typically, phantom stock is given to employees as a form of incentive. The employees receive stock as a bonus and the value of the stock grows as the company prospers. There is a contract, however, that upon the employees voluntary or involuntary termination, the company buys the phantom stock, usually at book value.

Employee Stock Option Plans (ESOPs)

You can utilize all the options just mentioned and still go another step by implementing employee stock option plans (ESOPs). ESOPs are one of the very few programs that continue to receive favorable tax treatment. These plans are often misunderstood because there is an underlying worry that stockholders are giving away control of their company.

Let us outline some of the major features of ESOPs. Think of the ESOP as a profit-sharing trust where the voting rights of the trust are controlled by the trustees appointed by your board. The trustees can be members of management or be major shareholders.

An evaluation of the company's worth is made objectively. This establishes the value of a share of stock. The ESOP then goes to a bank and borrows money to buy stock. The loan is guaranteed by the company. The bank lends the money to the ESOP at a lower than market rate since they are not obligated to pay taxes on earnings from a loan to an ESOP.

If the ESOP buys 30 percent of the stock, the shareholders might take the money and reinvest it in the corporate stock or bonds of an American company. The American company need not be traded; that is, the shareholders could actually take the money and start another company. The shareholders do not have to pay any capital gains tax until they sell the second investment.

The company makes contributions to the ESOP that are at least adequate for the ESOP to pay the principle and interest on the loan at the bank. These contributions to the ESOP are tax deductible to the company. Figure 11-2 traces the flow of cash in an ESOP transaction.

In addition to the significant tax advantages created by ESOP for both the corporation and the shareholders, you can see that an ESOP allows the control of business to remain in the right hands.

An ESOP is also an ideal solution if you have some emotional hangups about selling the business that you've built from scratch or where you have loyal employees or family members active.

A recent change in the tax law provides an estate with a 25 percent credit on estate taxes for any sale of stock to an ESOP after death.

If you have an existing profit-sharing plan, you can roll it over into an ESOP. This, of course, reduces the amount of borrowing required. If you are interested in an ESOP, it is a simple process to determine if your company can afford it. Make a rough appraisal either in terms of multiples-of-book or multiples-of-earnings in order to place a value on your business. Multiply that by 30 percent. The result is the amount of money the ESOP will have to borrow, less anything that will be in your existing profit-sharing plan. This is the amount that will be needed to redeem 30 percent of stock. Calculate the principle and interest payments for a 6 year loan conservatively at the prime rate. Ask yourself if your company can afford to make a tax deductible contribution of this size annually.

Employee Stock Option Plan (ESOP) Transaction Cash Flow

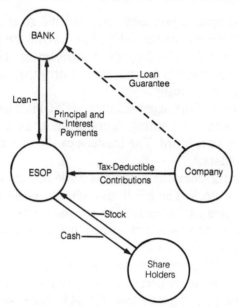

—— means that no cash actually flows.

Fig. 11-12. Employee Stock Option Plans (ESOP) transaction cash flow.

Again, as with all of the options listed, you should solicit expert advice. There are reputable companies who specialize in ESOPs. They offer seminars and training on the subject.

Keep in mind that an ESOP is only as good as the company itself. If the company fails, an ESOP provides the individual with nothing. If a person's personal wealth were invested with the hope of bringing retirement income, the person could lose everything if the firm fails. This situation actually occurred in some recent bank failures.

Going Public

By definition, this book is designed for the emerging company that we feel, in most instances, would be classified as small business, i.e., under 500 employees. Even though it might appear to be a good idea and an opportunity for the owners of your business to make a lot of money, the propriety of trying to go public with an initial issue is definitely not the best alternative for the majority of emerging companies.

To make an initial issue of stock is very expensive and time consuming. In addition to legal and accounting fees, there are expenses in satisfying the federal, state and local regulatory agencies. A public offering is going to take a significant amount of management time away from the efforts of running the business. Timing is of the utmost importance, and should you miss the window of opportunity—new industry in vogue, industry that has good multiple, escalating stock market, and other facets—you might have to abandon your attempt.

In every case, caution is advised in evaluating the opportunity to go public, even if you choose to buy an existing public shell.

A Strategic Cash Out Alternative

Another aspect of cashing out is subdividing your business. If you have already reached the decision to cash out *now*, it is probably too late for you to use this alternative.

For those still looking to the future, consider the following alternative. If your total business is worth one million dollars or more, consider ways of subdividing it. For example, could your real estate holdings be taken out and put into a separate corporation? Can your operations be divided into a core business and supporting operations? (Table 11-2). Do you already have subsidiary corporations that could be spun off?

If the answer to any of the above questions is yes, you might want to consider converting one of these separate businesses to a subchapter S Corpora-

**Table 11-2. Potentials for Subdividing
Your Business for Partial Cashing Out.**

Type of Business	Subdivisions
General Contractor	Concrete work excavating brickwork Real estate
Retail Company	Service Parts Financing Real estate
Restaurant	Catering Banquets and Entertainment Real estate
Manufacturing	Service Distribution Transportation Leasing Real estate

tion. You might also want to consider a limited partnership, particularly for the real estate.

The bottom line is: if you can subdivide your holdings, you have the potential to cash out of a noncore business to increase your personal liquidity. All the while, you maintain your core business. This spin-off does not affect your employees nor do you retire. The nature of the spin-off depends on the business you are in.

Index